STRATEGIES FOR LEARNING

STRATEGIES FOR LEARNING

Small-Group Activities in American,
Japanese, and Swedish Industry

ROBERT E. COLE

UNIVERSITY OF CALIFORNIA PRESS
BERKELEY   LOS ANGELES   LONDON

University of California Press
Berkeley and Los Angeles, California

University of California Press, Ltd.
London, England

© 1989 by
The Regents of the University of California

Library of Congress Cataloging-in-Publication Data

Cole, Robert E.
    Strategies for learning : small-group activities in
American, Japanese, and Swedish industry / Robert E.
Cole.
        p.   cm.
    Includes index.
    ISBN 0-520-06541-7 (alk. paper)
    1. Work groups—United States.   2. Work groups—
Japan.   3. Work groups—Sweden.   4. Comparative
management.   I. Title.
HD66.C54   1989
338.6—dc19   88-36949
                                                               CIP

Printed in the United States of America
1   2   3   4   5   6   7   8   9

To Lillemor

"Every man is a valuable member of society, who by his observations, researches, and experiments, procures knowledge for men." . . . The long run health of science does not rest exclusively with a small professional elite . . . seeking to advance knowledge. . . . The diffusion of knowledge, a valid goal in itself, is also a means to a further end. It multiplies the number of researchers, widens the range of inquiry, assures the public's readiness to support their work, and hence powerfully enhances the chances for new discoveries. The increase and the diffusion of knowledge are in some respects ultimately bound together. . . . In the long run, each can flourish only as the other flourishes.

> Robert McCormick Adams at his installation as the ninth secretary of the Smithsonian Institution on 17 September 1984, reflecting on the remarks of its founder, James Smithson.

Contents

Figures and Tables

Figures

Tables

Acknowledgments

This book has a longer history than I care to disclose publicly. As a consequence, the list of those whose support made it possible is quite long. Data for the sections on Japan were largely collected during my tenure as Fulbright Research Scholar in 1977–78. I am indebted to the Fulbright Commission for its support and to the Japan Institute of Labour for providing research facilities. I also wish to express my appreciation to the German Marshall Fund, which provided a grant for collection of Swedish data. Sigvard Rubenowitz provided research facilities at the Department of Applied Psychology at Gothenberg University. I am especially indebted to the countless business organizations and associations in Japan, Sweden, and the United States whose executives gave freely of their time in an attempt to educate me in the intricacies of organizational change. I would particularly like to thank the members of the board of directors and the staff of the International Association of Quality Circles, where I conducted participation observation research since its inception.

A grant from the East Asia Program of the Woodrow Wilson International Center for Scholars in 1984–85 enabled me to spend a year doing my initial write-up in the congenial environment of the "castle." The Center for Japanese Studies and the School of Business Administration at the University of Michigan both provided substantial financial support as well. None of these institutional benefactors are responsible for my findings.

As a result of the long period taken to complete this study, I had occasion to come back again and again to some of my informants

xv

with new questions about old and new developments. In this connection I would particularly like to thank the following for their extraordinary patience: Inge Janérus of the Swedish Trade Union Confederation; Berth Jönsson, previously with the Volvo Corporation; Jan Helling of Saab-Scania; and Junji Noguchi of the Japanese Union of Scientists and Engineers. Andy Walder, William Whyte, Shimada Haruo, and Kōshiro Kazutoshi were especially helpful in getting me to frame some of the key ideas developed here. Howard Aldrich, Ellen Auster, Mayer Zald, Stanley Seashore, and Bertil Gardell read selected chapters. Still other readers prefer to remain anonymous, but I am no less in their debt for that. I also owe special thanks to Steve Fraser of Basic Books.

The way I evaluate this subject and its significance has changed dramatically since the initial data collection in the late 1970s. Rather than lament the long gestation period of this book, I would rather focus on the added enlightenment that has come my way during the long period I have had to think about the material.

Part One

Chapter One

Culture and the Emergence of Small-Group Activities

Over the past twenty-five years in the advanced market economies, and even among some of the command economies, a movement has grown for building small-group activities among lower-ranking production and office employees. The term *small-group activities* refers to workshop- or office-based groups that are given a greater opportunity to exercise direct control over everyday work decisions and the solving of workshop problems. In the United States the rise of quality circles (employee-involvement groups) and, of late, self-managing teams has come to symbolize this movement, which has been associated in varying degrees and ways with a broader effort to expand employee participation in managerial decision making. In many countries this movement arose as a response to a crisis in management confidence that in turn derived from the need to respond to a threat to or loss of a competitive ability. The idea was to find a more effective way to recruit and make better use of employees to achieve organizational goals while satisfying the needs of individual employees for control over their immediate work environment. There were significant national variations in this regard, and indeed such variations are central to this book's strategy of analysis.

In some nations powerful currents have sustained spring tide conditions. In others the ebb tide has come quickly, and only scattered debris is left to show small-group activities having been present. In still others a riptide churns the currents in opposite directions. These disturbed currents obscure underlying movements, which only the passage of time will clarify.

The task I set myself was to analyze and understand these different currents. I wanted to understand how these activities spread—diffused—in given nations. Why had they spread more rapidly in some countries than in others? What were the channels of diffusion? Through what mechanisms and with what effect? Analysis of these movements is more complex than might initially appear to be the case; a variety of environmental factors affect the course of development of small-group activities. Moreover, management commitment to these small-group activities often displays a faddish quality.

What Is So Important about Small-Group Activities?

There are compelling practical reasons for focusing on small-group activities. The failure of American business to fully use its human assets inhibits growth in quality and productivity, thereby undermining national living standards. There is good reason to believe that some competitor nations make better use of their human assets, thereby developing a competitive edge in the fierce struggle for international markets. Small-group activities allow individual workers to share their knowledge and skills and to develop them in ways that enhance economic success. This helps not only to assure the firm's success but to ensure employment security as well.

A more recent line of reasoning stresses the impact of the new technologies of flexible manufacturing and microelectronics, combined with growing worldwide competition in price and quality. In practice this means heightened pressures to produce more custom-made high-quality products and services to meet more volatile and sophisticated customer tastes. These developments are said to lead to further payoffs for increased teamwork, employee discretion, and participation to get the most out of the technology and to better respond to customer demands.

Some advocates take a different tack, starting from the proposition that small-group activities give individuals significant participation in organizational decision making. This in turn is said to be a strong democratizing force that finally brings the benefits of political democracy into the workplace. Notions of self-governance and self-determination underlie this perspective (see Dachler and Wilpert 1978:5). This claim contrasts with the neo-Marxist view that small-group activities are just one more management technique to control workers. The neo-Marxists see these evolving practices as part of a new corporatist strategy that, by fostering a sense of participation in the organization on the part of employees, destroys collective solidarity among workers and makes them vulnerable to a higher level of management control (Edwards 1979; Burawoy 1983).

Still another view stressing the participative aspects of small-group activities emanates from the moral arena. Secular humanitarian and religious leaders focus on the significance of participation for increasing the control of individual employees over their own lives and providing an outlet for their creative talents, thereby elevating individual dignity and self-respect. The draft of the bishops' pastoral letter "Catholic Social Teaching and the U.S. Economy" (National Catholic News Service 1984), for example, states that economic activity should be an expression of the distinctive dignity of human beings and that work should enable people to find a significant measure of self-realization and creativity in their labor.

Theories of human growth and development, with their stress on self-actualization, are a related perspective deriving from social science. Theorists working in this tradition talk about the "humanization of work" and tend to see participation as a key strategy for improving employee motivation and allowing individuals thereby to achieve their true potential. The focus tends to be on the individual's relation to the work task itself rather than on questioning the broad distribution of power and decisions.

There is now significant evidence to show that Japanese firms in particular have made better use of their human resources than have the Americans; this has significant consequences for living standards and the quality of life at work. Furthermore, by effectively conducting small-group activities, Japanese firms achieve a variety of economic benefits. These involve flexibility, speed, economizing on resources, and the execution of decisions based on accurate information (see Aoki 1987). Just as it is naive to think that small-group activity inevitably leads to self-actualization and democratization, it is unduly cynical to think that it is always a corporatist strategy designed to destroy the collective solidarity of workers.

What consequences small-group activities have is above all an empirical question. In focusing on the spread of small-group activities across firms and the role of national infrastructures in promoting this, I concentrate more on management than on workers' behavior. The preceding discussion is designed simply to show the reader that the content of what is being diffused is important.

Why a Comparative Study of Small-Group Activities?

What is the contribution of a comparison of different national experiences with small-group activities? First, it is clear that there are distinctive national approaches to small-group activities. The American model stresses direct, informal participation and provides relatively limited scope for those at the bottom of the organization to participate in decision making. This is strikingly different from the more formal representational approach to participation taken in continental European nations (see Dachler and Wilpert 1978:23–25). To be sure, collective bargaining arrangements in unionized U.S. firms should rightly be seen as providing representative participation, but relatively few of these arrangements have been used explicitly to pursue individual participation in work decisions per se.

From a social science perspective, a comparison of different national experiences permits one to begin identifying the characteristic elements of successful diffusion processes. It also helps us identify those elements of the diffusion process that are unique to particular nations; such unique elements are hidden when one studies one nation's experiences. The role of culture provides a dramatic example. It is impossible to estimate its effects when examining only one culture, but in comparison with others, we have the opportunity to clarify its significance. Given the attention paid to cultural effects in the analysis of small-group activities, this leverage appears to be of considerable benefit in furthering more robust explanations. By our knowledge of unique national characteristics, we in turn enhance our understanding of contrasting social structures. As Reinhard Bendix (1956:445) has argued, if different societies over time confront and resolve a similar problem, then a comparative analysis of their divergent solutions will help us understand the divergent character of the respective social structures in a process of change.

Finally, from a policy perspective, it is instructive to see how other nations "do it," so that we may learn from their experience. There is ample evidence of cross-national flows of information about small-group activities. I shall examine how social actors in different nations have perceived and responded to such information flows. There are a great many misunderstandings, colored by national ideology and cultural traditions, about how the borrowing process operates.

At a minimum, the very fact that small-group activities in one form or another have landed on the agendas of all the market economies over the past twenty-five years is remarkable. How did this happen and why? How is it that in 1984 a draft OECD report on the worldwide automobile industry could conclude:

Although there seems to be a diversity of managerial technology development and practice in the automobile industry in various countries, the general trend is towards increased worker participation in production decision-making. The quality circle approach, involving more off-line input and cooperation between workers and management, is considered important and is being experimented with and implemented by practically all major automobile companies around the world. . . . There is also a trend towards giving more on-line responsibilities to the workers, ranging from preventive maintenance to quality control, and to multi-process handling. . . . The strongest general trend is the introduction of *group work*. . . . There is a trend away from "man-machine relations" towards "team technological system relations." This involves restructuring the production process by setting teams which often number from three to eight people. It represents a move away from assembly-line structures with their isolating and alienating effects.

(OECD 1984a:37, 39)

The common trends described in the OECD automotive study are really quite extraordinary. In varying degrees, they have been reported for other industries as well. Are there common driving forces in each country, or is it simply a matter of "international faddism"?

A second question recognizes some of the variation internationally and leads us to ask why small-group activities ended up on the agenda earlier in one place and later in another. A focus on national differences also leads us to ask why the nature of the response has varied from one place to another. This kind of specific research is far more likely to yield useful information to makers of public policy and scholars than the recent vogue for writing vague popular treatises on how one nation's management system is generally superior to another's.

My focus is on the evolution of small-group activities in the United States, Japan, and Sweden between the early 1960s and the mid 1980s. The stress is principally on why developments have taken the direction they have, but I also explore what paths have not been taken and why. The comparative strategy has been developed for a variety of personal and intellectual reasons. I have long believed that explicit national comparisons are to be preferred to specific national studies of work organization (which often contain implicit and unverified comparisons). As a long-term student of the Japanese situation, I noted that even when comparative studies were carried out by American scholars, they commonly compared Japan to the United States. An ethnocentric bias commonly led to the implicit judgment when explaining observed differences that we were "normal" and they were "different." Japan's recent economic ascendancy has led to some reversal of this assessment, but bias is no less apparent.

It was these kinds of reflections that led me to conclude that a well-grounded study of small-group activities that included a European country would be of considerable value in casting new light on work organization and the various options open to national actors. In fact, I was raising the N from two to three. While some would emphasize that this is still a very small number of cases, I sensed that with proper selection for maximum variation, one could get a lot of leverage from that additional case. Sweden has a strong reputation as an innovator in work organization and its selection as a third country to be compared seemed ideally suited to my aims.[1]

1. By limiting the analysis to the United States, Japan, and Sweden, I ensured linguistic competence in the three countries to be compared. This made possible field and archival research based on primary source materials, as well as interviews with key informants in their native language, and facilitated survey research on "early adopters" of quality circles in the United States and Japan.

In the case of Sweden, in addition to the voluminous scholarly and management literature on the subject in Swedish, the newspaper coverage was also extensive. This allowed a different vantage point on developments. These data sources were supplemented by interviews with key informants and recognized experts in the unions, companies, universities, the employers' confederation, and research institutes. Volvo and Saab, two major innovators, were particularly receptive to my initiatives.

For the United States a large scholarly and management literature on direct

Some Introductory Thoughts
on the Role of Culture

In speaking of small-group activities, the question inevitably arises of whether one nation can learn from another's experiences. This in turn raises the issue of culture as a potential barrier to the learning process. Powerful cultural stereotypes in each country bias how one assesses the impact of culture on the cross-national borrowing process. These stereotypes, themselves part of powerful societal ideologies, constitute an important set of resources and constraints on the learning process. As ideologies, moreover, they also distort our understanding of actual social behavior and thereby conceal important resources that are available to the learning process.

Americans and Japanese have an image of Japan as a group-based culture and of the United States as one based on individualism. Many go on to conclude that a group-based activity such as quality circles will not work in the individualistic American culture. Such stereotypes clearly have a basis in fact; Americans do have a strong tendency to assign tasks to the individual and to hold the individual accountable, while the Japanese are more inclined to assign tasks to the group and make the group accountable for performance.

These differences do have their roots in the respective national histories of the two countries, and thus constitute different cultural constraints. In the case of Japan, for example, the legal system during the Tokugawa period (1603–1867), which was based on the principle of collective responsibility, allocated complete authority and responsibility for the performance and conduct of group members to group representatives such as the village headman (see Smith 1983:38). In practice, the system operated over time to assign a high degree of autonomy to village communities and urban neighborhoods alike.

---

participation on the shop and office floor level exists. In addition, the author, through lecturing, consulting, and participating in professional associations, has been an active observer of, and sometimes participant in, the process of diffusing quality circles.

In the case of Japan, a significant scholarly and management literature exists on the subject in Japanese. Selected company visits and interviews supplemented this literature, as did interviews with employers' confederation officials and union leaders. The Japanese Union of Scientists and Engineers (JUSE), a key actor in the diffusion of quality circles in Japan, was particularly forthcoming in its cooperation and arranged for a variety of meetings with key informants.

Nevertheless, these stereotypes and generalizations can be terribly misleading when it comes to assessing the practices of individual companies, whether in Japan or the United States.[2] First, there is ample evidence from social science that under certain conditions, group activities and decision making can be stultifying. Consider the observations of Karl Weick (1984:22), a noted student of organizations:

Take the common demonstration that groups, in the interest of coordination, often accommodate to the least accomplished member. When this happens, members set in motion a mechanism that winnows some intelligence out of the system. In fact, most group mechanisms that have been uncovered (e.g., groups promote polarized beliefs; groups are solution centered rather than problem centered) imply that groups and organizations seem to be exquisitely organized to vulgarize their own minds.

Seen in this light, the question is not whether groups are superior to individuals or vice versa, but under what conditions and in what environments groups perform effectively.

Moreover, in the extent and nature of group activities, there is tremendous variation between firms in Japan and in the United States. Nor are group activities foreign to many American firms. In some cases, the nature of the technology or the service to be provided almost dictates group organization. Yet the teamwork imposed by management policy or dictated by technology must be distinguished from the attitudes internalized by employees. In their recent large-scale survey of workers' attitudes in Japan and the United States, Arne Kalleberg and James Lincoln (1989) report that the Japanese employees are only slightly more inclined to "favor working in groups" than their American counterparts. While the data lend themselves to a variety of possible interpretations (perhaps the Japanese respond the way they do because they have "had it" with group activity), they do suggest caution in embracing popular stereotypes too closely.

To look at the matter differently, consider the practice of individual reward and recognition. One can make the strong argument that in U.S. manufacturing firms the individual blue-collar worker is typically treated in the mass (that is, as a member of a large group) in the sense that he or she receives little recognition in the wage sys-

2. A biting critique of the groupism model as applied to Japan appears in Mouer and Sugimoto 1986.

tem or informally as to individual performance. The auto worker who told me during an interview, "Nobody gives a damn whether I do my job well or not!" captured this situation all too well.

Conversely, in Japan, there is tremendous effort made in personnel policy to individualize treatment of blue-collar workers and tailor training and wage increments to individual performance.[3] Now in which economy is the individual "king" and in which does the group dominate? One of the major implications of this focus on the individual in the Japanese reward system for lower-ranking employees is that it leads to tremendous competition among individuals. This means that the highly publicized teamwork among Japanese workers gets played out in the context of a delicate balance between cooperation and individual competition. Such subtle relationships are notably absent from typical Western treatments of the subject, with their overwhelming focus on groupism. Yet they have been a major component in the engine driving continuous improvement activities in postwar Japanese firms.

Similarly, there is the Western image of the Japanese individual subjugating himself or herself completely to group-defined objectives. Such a view does not allow for the real life subtleties whereby individuals seek to control the definition of group objectives in ways that serve their individual interests or values. Nor does it allow us to grasp the changing situation reported in Japan whereby the individual increasingly appreciates the group to the extent that it responds to individual needs (Cummings 1980:197).

Much of our image of the Japanese group model is an account of how human relationships ought to be. That is, it is ideology. The reality is that groups are often subject to competition and conflict, with even the appearance of harmony being quite deceptive. Moreover, Americans are misled by Japanese stereotypes of themselves as group-oriented and harmonious, just as we are misled by stereotypes of ourselves as exclusively individualistically oriented.

Americans have, in fact, conflicting cultural stereotypes. There exists a communitarian ethic in the United States that has powerful roots growing out of our traditional agricultural society. While we highlight the role of individualism, we also have a set of stereotypes, commonly emanating from the sports metaphor, that point to the powerful benefits to be achieved from teamwork. Only with

3. These differences do not need to be large to be significant in the eyes of the employee.

the close coordination of individual assignments are the individual talents on a football team channeled to bring about maximum group performance. These analogies are in common use in our business firms, and motivational speakers from the sports world who invoke such comparisons, like Fran Tarkenton, are in great demand for speaking engagements.

Consider also the contradiction involved when observers applaud teamwork but criticize meetings as wasteful! Again, the issue is what kinds of teamwork or meetings, under what kinds of conditions, produce what kinds of outcomes? To argue that group-based activity such as quality-control circles will not work in American firms because they violate our individualistic ethic hardly reflects the reality of competing values and circumstances.

Some Japanese scholars go so far as to argue that Japanese firms succeeded with small-group problem-solving activities *in spite of* not because of culture. This turns the conventional wisdom of Westerners, not to speak of Japanese traditionalists, on its head. Fujita Yoshitaka argues that only through a strong commitment and strategic and long-term efforts were Japanese managers able to overcome cultural constraints (Fujita 1982:77–86). He notes that traditionally Japanese workers were accustomed to a "do as you are told" style of work in which they had little incentive to think creatively. He sees such practices as deriving from the permanent employment and seniority wage systems, practices often associated with Japanese culture.

Similarly, Shimada Haruo argues that the cooperative labor-management relations upon which small-group activity, information sharing, and other contemporary worker-manager relationships are based, were not bestowed upon Japanese corporations from the beginning. "Rather they were constructed deliberately and at considerable cost." By cost, he refers to the difficulty of coming to terms with a hostile and aggressive labor movement in the early postwar period (Shimada 1982:246). Support for this interpretation can be found in the detailed accounts of individuals who established postwar Japanese employment practices. The Japanese Institute of Labour published a set of interviews with key figures of the postwar period in the personnel departments of major companies such as Nippon Steel and Toyota Motors. What comes through strongly in these presentations is the sense of struggle and personal hardship (expressed in rather typical Japanese melodramatic fashion) experienced by those trying to create new personnel practices during a period of tumultuous upheavals (see, for example, Tanaka 1982). These perspectives provide a healthy corrective to the conventional Western view that simply sees quality-control circles as coming naturally to the Japanese by virtue of their group-oriented culture—a gross distortion of what actually happened and the amount of "sweat" involved in making it happen.

That is not to say that culture does not bestow some advantages—to be read as providing resources—on Japanese managers seeking to introduce small problem-solving groups. It is apparent as one examines the training packages of the Japanese Union of Scientists and Engineers and the typical packages produced by American organizations that the Americans put far more stress on group dynamics. There is an implicit assumption that Americans need more help in navigating these problems. Our supervisors seem less well trained in such techniques as individual motivation through group activity and group problem solving than are the Japanese. Small-group organization is pervasive throughout Japanese society in a way that suggests it provides a basic "code" for how contemporary Japanese think about organizing to solve problems. For example, the group organization of normal learning activities and student responsibility for classroom maintenance tasks documented in Japanese schools stands in sharp contrast to practices in American schools (Cummings 1980). It is reasonable to believe that such experiences during one's formative years provide a strong foundation for subsequent group-oriented activities.

Yet even in Japan tremendous investments were made in training and organizing to get these groups operating effectively in a new problem-solving mode (see Lillrank 1983). After all, you can have close teamwork that is not particularly task-oriented or, worse yet from management's perspective, close teamwork that operates in a way that works against formal organizational objectives. There is, in fact, a large social science literature in the United States on the way in which informal organization at work functions in exactly that fashion.

Basic Arguments

The central questions raised in this book rest on the observation that, in the main period under investigation, 1960–85, American firms moved more slowly and less effectively in adopting small-group activities than Swedish and, especially, Japanese ones. Why was this the case? Generally speaking, the answer is to be found in a confluence of factors, ranging from different labor-market circumstances, labor-management traditions, and the predispositions of major institutional actors (especially the degree of top management consensus) to the willingness of these institutional actors to take joint action to build national infrastructures for diffusing small-group activities.

Through various comparisons I elaborate below on the relevance of these various factors and the linkages among them. Moreover, I also show how the small-group-activities movement took different forms in each country, reflecting the labor-management balance of power, cultural traditions, and, above all, the degree to which national infrastructures developed and operated to diffuse innovations effectively. I focus particularly on the evolution of these national infrastructures, for they tell us much about the commitment of various national interest groups.

The reader will note in examining the above list of causal factors that I take a decidedly "macro" approach in trying to understand what happened, or did not happen, to the small-group-activities movement in each country. It is only in this fashion that one is able to distinguish the forest from the trees. Much contemporary theorizing and empirical research on small-group activities involves researchers, especially industrial or organizational psychologists, reporting factors within organizations that inhibit or enhance the probability of success (Dachler and Wilpert 1978:29–35). Success is typically measured in terms of survival of the innovation or contributions to improved quality and productivity, increased participation, job satisfaction, or reduced employee turnover and absenteeism. The critical factors typically identified as responsible for these outcomes include the mode of innovation, the amount of authority given to group sponsors and leaders, the makeup of the group, its leadership, the group's procedures and objectives, the nature of the organization's technology, how the small-group activities fit in with wider organizational practices, and so forth.

A pattern emerges (also seen in other domains of organizational research) of a variety of often contradictory studies showing how under different conditions one or another micro variable contributes marginally to affecting outcomes. Charles Perrow (1979:96–112) documents just such a pattern in his scathing critique of the accumulated human-relations literature, showing how it fails to demonstrate a clear link between leadership and morale on the one hand and productivity on the other. The application of increasingly complex research methodologies and causal models has only resulted in a loss of applicability and theoretical power. The variables become so numerous that one can hardly generalize to organizations or even to types of organizations.

By shifting from the micro analysis of the social phenomenon under examination to a macro analysis, the opportunity develops for grasping the broader environmental factors behind innovation. As Perrow (1979:110) puts it, "It may be, hopefully, that any theory that has the power to explain a good deal of organizational behavior will have to deal with more general variables than leadership and small-group behavior." In emphasizing such macro explanations as I do, I further assume that the micro variables associated with small-group behavior are randomly distributed and thus have little effect when a large number of organizations are being studied.

In keeping with this vision, I show the importance of understanding the position of the national business leadership toward such innovations. Also to be considered is how these positions interact with national labor-market conditions as well as other variables. In summary, the overall perspective adopted in this book is that this macro approach will produce a far better and more generalizable understanding of the spread of small-group activities across and within firms than a detailed analysis of what makes small-group activities work or not work in particular organizational settings.

This is not to say that I ignore all the micro factors on which many of these outcomes rest. The decision by individual firms to invest in building a national infrastructure rests on the trade-offs these firms perceive, and they will be the subject of further discussion.

Chapter Two

What Is Small-Group Activity?

To say that one is going to study the spread of small-group activities in three countries requires that one identify the phenomenon being spread. The careful reader will have noted some ambiguity implied by the different terms *small-group activities* and *participatory work structures*. Clarification of the relationship between the two terms is central to any serious understanding of the subject.

There are many types of what Europeans, Americans, and Japanese alike usually call "worker participation" (Dachler and Wilpert 1978). It can take the form of representative democracy, with workers' representatives serving on boards of directors (for example, the German co-determination model). It can manifest itself in councils of workers having the dominant decision-making role in firms, as in Yugoslavia (that is, workers' control and self-management). Typically, these types are formal in the sense that the arrangements are prescribed in government rules or collective bargaining arrangements.

Participation can also, however, take the form of direct participation of employees in the everyday decision-making process on the shop or office floor. This may be either formally prescribed by management rules or collective bargaining arrangements or of a more informal nature (the voluntaristic model). In this book, I focus on direct participation, first, because this is an area in which the Swedes and the Japanese have been most innovative; second, because scholarly research suggests that it is the area that matters most to workers (see, for example, Kohn 1976: 111–30); and, third, because direct shop and office floor participation is the primary focus of organized participatory work practices in the United States.

My examination of participation focuses on efforts to directly expand employee control in the everyday decision-making process on the shop and office floor. While the topic is direct participation, it is important to examine the process by which these "solutions" emerged in competition with potential alternatives, such as board representation. It is also important to ask why some forms of direct participation were selected over others and what the implications for the diffusion process were. Finally, it is important to keep in mind that these various approaches to participation are not mutually exclusive. Often we find mixtures of representative and direct participation, as well as formal and informal modes, within the same system of industrial relations.

To examine only part of the participatory system operative in a given country invites distortion. The benefits involved are, however, considerable. One is able to pursue an intensive study of a limited number of cases. Limiting the study to countries that have all emphasized small-group activities enhances the search for explanations of their similarities and differences.

Japan, Sweden, and the United States span a range of variation favorable to the task of comparison. The United States is an example of limited change relative to the other two, both of which have experienced a significant, although varying, degree of institutionalization of small-group activities. There is also variation in their social, economic, and political systems; Sweden may be characterized as social democratic, the United States as liberal capitalist, and Japan as liberal capitalist with a strong developmental thrust. These different political systems vary considerably in their dimensions: group interest, labor-market conditions, managerial problems, political organization, and institutional mobilization. Insofar as culture is a variable partially explaining small-group behavior, one might anticipate that Sweden and the United States, as heirs to the Western cultural tradition, would have more in common with each other than they would with Japan. This is a theme to which I shall return.

What's in a Name?

My analysis thus far is a bit too neat. What are we actually comparing when we say that we are trying to explain the spread of direct shop and office floor participation in decision making in the three countries? It is hard to get a grip on the concept of participation in decision making.

This is because participation can occur in many work domains and in different parts of the decision-making process. There are small-group activities with greater and lesser degrees of employee participation. I selected *small-group activity* as a generic term that would not be weighed down by the specific connotations of *direct participation*. Such a neutral term makes it possible to examine the processes operating in the three countries with less likelihood of attributing values and intentions to actors that do not apply. While *small-group activity* is hardly a household term, at least one U.S. company, Hughes Aircraft Co., has created the title of manager of small-group activities.

In any case, my focus is on *the introduction and spread of small-group activities at the workplace*. Specifically, I examine quality-control circles in the United States and Japan and what were once known as semi-autonomous work groups in Sweden. As implied above, the small-group activities represented by these labels vary in structure and process across the three nations and indeed over time in a given nation.

What is involved in quality-control circles and self-managing teams? Since QC circles were introduced in Japan under the auspices of the Japanese Union of Scientists and Engineers (JUSE) it is appropriate to use its definition:

The QC circle is a small group within the same workshop that voluntarily carries out quality-control activity. The small group continuously conducts control and improvement of the workshop as one part in the chain of companywide quality-control activity. In this fashion, utilizing quality-control techniques, the small groups carry out self-development and mutual development.

(JUSE 1970:1; my translation)

The circles are relatively autonomous units composed of small groups of workers, usually of common status, in each workshop. A 1983 JUSE survey reports that typically circles had five to eight members. Some 60 percent of the groups choose their own leaders, and some 20 percent rotate the leadership; still others have staff specialists as leaders, or leaders are appointed by the supervisor (Lillrank 1984). The circles usually meet once a week for an hour or so; they are parallel organizations in that they are not directly a part of the work process. The workers are taught fairly simple statistical techniques and modes of problem solving and are guided by leaders in the selection and solving of problems. The circles concentrate on solving job-related quality problems, broadly conceived as improving methods of production as part of companywide efforts. The circle solutions are presented to management for action, with the circle members having no authority to implement the solutions on their own. Quality-control circles are supposed to allow for the acquisition of skills by workers, the development of career potential, cooperative activity, and the like. If functioning properly, they should give workers a sense of control over their everyday activities on the shop floor.

As the concept of the circles spread to the United States, they became separated from their quality-control foundation in Japan. As a consequence, they also became less concerned with statistical methods and more focused on building process skills (for example, how to run an effective meeting). Thus, a case can be made that the circles themselves are not the same institution in Japan and the United States. Reflecting this difference, they are known in Japan as quality-control (or QC) circles, while in the United States they are generally known simply as quality circles.

The Swedish idea of self-managing teams or autonomous work groups[1] is that workers make their own decisions regarding work allocation, recruitment, planning, budgeting, production, quality, maintenance, and purchasing. The group members are not merely carrying out a certain number of tasks. They are working together on a continuous basis to coordinate different tasks. They take responsibility for the organization of work and take the necessary measures to cope with the work of the entire unit. Job rotation among members at their initiative is seen as a normal part of work activity. A great deal of mutual help, joint responsibility for the total operation, and continuing opportunities for learning are expected.

This ideal has seldom been fully realized in practice, but it constitutes a set of objectives toward which many Swedish companies have made partial progress. We can see that even modest implementation of the concept of autonomous work groups would give workers greater control over the work process than is the case with

1. I use the terms *semi-autonomous work teams, autonomous work teams,* and *self-managing teams* interchangeably.

quality circles. Workers in such groups can not only make recommendations based on their analysis, but can make decisions about their work and implement them in a broad framework established by management and unions. To be sure, such action tends *in practice* to have been focused on working conditions, task assignment, work methods, personal equipment, and establishment of daily routine, while broader management issues tend to be left to higher-level management and union officials. The former are the same work domains that occupy quality-control circles, but the self-managing teams, unlike circles, in principle involve themselves in personnel matters and budget decision making as well. In practice, too, self-managing teams often seem to have greater access to decision-making processes than do quality circles. Moreover, they are part of the work process, not a parallel institution.

In contrast to self-managing teams, there tends to be less of a gap between the ideal of quality circles and how they actually operate. This relatively close correspondence suggests that quality circles represent a tighter (better-defined requirements) and less demanding (more realizable in terms of fewer required changes from conventional practices) package than self-managing teams.

Some Differences among
the Three Countries

Consider the following differences: in Japan the key term used to explain the innovation as it began to be applied was *decentralization of responsibility*. By decentralization the Japanese do not generally mean delegation of authority to offices down the hierarchical structure. Rather, for them decentralization means the taking of responsibility for objectives by large numbers of people (cf. Kalleberg and Lincoln 1989). Generally, the Japanese simply speak of small-group activities (*shōshūdan katsudō*). In Japan quality-control circles have allowed workers to play a greater role in the input phase of the decision-making process, but management retains control of the decision itself. The term *decentralization of responsibility* does not suggest a voluntaristic process in which workers organize to obtain greater participation for themselves or choose to democratize the workplace. Rather, we get a sense of small-group activities being imposed by management as part of its personnel practices. The extraordinarily high rates of participation in small-group activity in Japanese firms support this interpretation.

Small-group activities were commonly introduced as part of a corporate strategy to mobilize all the resources of a firm to overcome foreign and domestic competition. In this sense, management sought to make participation a responsibility, an obligation, of employees rather than to provide an opportunity for them to express their individual talents or "self-actualize," California style. Moreover, the term *democratization* was seldom heard. It was not until the late 1970s that one even began to hear of a stress on participation in management (*keiei sanka*) in a sense even approximating American usage. Rather, the focus initially was on engineers aiming to solve quality and cost problems in the workplace; the motivational aspects were an afterthought that only came to be explicitly discussed many years later.

One of the first scholars to talk about small-group activity in the context of participation was Ueda Toshio, whose 1975 book with Hirota Kimiyoshi (Hirota and Ueda 1975:25) discussed the newly raised expectation that small-group activities might lead to greater participation (*sanka*). This was some thirteen years after the first quality-control circles were formed. The increasing tendency of interpreters of the movement to link it to participation occurred partly in response to positive American definitions of what they were doing. Prior to this time, when the Japanese used the term *keiei sanka* and spoke of democratization of management, they were not even thinking of small-group activities. This remains true to a great extent even today. Rather, the Japanese think primarily in terms of systems of indirect participation, such as the widely diffused labor-management consultation system. Internationally, the term *keiei sanka* conjures up for them images of the German co-determination system and other formal representational approaches in continental Europe.

There is another sense in which the term *participation* has been used by the Japanese, and it is quite revealing. This usage refers to the *necessity of the act of participation* in small-group activities. Shiba Shoji summarizes this perspective well when he bluntly states that the real meaning is that:

Every worker participates in the same workshop. Let us say there are seven workers in the workshop who work together on the same production line in the workshop. All seven workers have to participate in the circle activities. Isolation of workers in the workshop is not allowed. Small-group activity with the participation of every worker is aimed at improving the work in which they are engaged. QCC activity is not an activity for amusement but an activity for the improvement of work.

(Shiba 1983a:13)

We see clearly here just how Japanese use of the term *participation* contrasts sharply with how Americans have typically used it.

In the United States, managers often speak of participation in management, quality of work life, and employee involvement to explain what they are doing (Kanter 1983:44–46). It is precisely for this reason that we mistakenly equate participation in the American sense with what the Swedes and the Japanese have been doing in the area of small-group activities.

To a somewhat greater degree than in Japan, the terms *democratization* and *humanization* have been used—and often confused—in the United States. Nevertheless, this is a rather subdued theme relative to other terminology. One leading academic consultant explained to me in 1985: "I used to use the term *democratization*, but I don't anymore because I find it gets in the way of operational objectives." There appears to be considerable confusion about what is meant by the terminology used in the United States. A 1982 study by the New York Stock Exchange that focused on the concept of quality of working life (QWL) and investment in human resources (Freund and Epstein 1984:120) defines QWL as "the effort to encourage employees to participate in the key decisions that affect and determine day-to-day work patterns" (for more elaborate definitions of QWL, see Walton 1975:91–97). The concept of participation appears to be central to how most American managers have understood what they are doing. Management sees itself as developing tools to tap unused human resources through participation. The motivational consequences in terms of job satisfaction and worker morale are commonly highlighted.

In Sweden the early movement was strongly punctuated by expressions stressing joint influence and democratization of the workplace. In an influential book entitled *Form and Content of Industrial Democracy*, originally published in Scandinavia in 1964, Fred Emery and Einar Thorsrud argue that the objective of industrial democracy cannot be attained solely by worker representation on boards of directors. Rather, this must be supplemented by an approach at a level where "a large proportion of employees are both able and willing to participate" (Emery and Thorsrud 1969:86). They have in mind, of course, direct shop and office floor participation. The Swedes have stressed changing power relationships between managers and employees at all levels. As one Swedish commentator notes, even when the North American advocates talk about workplace democracy as a goal of new work structures, they commonly have in mind "democratic leadership styles" rather than a transformation of structural relationships as envisioned by many Swedes (Leymann 1982:47).

A central element of the democratization theme in Sweden has been the focus on work group autonomy as an end in itself. The contrast here with the Japanese case is particularly stark. The Japanese version of participation emphasizes teaching workers conventional and nonconventional engineering and statistical skills to design and improve their own jobs under close managerial direction and control. Japanese managers have achieved a more thoroughgoing implementation of scientific management to an extent that its founder, Frederick Taylor, could not even have imagined. Whereas Taylor stressed the importance of managers' getting to know worker capabilities, in the relatively uneducated immigrant America of his time, managers saw these capabilities as quite limited. In contrast to that situation, Japanese managers have gotten increasingly well educated workers to participate in their own job design, thereby tapping powerful motivational principles associated with challenging workers' individual abilities and providing them a limited sense of control over the workplace (see Shimada 1988). To be sure, to accommodate worker interests, managers made some important modifications of traditional hierarchical control structures and scientific management practices. They moved toward decentralized operational decision making. This meant that workers together with production engineers could make many decisions with regard to organizing production as long as they met the demanding improvement goals set by management. It was in this context that circles emerged. Finally, in contrast to traditional scientific management, Japanese management aimed at building a broader rather than a narrower range of individual job skills for its labor force.

The popular symbols and choice of language used to characterize a social movement tell us a great deal about the motivation of actors and the kinds of constraints they impose or have imposed on them. In the case of Japan, the focusing of the debate on *decentralization of responsibility* tells us that management was pretty much in charge and could impose its own categories and labels on developments. In the case of Sweden, the focus on *industrial democracy* tells us first that management did not have full control of the agenda. Moreover, the Swedes had a highly centralized labor-management decision-making system. This meant that advocates of semi-autonomous work groups in labor, management, and academic circles could argue forcefully and believably that there was something missing at the shop and office floor level in terms of democratic decision making. Based on that view, they further maintained that semi-autonomous work groups could fill that vacuum. In the United States, unlike in many Western European countries, there is a labor movement with an active shop floor presence, at least in the unionized sector. This has to a considerable extent preempted the industrial democracy theme. Instead, in the United States there is a rather more modest focus on *participation and employee involvement*, with the motivational consequences being given great emphasis.

The major implication of this extended discussion is that in examing small-group activities cross-nationally, there is inevitably an element of comparing apples and oranges. Small-group activities are not the same across nations. Rather than try to eliminate this difference in what is being compared—which I judged to be a futile exercise—my strategy has been to acknowledge those differences. The task then is to try to develop plausible explanations for the way these practices developed and the effects they might produce.

Three Snapshots

The United States

In the early 1970s extensive discussion of the need to humanize work began in the United States. We heard of job redesign, job enlargement, and job enrichment. Although the terms are often used loosely, the job humanization movement has focused primarily on the redesign of jobs, envisioned as occurring either horizontally (job enlargement), creating more variety in the job, or vertically (job enrichment), expanding the domain of employee decision making. Although there are numerous similarities with the earlier human-relations movement (Berg, Freedman, and Freeman 1978), a distinctive characteristic of the new movement is its focus on changing the job itself.

Whatever the forms, the programs and proposals designed to humanize work have one common denominator: they all involve attempts to reduce alienation and increase job satisfaction by increasing employees' participation in workplace decisions and job variety, thus making more effective use of workers' potential. Ideally, these changes are supposed to improve organizational efficiency and productivity while enhancing the quality of work life. Improved quality of work life involves workers controlling those aspects of their work that directly affect their everyday lives.

When one examines the adoption and diffusion of small-group activities of this sort in the United States over the period 1960–85, one is hard put to say that many of the noble ideas outlined above have been institutionalized in large numbers of American corporate entities. In the 1970s self-managing teams won only very limited acceptance here. In companies like General Electric, where a number of plants adopted some version of self-managing teams, they had all died out by the 1980s. Generally, the number of plants adopting them was small, and the labor force of such plants was often atypical as a result of special recruitment procedures. The little that was accomplished in the 1970s was commonly done in nonunion plants. Generally speaking, more was done in new plants; far less was tried or succeeded in established plants. Even less was accomplished in office work. In addition, even in allegedly "successful" experiments, such as the General Foods plant in Topeka, Kansas, the innovation was slow to diffuse to other plants in the company, not to speak of its offices (Walton 1978).

Finally, there is more form than substance to many of the announced programs of U.S. companies. Given the ambiguity of goals and technology, it is not surprising that it is often difficult to judge what has actually happened, why it happened or did not happen, and whether what happened is good (see March and Olsen 1976). Organizations often develop myths about what they are doing in small-group activities, and, because of the lack of agreement over what constitutes participation, they have a great deal of latitude to do just that. This can be used as a vehicle to encourage or discourage the diffusion process. Small-group activities can be adopted ceremonially, but in practice be buffered from actual work, so that little substantive change occurs (Meyer and Rowan 1977). This allows forms to be adopted without producing significant change. With their stress on "off-line" activity, quality circles lend themselves to this outcome.

I attended a number of company presentations in the late 1970s in which, once all the rhetoric was stripped away, the bulk of the participation program consisted of workers being able to have lockers near their work sites or the plant management having established a recreation program. In general, one sees many "programs" in the United States that have beginnings and ends, but relatively few instances in which small-group activities are highly institutionalized.

Notwithstanding these observations, there is a way in which, as Rosabeth Kanter reminds us, talking about innovation often serves as a precursor for it. She documents the transformation of topics and treatments in business periodicals between 1960 and 1980, noting the rise to prominence of "human resource management" and "participative management" (Kanter 1983:44–46). It is a sign of our times that a company such as Motorola used the slogan "Quality and productivity through employee participation in management" as part of its newspaper advertising in 1985.

The 1980s have indeed produced a burst of experimentation with small-group activities by U.S. firms. Inspired in part by the rapid internationalization of the economy, and in particular by the powerful competitive threat posed by the Japanese, both management and labor have been forced to reexamine the contributions of small-group activities. The New York Stock Exchange national survey of human-resource programs and QWL in 1982, based on a sample of 49,000 U.S. corporations (27 percent response rate), and including both manufacturing and nonmanufacturing firms, documents this explosive growth. Of the firms sampled with 500 or more employees, 15 percent had initiated quality circles. The figure rose to 22 percent in firms of over 5,000 employees. Overall, 19 percent of manufacturing firms reported adopting quality circles, compared to 9 percent of nonmanufacturing firms. In keeping with my observations about the suddenness of this growth, the study reports that in corporations of over 500 employees, quality circles were the most rapidly growing human-resource activity. Indeed, the report states that quality circles had come to epitomize the QWL concept. Some 74 percent of the quality circles surveyed in firms of over 500 employees in the spring of 1982 had been established for less than two years, with 85 percent reporting less than five years' experience (Freund and Epstein 1984).

Yet caution is necessary in interpreting these data. For a firm to say it has initiated quality circles does not mean that a majority of its employees, or even a significant minority, are in fact participating in them. Indeed, one seldom finds large plants or offices, much less companies, in which more than a minority of the labor force are participating in quality circles. In my 1985 survey of 236 circle adopters, only 24 percent of respondents reported more than 25 percent of their workforce participating in quality circles, and only 11.9 percent reported more than 35 percent of their workforce doing so. Moreover, there are no data at the national level to indicate that quality circles have been institutionalized in American corporations. Circles also have a more limited impact and pose a more modest threat to management's hierarchical decision-making structure than self-managing teams.

Despite the initial excitement over quality circles in the United States in the early 1980s, by the mid 1980s the amount of attention being devoted to them in the business press and management journals had fallen off dramatically. Inside companies they were less and less a topic of conversation. They were now being publicly described as a fad, with discussion focusing on what would succeed them (Lawler and Mohrman 1985: 65–71). For many companies, self-managing teams became the new game in town.

Japan

The Japanese movement for small-group activities began in the early 1960s and accelerated thereafter. There was an increasing emphasis on decentralization of decision making; employees were to take responsibility for a variety of everyday decisions for which management representatives had hitherto been responsible (functions like maintenance, quality control, and safety). The vehicle for these efforts was "small groupism" (*shōshūdanshugi*), as the Japa-

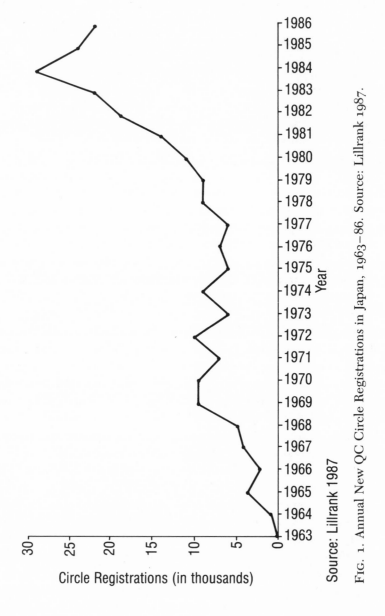

Circle Registrations (in thousands)

Year

Source: Lillrank 1987

FIG. 1. Annual New QC Circle Registrations in Japan, 1963–86. Source: Lillrank 1987.

nese called it. The idea was to make the small group the responsible unit in this decentralization effort.

A variety of surveys suggests that these practices are now widespread. The Japanese Union of Scientists and Engineers, which registers QC circles, reported some 250,000 circles, with over two million members, in early 1987. In addition, JUSE "conservatively" estimates unregistered QC circle members to total an additional five times the number of those in registered circles. I would suggest the more conservative figure of three times that number, which would nonetheless bring the total to about eight million employees, or roughly one out of every six Japanese employees.

Figure 1 depicts annual new quality-control circle registrations from 1963 to 1986. There was one relatively short burst of increases in the registration rate and one major sustained one. The first was from 1966 to 1969, when registrations rose from roughly 2,000 to almost 10,000 circles a year. The second occurred between 1977 and 1984, when new registrations rose from some 5,500 in 1977 to almost 30,000 circles a year in 1984. This latter point represents the peak of the diffusion rate; growth has since slowed, as befitting a mature movement.

The difficulty of estimating the amount and spread of QC circle activities arises in large part because many firms do not use the term *quality-control circle*, but rather engage in a variety of related small-group activities (typical categories of small-group activities in Japanese surveys in addition to circles include zero-defect groups, improvement groups, and Japanese versions of management by objective).

A survey of small-group activity by the Japanese Ministry of Labour in 1972 reveals that some 40 percent of firms with over 100 employees then reported such activity. For firms with over 1,000 employees, the figure was 70 percent, and in every size category firms with unions were more likely to have small-group activity than those without unions. About half the establishments reported that they established their small-group activities on existing organizational arrangements, with the rest stating that they had created new structures (Japan, Ministry of Labour 1973:36, 138). A 1977 follow-up Ministry of Labour survey reports strikingly similar findings, with 40 percent of the establishments with over 100 employees again reporting small-group activities (Japan, Ministry of

Labour 1978:166–71). By 1984, however, 60 percent of establishments with over 100 employees reported such activities, with the figure rising to 84 percent for firms with over 5,000 employees (Japan, Ministry of Labour 1985:14). These and other survey data suggest again that the growth of small-group activities in manufacturing has peaked. Manufacturing and utilities record the highest levels of small-group activity with services and the wholesale and retail trades recording significantly lower levels.

Although it does not show up in the aggregate data, JUSE reports that QC circles have spread rapidly in recent years to the nonmanufacturing operations of manufacturing firms (for example, sales and administration) and to the service sector, particularly banking, insurance, and hotels, and including even restaurants, nightclubs, and bars. Finally, in contrast to the United States, it is typical to find firms and plants and offices reporting over 90 percent participation in small-group activities. Just how typical can be seen from a JUSE survey that found that 74 percent of the companies with quality circles had a policy requiring all employees (*zenin sanka*) to participate (Lillrank 1984:8). That many of these small-group activities have survived for twenty or more years suggests that reasonably high levels of institutionalization have been achieved. Relative to the United States, there is little basis for thinking of the quality-circle movement in Japan as a fad.

Consistent with earlier discussions, a major characteristic of QC circles is that they tend not to threaten the hierarchical structure of authority as much as some other forms of direct participation. First-line supervisors tend not to be threatened by the circles, and indeed in the initial stages of the movement, they often served as leaders of them. In my survey of the 267 early adopters of QC circles in Japan, I asked managers: "Is it the experience of your company that the scope and/or content of the first-line supervisor's authority must be changed significantly in order to have this form of small-group activity function properly?" Only 6.5 percent of the respondents answered yes, with the remainder answering no.

Sweden

Swedish efforts to develop small-group activities crystallized in the late 1960s with emphasis on autonomous or self-steering work groups (*självstyrande grupper*) as the unit of production. These ideas about decentralization of decision making spread rapidly. There was a long and intensive public debate centering on broad issues of democratization and social justice. It is more difficult to evaluate how well these activities are actually diffused in Sweden than in the case of Japan. The reasons are themselves revealing; they reflect the Japanese penchant for national surveys and systems of formal registration. On the Swedish side they reflect, in part, the strategy of diffusion adopted by the technical department of the Swedish Employers' Confederation (SAF).

As noted earlier, the goal of autonomous work groups is for workers to make their own decisions regarding work allocation, recruitment, planning, budgeting, production, quality, maintenance, and purchasing. It is an ideal seldom, if ever, realized in practice, and certainly far less commonly achieved than the English-language public relations efforts of SAF and of companies like Volvo would suggest (Gyllenhammar 1977; Swedish Employers' Confederation 1975). Yet considerably modified versions of this decentralized work system did come into effect in most large Swedish firms, and, unlike in Japan, they spread rapidly to the public sector as well. Gunzburg and Hammarström (1979:39–40) report estimates of well over one thousand firms with significant work reorganization efforts in the mid 1970s. Albert Cherns (1979:360–61) ranks Sweden first among European countries in the extent to which the "quality of working life movement" had been diffused. Volvo, the most prominent Swedish innovator, points out that since the opening of the revolutionary and much-discussed Kalmar plant, with its group work organization, in 1974, it has built nine new plants whose design has been strongly influenced by the Kalmar experience.

Yet it has not been easy to maintain the early momentum of shop and office floor innovation. During the 1970s some twenty new laws relating to labor and national collective agreements came into effect, mandating representation for employees on boards of directors, new labor welfare measures, changes in working conditions, and a co-determination law among other things. There was a shift toward working out the implications of this new legislation, particularly the co-determination law. Many shop and office floor participatory efforts dried up or failed to diffuse from experimental units to the wider organization. Such was the case with Atlas Copco, a large manufacturer that figured prominently in the early days of experimentation. The uncertainty surrounding the loss of power by the Social Democratic government in the late 1970s also contributed to a wait-and-see attitude on the part of many employers. The struggle over the "wage earners' fund" proposed by the Social Democrats further diverted attention from small-group activities.

It was not until the 1982 agreement between the unions and the employers' federation, not long after the Social Democrats had again returned to power, that the framework for the application of the co-determination law was put in place and one began to see new life in the shop and office floor small-group-activities movement. But it is an approach chastened by past experiences. Managers no longer talk about autonomous or self-steering groups; instead their vocabulary stresses group work (*grupparbete*), group organization (*grupporganisation*), teamwork (*lagarbete*), and "the little factory in the large factory," with a renewed stress on productivity and quality improvement and new concern for flexible manufacturing systems and proper use of databases.

Based on the above observations, it seems reasonable to conclude that in the three countries surveyed, small-group activities have spread most rapidly and broadly in Japan, followed by Sweden and then the United States. However, we must constantly remind ourselves of the partial character of such observations. We are recording the tip of the iceberg. Much small-group activity is of an informal nature that is not easily recognized even by participants, much less recorded by outsiders.

Moreover, these observations do not mean that Japan has the greatest amount of employee participation in the American sense of that term or the most democratized workplace in the Swedish sense of that term. Consider the findings of the 1983 cross-national study of workers' attitudes sponsored by the Aspen Institute for Humanistic Studies and the Public Agenda Foundation, which surveyed the amount of workplace discretion (freedom to make decisions about work) employees said they had. Across industries, and for both white-collar and blue-collar jobs, the researchers found that Swedish employees consistently scored higher on their scale of employee discretion than did Japanese employees (Yankelovich et al. 1983:44–45; Zetterberg et al. 1983:140–41). Clearly, the amount of discretion employees have at work is a major factor in how much control they have over their immediate work environment.

These findings underscore my earlier observation that the spread of small-group activities in Japan was tied to management decentralization of responsibility rather than to voluntary employee participation in decision making per se. One can assume more responsibility without necessarily having a sense of more discretion. We should not impute increased employee participation and control to the spread of small-group activities without sound empirical support. Moreover, the amount of discretion at work that employees report arises not only from small-group activities but from other sources as well. Not all cross-national differences in work relationships result from recent experiences with small-group activity.

Chapter Three

Decision Making and Research Strategies

Central to this study is the concept of innovation. I am interested in how managers, union officials, and employees came to conceive, introduce, and spread the novel approach of using small-group activities in industry—a social technology—to solve problems and sometimes to organize production. I define *innovation* as a technology new to a given organization and *diffusion* as the process by which this innovation spreads to different organizations and to different parts of the same organization (see Tornatzky et al. 1983:2). Although the rate of diffusion may be faster in one country than in another, they may all end up in the same place over time. This represents a convergence perspective based on the assumption that there are functional forms of diffusion models, an approach that would leave little room for the long-term influence of cultural factors.

I shall examine the incentives to adopt such new practices and the nature of the obstacles that stood in the way of such adoption. In examining the spread of new ideas from one location and set of individuals to others, I ask: What are the patterns regulating the flow of ideas? How is it that some social strata get identified as carriers of these new ideas? Are there special agents of diffusion? How does one set of ideas get established, if it does, as "best practice"[1] and come to be seen as a general solution to a particular set of prob-

1. *Best practice* is a term used in economics to suggest that there is one specific best way (best technology) to accomplish a particular objective.

34

lems? Many of these questions, though sometimes expressed in different terms, have been asked in typical studies of the diffusion process, and this book will be no exception (cf. Rogers and Shoemaker 1971).

Still, there are a number of problems with the traditional social science literature on diffusion that need to be addressed. In dealing with the political sphere, the classic literature on diffusion centered on the development of an appropriate infrastructure for diffusion and the receptivity of adopting units, rather than on how these factors are influenced by the interplay of interests in the broad political and economic arenas (see, for example, Rogers and Shoemaker 1971). It is for this reason that I shall weave the perspective of political economy into my analysis.

Most important, one needs a causal model of decision making to order and explain the process of social change. It has often been pointed out that studies of the diffusion process seem to lack theoretical content and therefore ultimately reach a dead end. What kind of theory of decision making will help us understand the diffusion of small-group activities?

Small-group activities take place, or do not take place, in specific local organizations, which may create organizations at the national level whose mission it is to spread these new practices. In the end, the latter organizations are the main focus of my analysis. We need a mid-range theory of decision making that provides an explanatory framework for these organizational and interorganizational activities.

The test for a useful theoretical framework is what provides the best fit with the data and forces the researcher to ask novel questions, thereby revealing fundamental characteristics of the phenomenon under investigation. Theories of "loose coupling" partially fulfilled these objectives for this research project. It is a decision-making model that allows us to flesh out the skeletal characteristics of the diffusion process through a set of contingent decisions made by the various actors.

The Loose-Coupling Model

Social scientists developed the "loose-coupling," or "garbage can," model in the 1970s, primarily in the context of their study of educational institutions. In this model the stress is on more or less seren-dipitous combinations of problems and solutions. That is, decisions occur when elements from streams of problems, solutions, partici-pants, and opportunities come together. But they often come to-gether under conditions of great uncertainty, such that there is a weak correspondence between specific problems and particular solutions.

This model may be juxtaposed to the traditional rational model of decision making in which problems are identified and a search is instituted for the most suitable solutions. In the rational model, means are tied to ends in a logical fashion, actions are tied to inten-tions, solutions are guided by imitation of one's neighbor, prioritiz-ing of goals takes place, feedback and evaluation control subse-quent decisions, and past experience constrains present activity.

In the case of small-group activities, the rational model would work as follows. Managers identify a set of problems they are hav-ing, such as poor productivity, low worker morale, or lack of con-trol over the labor force, and after a search conclude that small-group activities will best address these problems. They learn what "best practice" is and they introduce small-group activities, con-stantly modifying their practices based on feedback so as to best achieve their objectives.

My research suggests that while such a rational model can be relevant to certain parts of the adoption and diffusion process, a fuller accounting requires a much more flexible theoretical model. For as managers and employees wrestled with the adoption pro-cess, what I often saw were ambiguity, uncertainty, ignorance, conflicting goals, and "solutions chasing problems." Managers don't know what they want until they see what they can get; in this sense, solutions are used to formulate problems.

How can this be? The early research on loose coupling and the garbage can model was conducted in universities, on school boards, and in local government institutions that were characterized by an "organized anarchy" in the sense that the objectives or participants often varied, best practices were hard to define, and responsibili-ties for decisions often unclear. We, however, are examining busi-ness firms in the private sector, where objectives can presumably be stated relatively clearly, where a technology associating alternatives with outcomes is reasonably well known, and where there is a stable division of labor by which specific individuals and groups specialize in certain decisions (Cohen, March, and Olsen 1976:24).

The resolution of this seeming paradox lies not in the characteristics of participation or small-group activities per se but in the fact that we are talking about innovation. Uncertainty and ambiguity are the central features of innovative activity, and they are resolved only over time through learning activity. Louis Tornatzky and his associates arrive independently at this same conclusion when they state that "a typical innovation process is likely to have many of the aspects of 'garbage can' decision sequences" (1983:18). Characterized by uncertainty and ambiguity, the innovation process is like a floating capsule within the organization, partially insulated from normal organizational rules and processes. Indeed, one of the areas of ambiguity is the extent to which it should be insulated from normal rules. Only with the passage of time and routinization of the innovation does the protective wall dissolve and "normal functioning" resume.

We can see the uncertainty operative in the introduction of small-group activity through examining the organizational choices it represents for a firm. Even allowing for significant national variation, we find that decisions to adopt small-group activities involve organizational choices in which goals are problematic and technologies are ambiguous and only partially understood. Participation in the decision to introduce small-group activities is itself often fluid.[2]

Consider first the issue of goals and objectives. For management, there are many possible diverse goals that can potentially be served by small-group activities. Among them are increasing productivity, increasing product quality, reducing the ratio of indirect to direct employees, improving worker morale and reducing alienation, democratization of the workplace, meeting public pressures, more effective utilization of the labor force, good public relations, reducing employee turnover and absenteeism, reducing worker grievances, weakening unions, and developing cooperative rela-

---

2. March and Olsen (1976:38–53) refer to this as "attention structures." Studying the process of participation in decisions about participation contains its own set of ironies.

tions with the unions. While some of these objectives are not additive and are achieved only at the expense of others, others complement one another. Moreover, a variety of measures other than small-group activity may potentially contribute to the solution of each of these "problems." In addition, action taken to achieve some of these objectives might have adverse consequences on the achievement of still other organizational objectives.

Management goals will vary depending on the level of management. Middle management often sees small-group activity as a threat to its authority and prestige, and top management may see small-group activities as an opportunity to cut out layers of deadwood in management. Other parties, such as unions and workers, will have their own objectives. In sum, the goals toward which small-group activity is directed are problematic, with management having difficulty choosing the objectives to be served.

A similar case can be made for the ambiguity of the technology, by which I mean the technique of conducting small-group activity. The dispute over technique has been considerable. Scholars have often introduced their ideas on small-group activities at a high level of abstraction, so that practitioners are at a loss as to how to proceed. Competing agents of diffusion will offer different solutions on which small-group activities to adopt and how to execute them, with the potential user again left in a confused state. If failure occurs, it can be attributed to poor technique or the inappropriateness of the overall approach. Moreover, various proprietary interests may limit and distort the flow of information between firms. The belief that every firm, plant, and office has a unique culture that requires a special adaptation of the technology makes it difficult to specify the same appropriate technology across firms.

The difficulty of measuring the outcomes resulting from use of the technology of small-group activities and relating these outcomes to specific inputs also contributes to its ambiguity. Although some of the specific models being advocated are presented as self-contained packages, many provide little in the way of detailed guidelines. This diffuseness makes unclear just how much of an impact adoption will have on the organization in the long run and how much and what else will have to change in the organization as a result of adopting small-group activities.

All this further reinforces the ambiguity of the technology.[3] Managers prefer packaged solutions whose cost and outcomes are, if not guaranteed, at least defined and limited (Cherns 1979). I shall examine how the three nations handled this ambiguity in technology, whether there were variations in the degree of ambiguity of different packages, how these ambiguities were resolved over time, and whether the resolution involved joint organizational activity.

The issue of who can, should, and does participate in the decisions by the firm to innovate in the area of small-group activity is also commonly unclear, at least in the initial stage. James March and Johan Olsen (1976) argue that this follows logically from a situation in which goals and technology are unclear.

Consider the case of the United States. My survey of American firms that have adopted quality-control circles shows that sponsorship was widely dispersed among a broad range of departments, from quality assurance to personnel. The personnel department often has an adversary relation with labor and a vested interest in conflict. Consequently, it is often ill-equipped to undertake such initiatives. Other departments, such as human-resource development and training and education, are possible candidates for the role of sponsor, except that, like personnel, they are commonly low-status departments without the necessary clout in the organization to ensure the acceptance of proposed work reorganization. Quality assurance sometimes took responsibility, but it, too, tended to have relatively low status, at least in the late 1970s and early 1980s, when much of the initial experimentation took place. Moreover, at a number of companies I discovered that small-group activities emerged in the late 1980s as disputed turf between the newly revitalized quality department and the labor relations managers. Finally, the relative obligations and rights of staff versus line operations personnel to make and enforce decisions about small-group activities were often unclear in many firms. Staff were given the responsibility of undertaking small-group activities, but only the line people could "make it happen."

The ambiguity of goals, technology, and who is to participate in

3. Sahal (1981:60) adopts a similar view on the ambiguity of technology transfer. He focuses on the "technical know-how" bottled up in the system of its origin and the need for painstaking adaptation of the technology to its new environment.

the decision to innovate all make the choice process surrounding small-group activity one in which loose coupling is the norm. Only with the passage of time and either the dropping of the innovation or its routinization do these conditions disappear.

Finally, in the context of the loose-coupling model, it is important to examine the process by which given models of small-group activities were selected over available alternatives, and by what criteria and with what incentives for individuals and interest groups. It is also important to investigate whether certain characteristics of specific organizational sponsors, such as their membership, constituency, prestige, or size of budget, aid significantly in explaining the success or failure of the diffusion of given models of small-group activity (see Hirsch 1972). Where possible, I specify how the agenda of opportunities for choice emerges among relevant interest groups and organizations. This is a major focus of my investigation, especially in part 2.

The Microeconomics of Decision Making about Small-Group Activities

Thus far, I have concentrated on the nature of the problems faced by individual firms considering the adoption of small-group activities. Problematic goals, ambiguous technology, and confusion about decision rights are characteristics of the innovation process and define the loose-coupling model. Now I want to address the question of whether there are ways in which these problems can be resolved more efficiently than through trial-and-error corporate activities.

The analysis in the second half of this book concerns the development of the national infrastructure for the diffusion of small-group activities. That is, it deals with the macropolitics of the spread of small-group activities. Embedded in this focus is a central premise of the book: that the building of a national infrastructure for diffusion has been central to the successful spreading of small-group activities. By "successful spreading," I mean that this infrastructure has the potential to contribute to smoothing the decision-making process, thereby resolving the various problems just described more quickly and efficiently.

Yet there are many innovations that spread through the market as firms adopt them without requiring the creation of a national infrastructure. What is it that distinguishes these alternative approaches? Why would the spread of small-group activities be strengthened through the support of a national infrastructure? Why can't firms themselves simply build or acquire the necessary expertise to conduct small-group activities? Here the macropolitical approach requires an understanding of the microeconomics involved in firm-level decision making.

Transaction cost analysis, the framework elaborated by Oliver Williamson, provides a basis for understanding the underlying principles involved (Williamson 1985). I provide a very brief overview to set the stage for subsequent analysis. Transaction cost economics maintains that the choice of institutional arrangements (governance structures) results from the underlying differences in the attributes of transactions. This involves "an examination of the comparative costs of planning, adapting, and monitoring task completion under alternative governance structures." The expectation is that the firm will adopt a strategy of economizing on transaction costs under conditions of uncertainty.

A key concern is identifying under what conditions a firm will internalize a particular function, as opposed to contracting for its provision. Attributes of the contracting process include above all asset specificity. Here the question is: Are the assets that are developed "dedicated assets" or can they easily be redeployed for use in other transactions with other firms? In the area of small-group activities, we are concerned primarily with human asset specificity and, by extension, with what I would call "organizational routine" assets.

The other two attributes of importance are the behavioral assumptions of bounded rationality and opportunism. *Bounded rationality* refers to the fact that human agents intend to be rational but are only partially successful. *Opportunism* is defined as seeking one's own interest with guile. Creating and taking advantage of an asymmetry in information with one's bargaining partner with regard to one's true expertise or costs is an example of opportunism.

The principal ways in which transactions differ are in asset specificity, uncertainty, and frequency of occurrence, and it is the nature of transactions that will determine which governance structures (types of organizations) are appropriate. We can clarify this most easily by turning directly to elaborating the case of small-group activities.

In all three countries, businesses faced the issues of whether to adopt small-group activities and, if so, how to go about acquiring the necessary expertise. They could choose to develop such expertise themselves, building their own internal competence and relying on sketchy reports in the public domain; they could choose to acquire much of that expertise through the market, primarily through contractual arrangements with consultants; or they could choose to join forces with other firms to build a national organization (or take advantage of an existing one) to serve as a forum for a dialogue among companies and develop and diffuse the necessary assets—human capital and organizational skills—to successfully implement small-group activities.[4] There were a variety of collaborative arrangements that could be considered, some of which I shall discuss in describing the various forms that developed in the three countries.[5]

Which governance structures should be selected to provide the organizational expertise required for introducing and operating small-group activities? Let us consider the abovementioned options in order. Firms could simply opt to develop the required expertise among their existing employees. But this would be a laborious task given the vast difference between these new practices and conventional practices, uncertainty about what is required, and the rapid evolution of best practices among the many firms experimenting with them in each country. There are large start-up costs associated with instituting small-group activities. The cost of creating state-of-the art quality-circle training materials for managers, facilitators,

4. This approach is broadly comparable to William Ouchi's (1984) application of Williamson's framework to his analysis of industrial associations. Ouchi, however, never works out the linkage to the specific elements of Williamson's theory that make such associations a logical approach to governance.

5. Other nonmarket collaborative solutions include, for example, visiting firms that have greater experience in the area of interest. This is widely practiced (usually based on a norm of reciprocity) even among firms in the same industry. While useful, such visits are typically of limited duration, and there is the possibility that information viewed by the lender as proprietary will be held back, that the information may not be adapted to conditions in the borrowing company, and that it may lack a "hands-on" quality.

leaders, and group members in the United States in the early 1980s, for example, easily ran to a quarter of a million dollars and more. Nor does this cover a variety of other start-up and operating costs, such as staffing, and opportunity costs, including time lost from production by group members.

Even large firms have difficulty recovering the extensive costs associated by spreading their application over a wide range of clients; small-group application is limited primarily to one's own employees. While small-group activities among one's employees may be frequent, the size of each transaction is small. In a few cases, especially in the United States, some large companies have tried to market the expertise of their small-group-activities staffs to recover their investments, but success has been limited. Notwithstanding, larger firms stand a better chance of recovering their investment costs than do smaller firms and thus have somewhat less of a need to contract for outside help.

One could use the market to replace existing employees with new employees with the required small-group activity skills were such individuals available, but this would obviously disrupt organizational performance dramatically if done quickly. After all, small-group-activity skills are only one of the many qualities that one would want employees to have. On the other hand, if such a substitution of employees is done gradually, one risks losing competitive advantage to other firms that are moving more rapidly to gain the productivity and quality advantages associated with effective small-group activity.

Yet the asset specificity of the human and organizational skills required to operate small-group activities is high. To be sure, there are generalized leadership, content, and process skills involved. Notwithstanding, the effective integration of small-group activities with an adaptive authority structure and flexible shop or office floor practices requires the development of specialized norms and practices. Individual employee "ownership" of these new practices is required for them to be effective, and that requires in turn that the expected users participate in their design. Thus it is ultimately firms that have to undertake and manage such activity. It cannot be farmed out.

We see, however, from this analysis that while firms have to do it themselves, they need help to acquire the necessary expertise.

They need help to obtain the general purpose investment in small-group activities that they can themselves later adapt through continuous experimentation to produce their own specialized version. They need help in clarifying goals, reducing ambiguity about the technology, and sorting out individual decision rights. There are two primary sources of such help: consultants and the pooling of corporate resources.

The consultants range from one-person companies to the specialized staffs of large consultant firms. Especially in the United States, these firms are often staffed by individuals who have acquired "know-how" from leading small-group activity developments in the private sector and then quit to try their hands at selling such knowledge. As we shall see, there is sharp variation among the three countries examined in the extent and type of consultant activity.

What is the appeal of contracting with such consultants for firms seeking to develop small-group activities? Most consultants in the United States offer an implementation package based on materials they have developed, purchased, or appropriated (from other consultants or firms using small groups). Consultants have typically had access to the experience of many companies and can therefore provide a pool of knowledge. It is in their interest to develop a generalized package that they can then market to a large range of companies. As we have seen, it is in the adopting companies' interest as well to acquire general purpose knowledge. Consultant companies typically offer implementation packages with known and fixed costs. For those companies that see small-group activities as a simple package to be slotted into existing structures and practices, this is particularly appealing. Such companies were more common in the United States than in Japan or Sweden.

An internal survey of managers at one large U.S. manufacturing company found managers giving the following reasons for seeking an external consultant for small-group activities in the early 1980s:

Need for expertise in how to implement employee involvement; nobody knew what to do to start the process

Perception that a consultant could help overcome local inertia in getting the process started

Belief that a third party would be credible to all parties involved in implementation (especially important in plants with strained union-management relations)

Feeling that an outside consultant could be candid to all parties

Perceived need for a coach as the process unfolded

Perception that a consultant could resist and buffer demands by higher management for premature evaluation of the process

Perception that it was division policy to use outside consultants

There are, however, considerable drawbacks to consultants. Above all, U.S. managers often reported concern about consultants being opportunistic. What is the nature of such opportunism? Above all, consultants may misstate their expertise. In the late 1970s and early 1980s, there was a bandwagon effect as new consultants entered this new and rapidly evolving field in great numbers. There was also tremendous uncertainty among managers as to what was involved in engaging effectively in small-group activity. Under such conditions, the cost of verifying the expertise of consultants was considerable.

The extent of these costs can be seen in the experiences of the Ford Motor Company, whose Personnel and Organization Staff designed a handbook in 1984 to help units decide whether they needed outside consultants, how to screen them, and how to deal with them in connection with their employee-involvement (EI) activities. The handbook itself was the product of fifty hours of interviews with Ford managers and union officials and required a task force of twelve managers. Suggested procedures:

First evaluate the adequacy of internal resources

Review external consultants certified for EI work within the company and choose a number of them for further consideration

Contact locations that have used consultants being considered

Compile a list of several candidates for review

Invite candidates in for on-site interviews with the steering committee or operating committee

Review the services each consultant provides

Determine consultant's range of resources that can be used to support the growth of the local EI process

Identify a consultant who can relate to employees at all levels of the organization and gain their trust and confidence

This list does not exhaust the factors that the handbook recommends local managers examine, but it does make clear that there are considerable costs in time and manpower associated with trying to determine the qualifications of consultants. As implied in the second item, Ford adopted corporationwide certification of consultants; this represents a centralized screening procedure to reduce costs and the likelihood of error. At Ford that certification process in turn necessitated a corporationwide panel to review the credentials of consultants, which conducted a ninety-minute group interview with prospective consultants.[6]

Beyond such general sorting activities, the costs to local units of finer screening to meet their specific needs are substantial. Smaller companies with more limited resources find it more difficult to evaluate, and therefore more expensive to screen, external consultants. However extensive the screening and however large the company, the danger that consultants may exaggerate their contributions and the company may not be able to see through self-serving claims remains significant.

Furthermore, managers may fear that consultant information and materials are slanted in ways that encourage continued dependence on consultants and their training materials. To rely on consultants to keep abreast of changes in best practice entails continued expense.[7] In practice, most companies reduce their use of external consultants as they gain experience with small-group activities.

Apart from opportunism, consultants have little specific knowledge of their client firms. There are thus considerable limits to

6. This corporationwide activity was eliminated in the late 1980s as reliance on external consultants diminished and the central staff developed greater confidence in the sophistication of local units in such matters.

7. It should be noted that the relationship is fraught with opportunism from the consultant's point of view as well. I witnessed a number of cases in which firms passed a rough rewrite of consultants' training materials off as their own, ignoring the (obviously weak) copyright protection. This enabled them to avoid royalty payments for each set of training materials purchased from a consultant. Other companies bought a few copies and then let their copy machines take over, again avoiding royalty payments.

their potential contribution to integrating small-group activity with shop or office floor practices. While some consultants are willing to acquire such knowledge with a view to building long-term relationships with a firm, this can be an expensive proposition from the firm's point of view.

For firms or unions that see small-group activity as part of a national movement (whether to gain competitive advantage or advance industrial democracy), such piecemeal efforts to acquire general purpose knowledge about small-group activities are inadequate. An alternative is to pool corporate and/or union investment (formally or informally) in industry- or nationwide infrastructure-building activities.[8] By absorbing what was going on in the field, refining it, and feeding back best practices to individual firms, the resultant associations could develop the general purpose knowledge required. They could conduct research on promising new directions and help forge a consensus on what these were, thereby smoothing the decision-making process within each firm. Such associations are instruments that allow competitors to develop a non-adversarial relationship for mutual advantage.

As agents of their constituencies, such associations are not very likely to engage in opportunistic actions.[9] Firms drawing upon their services can still develop competitive advantage through more effective tailoring of the association's outputs with their own norms and practices. Moreover, to the extent that a national association's general purpose knowledge is superior to the general purpose knowledge being generated by international competitors, cooperative action among domestic firms can still yield international competitive advantage for all. Yamazaki and Miyamoto (1987:313) make the same point in their comparative study of trade associations.

Such associations, with their wider network, in principle offer greater opportunities for keeping up with the developing standard of best practices than do individual consultants. For one thing, they are less likely to conceal failure and more likely to share learning that results from failure. Finally, such nationwide associations offer

---

8. These collaborative efforts may be seen as institutions midway between markets and hierarchy, to use Williamson's categories.

9. To be sure, there is a literature on the problem of accountability of agents to owners (see Jensen 1983), but relative to independent consultants it seems clear that the incentive for opportunism is likely to be limited.

the possibility of creating a national social movement for small-group activities. This can be organized in conjunction with unions under the banner of industrial democracy, but it can proceed without union involvement as well. These efforts can provide a motivation for employees to engage in small-group activity that neither individual firms nor consultants can offer.

This is not to say that such national associations do not have drawbacks. They may become caught up in bureaucratic procedures that strangle innovation, or they may fall victim to internal political struggle among member firms. Should the association stress developing new applications of small-group activities to better serve its more sophisticated members, or should it concentrate on innovative ways to get firms started on small-group activities?[10] Notwithstanding such dilemmas, associations on balance have tremendous potential for advancing the small-group-activities movement.

These are all issues addressed in the second half of this book. Central to consideration is the question of whether firms in any given country took greater advantage of the collaboration and pooling of resources in the associational framework to better spread small-group activities and capture their benefits. In so doing, there should have been less of a garbage can quality to their decision-making process. My purpose now is simply to demonstrate that the evolution of a national infrastructure can be crucial to the spread of small-group activities. This evolving infrastructure economizes on bounded rationality and minimizes opportunism.

Areas of Comparison

To provide a map for the subsequent chapter-by-chapter analysis, I take as a starting point the standard rational model of the diffusion process. It generally involves the following stages:

MOTIVATION → SEARCH → DISCOVERY →
TRANSMISSION → DECISION → IMPLEMENTATION

Such stage models are useful intellectual tools for simplifying a complex process. The complexity of the actual decision-making

10. Ouchi (1984:181–84) documents comparable conflicts in associational activity.

process, occurring as it does at many levels and involving many individuals, is such that it is, in fact, extremely difficult to see the innovation process as one in which decisions feed each other in a linear or logical sequence. One important piece of evidence in this regard is that decision makers themselves are often unaware of just what stage they are going through (Tornatzky et al. 1983:19). Indeed, this is the point of my using the loose-coupling model as a guide.

Notwithstanding, I shall follow the above model for the subsequent chapter divisions, always, however, keeping in mind the way the ambiguity of the problems and solutions suggests different processes. This latter consideration requires exploring the possibility that "latter" phases precede "prior" phases and in particular the conditions under which discovery and transmission precede the search stage. Exogenous developments also display an ability to transform the process. The political dimension operates as a cross-cutting variable that has an impact on all stages. To begin at the beginning requires an exploration of the motivation for small-group activities. This is the subject of the next chapter.

Once this exercise is complete, I shall turn my attention in chapters 8–13 to the nature of the national infrastructure for diffusing small-group activities in the three nations. This infrastructure has the potential to influence decision making in all phases of the diffusion process.

Chapter Four

The Motivation to Innovate

The greatest disservice that fashion does is
carelessly to turn life's most precious and
fragile assets into marketable products of tran-
sient worth.

Kennedy Fraser,
The Fashionable Mind

It might seem a simple matter to read the explanations of key
actors as to the central problems they saw themselves facing and
follow the problem-solving activity that led to the identification of
small-group activities as a solution to problems of work organization. The social reality is a good deal more complicated. Many possible incentives and precipitating factors are capable of producing
the set of decisions that lead to the introduction of small-group activities. Moreover, not all those factors are equally salient for the
many social actors involved in the process, and their importance
varies according to time and place.

Consider first the matter of the explanations given by key actors.
If we allow for the possibility that experience creates values, rather
than the conventional emphasis on value preferences determining
choices, the problem of reconstruction becomes far more difficult.
The diffusion of quality-control circles in Japan provides a textbook
example of how interpretations and explanations involving the value
of participation per se were called forth long after the initial innovations (March and Olsen 1976). As we saw in chapter 2, participation emerged in Japan as an ex post facto rationalization of the
small-group-activities movement. While Japanese managers were

indeed responding to a specific set of problems as we would expect based on a rational model of decision making, they were not necessarily the problems they now cite. Such rewriting of history is hardly unique to the Japanese.

Notions of democratizing the workplace, reducing worker alienation, and giving dignity to the worker are often given as motives for adopting small-group activities in Western countries. Sidney Harman, one of the early management pioneers of the new movement, spoke in 1972 of the need to see "work satisfaction—which is to say the attainment of a sense of purposefulness in his or her work, the achievement of a sense of personal worth and dignity— . . . as a fundamental right of employees and therefore a fundamental obligation of employers" (U.S. Department of Health, Education and Welfare, Special Task Force 1973:25).

Typical statesmanlike pronouncements are made on the subject by academics and high-level company and government spokesmen. Notwithstanding, one must establish whether there is an incentive structure in the organization that would encourage managers to identify alienation and lack of democratization, work satisfaction, and dignity as problems and small-group activities as a solution to these problems. By and large these incentives do not seem to have been as significant as the many public statements would suggest, except insofar as national political pressures were brought to bear. Even then because our cases are market economies, a focus on managerial incentives seems very much to the point.

None of this is meant to suggest that managers are any more disingenuous about the motives for their social behavior than any other group. Sociologists have often noted the need of individuals and organizations to rewrite their personal and organizational histories to fit current circumstances (Berger 1963). Rosabeth Kanter goes so far as to suggest this is necessary for organizational change to occur (1983:278–306).

An Analysis of "Structural Causes"

Apart from the difficulty of relying on the explanations given by key actors for their motivations, one may also question the ease with which we can identify the structural conditions underlying the decision to adopt small-group activities. Thomas Sandberg takes up this issue with an interesting analysis of how it came to be that small-group activities in the manufacturing sector diffused more widely in Sweden than in Norway in the 1970s. According to Sandberg (1982:93), the likelihood of adoption of small-group activities increases with:

the share of people employed in industry;

the importance of industry for the national economy;

the share of the engineering industry—including the machinery and transportation equipment sectors—in total industry;

the size of workplaces and firms;

the degree of work rationalization—efficiency brought about by introduction of productivity improvement machinery and work reorganization;

the level of welfare;

the level of employment;

the share of the population in the labor force; and

the share of women, immigrants, and other new groups in the labor force.

Sandberg recognizes that these structural explanations alone are insufficient for understanding the emergence of small-group activities, but nevertheless makes a plausible case for showing how these conditions facilitated developments in Sweden and inhibited them in Norway (Sandberg 1982:96–128).

What happens when we place the United States and Japan in the picture alongside Sweden? The utility of these structural explanations disappears; they cannot explain the speed of the Japanese in widely diffusing small-group activities relative to Sweden, much less the United States. By some measures, such as size of workplace, industrial concentration, the importance of industry, and degree of work rationalization, one might well have predicted that the United States would be the earliest and most successful adopter of small-group activities, with Japan coming last.

Consider the impact of labor shortage, which seems to underlie a number of Sandberg's measures, though he has relatively little to say directly on the subject. It might seem a simple matter to operationalize this structural condition in terms of employee-turnover data, the assumption being that high rates of voluntary employee separations are associated with labor shortage as employees exploit their superior bargaining power with employers. This, in turn, leads employers to search for new approaches to committing their labor forces to the firm. If we examine such data for the 1970s, we find that turnover rates, even allowing for differences in data collection and presentation, were high in Sweden and the United States and low in Japan. Kōshiro (1983:67) reports that monthly separation rates for workers in manufacturing in 1970 stood at 4.1 percent for the United States and 2.3 percent for Japan; they declined steadily thereafter in Japan, falling to 1.4 percent by the late 1970s, but held constant in the United States. In the case of Sweden, the monthly separation rates for private sector industry stood at 3.2 percent in 1970, but fell to 1.9 percent by 1976 (Statistiska Centralbyrån 1971; 1978). This puts Sweden squarely between the United States and Japan in 1970 and closer to Japan by the late 1970s.

These data do not support the belief that labor shortage provides a guide to explaining the emergence of small-group activity. If anything, the above figures suggest that U.S. managers had the greatest incentive and Japan the least incentive to innovate. This does not appear to have been the case, as reflected in the amount of diffusion that took place in the two countries.

We can also examine another measure said to be loosely associated with labor shortage, absenteeism. The assumption here is that under a labor shortage, workers can be rather cavalier about being absent from work, as they can always find another reasonable job. Yet here as well, we do not find much guidance if we compare absenteeism across the three nations (excluding annual paid holidays and national holidays). The absenteeism rates for employees in the nonagricultural sector are highest for Sweden, 13.8 percent (1978), and lowest for Japan, 2 percent (1977), with the U.S. figures standing at 3.5 percent (1978). Thus, even making ample allowances for differences in data sources, the data still suggest that Sweden would have had the greatest incentive to develop a new approach to employee commitment and Japan the least incentive. Again, this does not conform with the national experiences.

An approach focusing on the structural conditions leading to the adoption of small-group activities also requires that we understand the link that ties these structural conditions to the solutions arrived at by individual decision makers. This scenario presumes decision makers develop a set of articulated interests and have an ability to identify problems and formulate solutions and the political will and power to implement solutions.

Still, it is not my intent to suggest that structural conditions are not basic precipitating factors in the emergence of small-group activities. They operate according to my model as changing environmental conditions, thereby leading managers to question the efficacy of existing organizational arrangements. Keeping in mind the Sandberg list, and looking for common underlying factors that would distinguish the early adopters (Japan and Sweden) from the late adopter (the United States), we do find some suggestive patterns.

A fine-grained analysis does suggest indeed that the perception of severe labor shortage did create the conditions for the emergence of small-group activity in Japan and Sweden. How, the reader may ask, can this be, since such an outcome is not suggested by the comparison of objective measures discussed above? Before turning to that issue, we should note a further complication. Decision makers tend to see themselves as responding to specific manifestations of labor shortage, such as lack of control over the labor force (rising turnover and absenteeism and loss of competitive strength reflected in poor quality and productivity), rather than a labor shortage per se. As we shall see, "motivation" is a peculiar mixture of the driving forces leading managers to reexamine existing practices (thereby creating an occasion for making decisions) and their strategic responses to a problem based on finding and choosing possible courses of actions. They formulate their objectives in the course of carrying out these activities, and may reformulate them over time as they come to reevaluate accomplishments. Viewed in this light, we can see that motivation is not an event but a string of decisions over time.[1]

It is difficult to mobilize managers and employees in response to abstractions such as the labor shortage, so broader ideologies, involving the virtues of participation as leading to self-actualization, democratization, dignity, improved quality of work life, and so on,

---

1. This perspective builds on the early observations of Herbert Simon (1965: 53–54).

are often brought into play. A good example of the themes just discussed is a statement in the Volvo company report of the draft 1984 OECD study, which starts out in straightforward fashion listing as aims of work organization development in Volvo plants over the past ten to fifteen years the following objectives:

Increasing production

Improving quality

Reducing absenteeism

Reducing the turnover of personnel

Facilitating recruiting

The report then goes on to conclude that all these objectives can be summarized as increasing efficiency and improving the quality of working life. Of particular interest is the way in which the labor-shortage issue gets converted into a quality-of-working-life issue. To pursue this matter, we need a more detailed understanding of the identification of labor shortage as a problem and how small-group activities came to be seen as one of the solutions. For this, let us turn to an examination of each of the three national experiences.

The Japanese Case

In the late 1960s and early 1970s Japanese employers found themselves faced with an increasingly tight labor market as the economy grew rapidly and the agricultural sector could no longer serve its historic function of providing surplus labor (Minami 1973). It became increasingly difficult for the major manufacturing firms to recruit those select employees they desired, and management came to believe that it was increasingly difficult to retain such recruits. (The evidence for the latter proposition is somewhat problematic.) Even though, as reported above, turnover remained low by Western standards, it occurred in the context of a severe shortage of new male school graduates, especially middle school graduates, at a time of rapid economic growth. Replacement was both difficult and costly because of the absence of a pool of workers willing to take the most disagreeable jobs in the manufacturing sector. This situation threatened future corporate growth prospects and market share by restricting the ability of firms to meet market demand.

These observations make clear the limitations of relying on simple aggregate measures of labor shortage to capture the precipitating factors leading to the adoption of small-group activities. A meaningful model of decision making must build not only on structural conditions but on expectations based on past experience and perceived future prospects.

Between 1970 and 1973 momentum began to build to reverse Japan's long-standing policy of relying exclusively on domestic labor and to admit foreign migrant labor. However, the oil shock of 1973 and the deflation of Japanese economic growth, along with the decision to increase offshore equity investments, resulted in the issue being shelved. Rising educational levels led meanwhile to an increasing proportion of workers who were reluctant to accept the least demanding jobs. The educational system was producing more and more high school graduates who had been led to expect white-collar jobs commensurate with their educational achievements. Instead, an increasing number were being assigned blue-collar jobs. Management was greatly concerned about these trends. Many predicted an increasingly militant labor force unwilling to be satisfied with menial jobs. Surveys reported that workers wanted jobs that would allow them to develop their abilities and talents, whereas in the past workers had given priority to job security. It may be that management overestimated the problem, egged on as it was by exaggerated media reports and predictions that unrest on campuses would spread to the shop floor.

By the late 1960s evidence that supported management fears began to surface. The labor shortage was intensified for just those firms in the manufacturing sector that had the most standardized and routinized jobs. Industries still characterized by hard physical work under trying conditions and those requiring routinized job performance had a good deal of difficulty recruiting and retaining their labor forces. The auto and steel industries experienced great difficulties and had trouble meeting their expanded production schedules. A survey of 1,579 establishments in the machinery and metal-manufacturing industry reports that of the new employees in spring 1969, 50 percent of both middle and high school graduates recruited had quit within a three-year period (Japan, Ministry of Labour 1974:72).

These circumstances constituted a major motivational force for Japanese management to search for solutions to deal with what had become identified as a significant problem. Although the QC circle movement had come into being in the early 1960s, circles became immensely more attractive to firms outside the original early adopters in the materials industry (steel and chemicals in particular). QC circles became a key managerial strategy for making firms more attractive to highly educated potential recruits and reducing the likelihood of turnover and labor unrest. Those firms and industries that had the greatest recruitment problems, such as the auto, machinery, and other assembly industries, took the lead in introducing small-group activities during this time frame. They were also, of course, the industries that were growing most rapidly during this period and absorbing more and more labor. The growth in QC circle registration at JUSE took its first sharp spurt upward during this period, 1966–69 (see fig. 1 in chapter 2).

In the interwar period, Japanese firms had carried on discussion and study practices among work teams (see Cole 1979). They thus had experience with small-group activities in their behavioral repertoire (tradition), albeit on a more authoritarian model. This experience made the selection of small-group activities a reasonable solution to their problems. However, it was hardly the only solution. At the same time that managers were introducing small-group activities, the pace of technological innovation accelerated. That is, companies adopted the standard management response to labor shortage—capital investment. Kōshiro Kazutoshi develops a more complex causal framework for explaining the emergence of small-group activity, stressing that labor shortage and pollution problems led to large-scale capital investment (Kōshiro 1983:70–86). The costs associated with this large-scale capital investment to mechanize the production process and modernize work organization were very high; they could only be recovered by the introduction of small-group activity that would maximize the efficiency of the new arrangements.

It is important to note that Japanese managers generally do not see capital investment as a solution that permits them to avoid dealing with issues of work organization. Rather, their experience has taught them that to get the full benefits of capital investments in equipment, they must work to optimize the relationship between the new technology and human factors. They have not, however, embraced any formal way of representing these relationships such as that embodied in the sociotechnical framework adopted by many Swedish managers.

Still another approach to dealing with labor shortages developed in the late 1960s and 1970s; offshore equity investments in production facilities grew at a rapid pace as Japanese firms sought to break the bottleneck imposed by the shortage of labor, take advantage of lower costs, and meet the domestic content requirements of Southeast Asian nations. Small-group activities were thus only one of several measures designed to deal with the effects of the labor shortage, and some of the alternatives had multiple objectives.

Another strategy adopted in some industries, especially by auto manufacturers, was the recruitment of large numbers of agricultural workers as seasonal labor. A related and somewhat later strategy used in many industries involved the increasing use of part-time workers, especially women. Initially, this strategy developed to meet labor shortages, but after the mid 1970s it was increasingly used to provide greater flexibility to employers trying to limit their regular employment in the face of slower economic growth; part-time female employment more than doubled, from 700,000 in 1975 to 1,800,000 in 1982, rising from 2.9 percent of the labor force to 6 percent. Yet for the critical period in question, 1965–75, female participation in the labor force actually fell from 48.8 percent in 1965 to 44.8 percent in 1975. This primarily reflected the reduction of the labor force in the agricultural sector, where many female workers had traditionally been concentrated.

The slowdown imposed by the oil shock of 1973 and the subsequent recession in 1975 provided an external solution to the labor shortage. Small-group activities were thus only one of the answers to the labor shortage. Moreover, they were only partially successful in addressing it. A substantial case study literature focusing on the contributions of small-group activity to quality and productivity improvement developed, however, and many managers accepted that small-group activities were meeting their objectives even though they did relatively little to moderate the labor shortage. In a 1977 nationwide survey, in 61 percent of all establishments surveyed, management respondents reported that small-group activity produced "good results." The larger the firm, the stronger the positive evaluation—83 percent of all establishments with over 5,000 employees reported good results (Japan, Ministry of Labour 1978:168).

There were other problems relevant to the selection of small-group activities as a solution. Small-group activities were part of a corporate strategy designed to mobilize all resources to deal with heightened competitiveness in domestic and foreign markets. The growing internationalization of the Japanese economy, and the tremendous threat this posed for the survival of Japanese firms, was one of management's major themes in the 1960s. Better utilization of its human assets could make significant contributions to improved productivity and quality. With labor to a large extent a fixed cost under conditions of low turnover, it made sense to fully employ the abilities of that labor force. Small-group activities were a logical follow-up to the growing interest in improving the training and education of workers.

Finally, a quite important point, the Japanese had by the early 1960s identified decentralization as an important strategy for reinvigorating their large organizations, thereby improving quality and productivity. Movements to decentralize safety and maintenance responsibilities were followed by efforts to decentralize quality responsibilities, leading in the early 1960s to the birth of the quality circles. Kobayashi Shigeru's influential book *Sony Revitalizes Its Employees* stressed his efforts at Sony's Atsugi plant to increase employee responsibility at the level of the small work group (Kobayashi 1966). Efforts to decentralize and to build small-group activity through increasing employee responsibility were part of a common effort, with the same actors serving as sponsors. The attempt to improve competitive performance through decentralization and small-group activity was both a response to the labor shortage and an independent outcome of the decentralization movement.

Management devised a variety of responses to environmental changes (labor shortage, rising educational levels, public concern about pollution, and internationalization of the economy). The objective was to raise productivity and quality while bringing about better communication, teamwork, and motivation in the workplace. Much of the literature of the QC circle movement stresses the importance of not aiming directly for productivity and quality

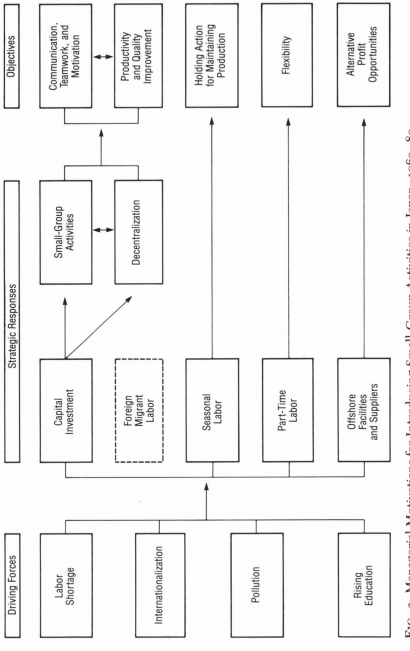

FIG. 2. Managerial Motivations for Introducing Small-Group Activities in Japan, 1960–80.

improvement, but rather letting them arise indirectly from the improvement in communication and teamwork among workgroups (Shiba 1983a:17). Japanese managers, being no more saintly than other managers, have tended in practice, however, to stress the productivity and quality-improvement side at least as much as, if not more strongly than, teamwork, communication, and motivation.

The preceding discussion of management motivation in Japan is summarized schematically in figure 2, which depicts the driving forces, the various strategic responses, and the objectives of Japanese management. Some of the strategic responses complemented one another; others represented clear alternatives, at least with regard to particular production outputs.

The Swedish Case

The labor-supply situation was even more serious in Sweden. By the 1960s a severe labor shortage developed. Swedish workers were increasingly unwilling to take jobs characterized by routinized tasks and poor working conditions. A number of studies in the early 1960s showed that many of the large industrial enterprises and public enterprises on Sweden's west coast were losing half of their newly employed Swedish labor within some seven and a half months of hiring. Overall, it is estimated that annual labor turnover at the beginning of the 1960s was running about 35–50 percent of the total number of employed workers (Berglind and Rundblad 1978:102–3).

Absenteeism also grew rapidly. Sick days per person were estimated to be running at 15.5 in the mid 1960s and rose to 19 days per person by the early 1970s (Jönsson 1981:10). This aggravated a growing labor shortage. Among new entrants to the labor force between 1970 and 1976, it is estimated, almost every second person was simply replacing working hours lost owing to absenteeism (Jönsson 1979:3).

At the same time, educational levels rose rapidly. In 1962 the government initiated the nine-year compulsory comprehensive school (ages seven to sixteen), raising the school attendance requirement two years over the old system. By 1968, moreover, 80 percent of sixteen-year-olds were continuing their education beyond comprehensive school. The growth in educational attainment led to new entrants to the labor force whose profile was dramatically different from that of the existing labor pool. Nowhere was the gap greater than in the manufacturing sector. Whereas 69 percent of manufacturing employees were graduates of primary schools in 1977, only 41 percent of the national pool of 20–24-year-olds fell into this category (Jönsson 1981:9). There developed a strong sense among employers that these new workers were not satisfied with existing working conditions and that heightened labor turnover and absenteeism were the result. Swedish employers sought to deal with these conditions through various approaches.

First, they welcomed more women into the labor market, a policy reinforced by a variety of government measures, including the establishment of a national network of day-care centers and labor-market training courses. The entire growth in the number of people in the labor market from 1965 to 1974, from 3.7 to 4 million, consisted of women, primarily married women. As a percentage of the labor force, women rose from 36 percent in 1968 to 42.5 percent by 1975 (Statistiska Centralbyrån 1978:56). Female participation in the labor force in Sweden rose from 46.6 percent in 1965 to 55.2 percent in 1975. These levels stand well above those recorded by the EEC nations, Japan, and the United States (U.S. Department of Labor 1983:422).

Interestingly, these increases did not especially accrue to the manufacturing sector, in large part because the traditional industries employing female labor, such as textiles, were rapidly losing employment. Women accounted for 24.4 percent of all manufacturing employees in 1965, increasing only fractionally to 24.7 percent by 1975. However, in those growing sectors hardest hit by the labor shortage, such as auto manufacturing and steel, the percentage of women in the labor force grew significantly. It rose in auto manufacturing from 13.7 percent in 1965 to 18.4 percent by 1975, and in iron, steel, and metal work from 12 percent in 1965 to 16 percent by 1975 (Statistiska Centralbyrån 1978:71, 73).

A second strategy has involved an increase in the employment of aliens. The number of aliens taking jobs in Sweden increased steadily from 121,747 in 1962 to 221,925 in 1973 (Statistiska Centralbyrån 1977b:257). The Scandinavian component of this migration has been approximately 65 percent, with the majority of foreign workers coming from Finland. Nevertheless, the Finns have presented substantial adjustment problems; for those who have not grown up in Swedish-speaking areas of Finland, the language hurdle is considerable. Yugoslav immigrants have come to constitute 10 percent of the non-Scandinavian inflow.

In 1977 approximately half these migrants (61 percent in 1971) were concentrated in the mining, quarrying, and manufacturing industries, as opposed to only 25 percent of the Swedish labor force; migrant labor constitutes 10 percent of the total employment in this sector (Statistiska Centralbyrån 1978:195). Moreover, within manufacturing, the migrant workers were concentrated in just those industries characterized by the most routinized jobs and poorest working conditions (Statistiska Centralbyrån 1977a:86). In the early 1970s only half the workers in these manufacturing sectors were Swedish and one-fifth were women.

By the late 1960s Swedish manufacturing employers became increasingly concerned that reliance on female and foreign labor was not solving their problem. They still had difficulty finding enough workers to do the least desirable jobs and found themselves relying on the lowest-quality labor. Doubts began to increase about the wisdom of relying on an increasingly larger number of foreign workers. In addition, absenteeism and employee turnover continued at high levels, with the rates being even higher for foreign and female labor than for male Swedish workers. Annual turnover by 1970 was running at about 50 percent in a number of large plants in metropolitan areas (Jönsson 1979:3). High unemployment and sick pay benefits made turnover and absenteeism relatively costless to employees.

As we saw with the Japanese, one strategy under these circumstances is to increase investment abroad, and there is indeed evidence of an increase of such investment in the early 1970s. Swedish assets in overseas manufacturing companies were characterized by high levels of employment, reflecting the concentration in transportation equipment and machinery. The pattern was for large Swedish manufacturing companies such as Volvo, Ericsson, and ASEA to establish overseas subsidiaries for parts manufacturing and assembly operations (Jones 1976:172–73).

Yet Swedish firms were hardly ready to abandon production in Sweden. Consequently, attention turned to strategies for restructuring work so that Swedish workers could be brought back into the factories and turnover and absenteeism reduced to manageable proportions. This restructuring of work had a number of dimensions, including the introduction of new technology and changes in the architecture of work organization. Small-group activities were an integral part of this response.

As in Japan, major innovations in small-group activities took place in just those industries suffering the severest recruitment, turnover, and absenteeism problems. Within Sweden, activities at Saab-Scania's engine plant and Atlas Copco's machinery assembly plant received great attention. Volvo experienced some of the severest problems and achieved fame internationally as one of the more adventurous firms in designing small-group activities (for a friendly assessment of its experience, see Jönsson 1979). Volvo's leadership role in Sweden needs to be fully recognized; its dominant position resulted from Volvo's status as the largest private firm in the Swedish economy. GM was the largest private firm in the United States until 1974, but it did not have the commanding role in the U.S. economy that Volvo did in Sweden. One estimate puts the impact of Volvo's operations on the Swedish economy at about twice that of GM's impact on the U.S. economy (Jönsson 1981:2).[2]

The Volvo company report for the 1984 OECD study summarizes its strategic responses from about 1975 as follows:

the introduction of new techniques;

modification of production systems/structures;

changed "architecture" of working conditions;

reformulation of tasks for supervision and production techniques;

modified arrangement of workers' tasks. (OECD 1984b:13)

With regard to the last item, the report identifies a "package" of activities, including delegation of responsibilities, integration of jobs where other skills are required, job rotation, participation in decision making about the job, and changes in physical working conditions. Volvo characterizes these responses as addressing the

2. This role has continued to grow. In 1985 the amount of capital associated with Volvo and its allied firms accounted for 20 percent of the capital of all firms listed on the Swedish stock market. See Per Afrell, "Fonder viskning mot Volvo-makt" (The [wage-earner] fund is a whisper compared to Volvo power), *Dagens Nyheter,* 10 February 1985, p. 10.

problem of integrating "hardware" with "software." That is, it asserts recognition of the need to properly prepare the "social" side of the organization for the introduction of technology. This represents a modified version of the original sociotechnical position, with its stress on changing both social and technical systems to better coordinate them. Small-group activity, while implicit in the above description, is also given a smaller place in the arsenal of company responses as compared to what it would have reported ten years earlier.

We see here a situation in which successive choices (recruiting women, recruiting aliens) were unsuccessfully applied to the labor-shortage problem until a new, "more attractive" choice, small-group activities, came along (cf. Cohen, March, and Olsen 1976). Rather than abandoning previous choices, however, employers simply added this new tactic to them in an effort to resolve the problem. As in the case of Japan, there were additional factors responsible for the identification of small-group activities as a solution. These factors were primarily political in nature and involved other interest groups. Such alleged motivating factors as the "postindustrial ethos" to which Cherns (1979) refers seem, however, to have operated more as legitimizing ideology than as causal factors in the adoption process.

A notable difference with Japan lies in the relation of the small-group activity movement to the decentralization movement in Sweden. As in Japan, a decentralization movement developed in Swedish industry in the early 1960s. It gradually gathered momentum over the next two decades, but was slow to merge with the small-group-activities movement. The focus for much of the early period was on the decentralization of functions such as marketing, and the advocates of decentralization, generally top executives, tended not to link their advocacy with the small-group-activities movement. Similarly, the sponsors of small-group activities, especially line managers, did not particularly connect their efforts with decentralization. Perhaps the gap was sharpest for union leaders (who assumed membership on boards of directors in 1973); they tended to oppose decentralization insofar as it might lead to independent subsidiaries that would limit employees' job transfer rights. At the same time, many firm-level union leaders tended to be supportive of the small-group-activities movement.

It was not until the appearance in the late 1970s of the Swedish

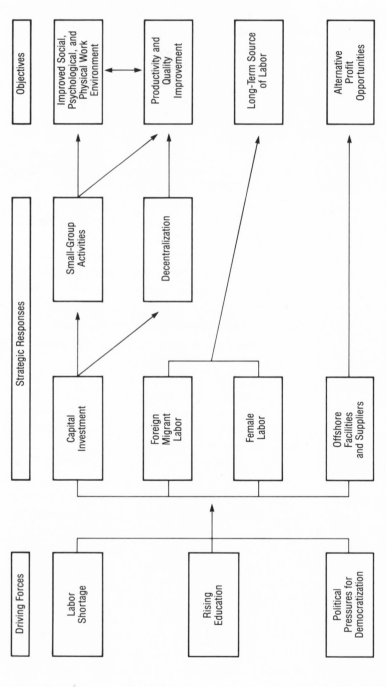

FIG. 3. Managerial Motivations for Introducing Small-Group Activities in Sweden, 1965–75.

Employers' Confederation's new version of decentralization (based on what it saw as starting to happen in a number of leading firms) that a firm link could be established between the two movements (Aguérn and Edgren 1979). With the publication of the results of its new factories (*nya fabriker*) project, SAF endorsed the "little factory in the large factory" concept and stressed a vision of relatively autonomous "product shops." This decentralization solution provided a better fit with the small-group-activities movement, but arrived on the scene at a time when that movement had already lost much of its steam and national politics was focusing on other solutions.

One can only speculate whether the consequences would have been different in Sweden if events had followed the same course as in Japan, where the two movements—small-group activities and decentralization—developed hand in hand, with the result that they strongly reinforced each other. In Sweden, however, middle-level staff and line management (quality, maintenance, production managers) found it easier to resist the movement for small-group activities when it was not reinforced by a top management push toward decentralization. These middle-level personnel had ample motivation to do so, since the small-group-activities movement was seen as threatening many of their prerogatives.

The failure of these two solutions—small-group activity and decentralization—to land on management's agenda at the same time in Sweden arose perhaps from the tumultuous political events of the 1960s. This reminds us of the serendipitous quality to problem-solving activity and the different effects resulting from different combinations of problems and solutions.

Managerial motivations in Sweden for adopting small-group activities are summarized in figure 3. There are striking similarities to the Japanese managerial motivations depicted in figure 2, as well as some significant differences because of political pressures in Sweden and the role of internationalization in Japan (Sweden already had a highly internationalized economy in the period under question). The turn to foreign labor and the relatively independent role of the decentralization movement in Sweden are also notable. While these differences had real impacts on the speed and shape of the new movement, one is still struck by the overall similarities. But such schemata tend to freeze motivation in time, when in fact it is constantly evolving. To deal with this, let us turn to an evaluation of efforts over time.

Evaluation and Goal Succession

As in the case of Japan, it is appropriate to ask what success the Swedes had in using small-group activities to address the various problems of turnover, recruitment, and absenteeism, as well as quality and productivity. The Swedish case is more interesting in this regard because of the changes that did and did not take place. Employee turnover has declined dramatically over the past decade. From the range of 35–50 percent in the 1960s, national annual turnover figures for production workers show a decline to the low 20s by the late 1970s (Statistiska Centralbyrån 1981:74). At the Volvo group (in which car manufacturing accounted for only 20,000 jobs out of a total of 76,000 in 1983), annual employee turnover fell from 20 percent in 1973 to 9.6 percent in 1981. Much of this decline can be attributed to a sharp weakening of the economy and the resultant tightening of the labor market. Thus, again, as in the Japanese case, small-group activities were at best only modestly effective in reducing employee turnover. Yet because the decline in turnover paralleled the introduction of small-group activities, and because it is impossible to separate the relative causal impacts of the different factors, it is possible for managers to proceed with the unchallenged assumption that some of the decline was attributable to the new work structures. This provides continued motivation and legitimation for pursuing small-group activities.

Some modest success has also been achieved in increasing the proportion of Swedish workers in the manufacturing sector. While the mining, quarrying, and manufacturing sectors accounted for 24 percent of the employment of all Swedish citizens (including naturalized citizens) in 1981 (down slightly from 25 percent in 1977), the proportion of foreign residents accounted for by these sectors fell from almost 50 percent in 1977 to 40 percent in 1981 (Statistiska Centralbyrån 1981:189). In the case of the Volvo group, the percentage of Swedish workers increased from 69.7 percent in 1978 to 73 percent in 1981 (of the 27 percent consisting of foreign residents, Finns accounted for 17.2 percent and Yugoslavs for 4.7 percent). At Torslanda, Volvo's largest plant, which employed some 10,000 workers in 1984, the percentage of non-Swedes fell from 50 percent in 1974 to 35 percent in 1984 (OECD 1984b:18).

The weakened economy was primarily responsible for a dramatic reduction in immigration to Sweden during the latter part of the 1970s and the early 1980s. The weakened economy and rising unemployment, the latter still low by American standards, led some Swedes to take jobs that they might have scorned a decade earlier. Again we see that small-group activities had, at most, a modest influence on developments. Again, even if the trends could not be used as dramatic evidence of the success of the new work initiatives, at least they could not be used to criticize them. It should also be noted that foreign labor is much less of a problem in Sweden in the 1980s for still another reason; most of the older immigrants have now learned the language and acclimated themselves to the Swedish work environment.

We turn now to an assessment of the impact of small-group activities on absenteeism. Unlike the changes in turnover data or the data on the proportion of Swedes in the manufacturing sector, the absenteeism problem has grown dramatically, rather than abated, over the past decade. Experts generally attribute much of this to the further improvement of sick leave benefits. Moreover, the reduced opportunities for voluntary job changing may be channeled into higher absenteeism. Others see the growth in absenteeism more positively as a new welfare society benefit, contributing further to employee flexibility.

Temporary absenteeism for a full measured week, including illnesses, vacations, military service, service leave (for example, for pregnancy or educational purposes), and strike activity, as a percentage of the number employed, rose from 9.6 percent in 1965 to 11.6 in 1970, 14 percent in 1975 and 17.8 percent by 1980 (Statistiska Centralbyrån 1981:44). It has since moderated somewhat. A 1985 report states that on the average 10 percent of the work force are away from work every day on grounds of sickness.[3]

Small-group activities were apparently powerless to arrest the growth of absenteeism because of improved sick leave benefits. In-

---

3. "Nyttigt att vara sjuk ibland" (Useful to be sick sometimes), *Dagens Nyheter*, 24 February 1985, p. 7. It was with some amusement that I read a telex message from the Central Bureau of Statistics apologizing to staff at the Swedish Embassy in Washington for a month-long delay in sending data I had requested on absenteeism and labor turnover. The responsible official explained that owing to absenteeism resulting from sickness and the press of other work, the bureau had been unable to get the request processed earlier.

stead of being used as an argument against small-group activities, however, the growth in absenteeism has been used from the beginning to justify the use of group work methods! Group work has been seen as a strategy to avoid the disruption introduced by absenteeism under traditional work methods. The reasoning is that through teamwork based on broad skills and job rotation, one can avoid the disruption caused by the loss of any one worker. The more absenteeism you have, the more useful group work thus is, not in reducing absenteeism but in cushioning its impact. By contrast, Japanese managers have typically used employee teamwork in conjunction with a tight (no slack) production system to reduce absenteeism by mobilizing peer pressures against workers "who create hardship" for their workmates by not coming to work. Here in microcosm we see a display of relative managerial and worker power in the two societies.

Moreover, using group work to cope with absenteeism in Sweden has its limitations. At its showcase Kalmar plant, Volvo was forced in the late 1970s to add still another reserve pool of workers to its existing absentee pool "to resolve the problems arising from absenteeism, which affects the different work teams quite unevenly" (Efficiency and Participation Development Council 1984:44).

What can we conclude from this assessment of the factors that provided much of the initial impetus to the small-group-activities movement? As we examine what has happened to turnover, recruitment, and absenteeism over time, we see that performance has been influenced by a variety of factors and allows for a variety of interpretations. While this does not allow proponents of small-group activities to decisively rout doubters and nonbelievers, it does, given continued top management support, allow them to pursue their efforts without being subject to severe criticism.

With such tenuous claims, however, new objectives for small-group activities are needed to sustain top management support. We can see this transition at Volvo. When Volvo initiated its Kalmar plant in 1974, Pehr Gyllenhammar, the corporation's president, stressed that it would be a factory that, without any sacrifice of efficiency or the company's financial objectives, would give employees the opportunity to work in groups. By 1984, with heightened competition in the worldwide automobile market, the stress was no longer on small-group activities *not leading to any disad-*

vantage but rather that they *should confer competitive advantages* in quality and productivity.

When viewed over the perspective of a decade and a half, there is considerable ambiguity about how to interpret the results of introducing small-group activities. This returns us to one of the early themes in chapter 3. Ambiguity is pervasive in this process, and the simple notion that it is reduced through learning over time hardly does justice to the complexity of the matter. What rather happens for many managers and workers is that new practices may gradually become institutionalized as normal organizational responses without much thought being given to what the original results were supposed to be. In the process managers assign new objectives to small-group activities. In short, a process of goal succession has set in whereby the original objectives are supplanted by new ones.

The U.S. Case

To contrast the situation in Japan and Sweden with that in the United States is revealing. A large reserve pool of unemployed labor is available in the United States to fill the most disagreeable jobs. Although labor turnover is remarkably high by world standards, an ever-ready source of replacements is thus available. This constituted a major barrier to the introduction of small-group activities in the United States, *particularly in a context where most domestic firms were insulated from foreign competition* (see Wool 1973).

The differences are most obvious in a comparison of the automobile industries. Gyllenhammar recounts how he came to the United States in the early 1970s and found that some American automobile plants had turnover figures similar to those of Swedish car factories—that is, "at the worst, half the employees left every year." At General Motors, it is reported that between 1965 and 1969, absenteeism rose roughly 50 percent, turnover rates were up more than 70 percent, grievances rose 38 percent, and disciplinary layoffs rose more than 40 percent (Kanter 1983:315).

Gyllenhammar was astounded that American managers typically did not perceive this as a serious problem. Rather, the American managers were accustomed to greater mobility of workers and reasoned that they could train people and put them on simple jobs so quickly that the turnover figures did not matter, even if they did make extra planning necessary (Gyllenhammar 1977). In short, because of this reserve pool of labor, management tolerated high turnover and absenteeism rates and had only modest incentives to engage in searches for new ways of organizing work. Indeed, the assumption that they had large quantities of unskilled labor being processed through the firm at regular intervals to a significant extent determined the simplifying job design specifications produced by engineers. It led them to expect less, rather than more, from their blue-collar employees, the opposite direction to that being taken by the Japanese and Swedes.

A similar argument can be made about rising educational levels. Although a number of scholars pointed to the rising level of education on the part of the American labor force, most of the change related to the rapid rise in those going on to higher education. The concern was whether there would be enough jobs for them. This was not seen by managers as affecting the supply of labor for lower-level shop and office floor jobs, and few American managers therefore saw a need to restructure their work organizations.

In the important book *Work in America*, published in 1973 as the report of a special task force to the Secretary of Health, Education and Welfare, the authors endorse participative management as one of the solutions to American work ills. Interestingly, the primary treatment of education in the report is as a means (through retraining) of improving work in America rather than as a force requiring management to reorganize work. The authors also point out that raising the educational level (credentials) is not terribly helpful, since there is little correlation between educational achievement and job performance (U.S. Department of Health, Education and Welfare, Special Task Force 1973:121–52).

Notwithstanding the stabilization or decline in college enrollment rates for the young in the early 1970s, the overall educational attainment of the labor force has continued to grow simply as a function of the retirement of older employees and their replacement by younger, better-educated workers. This gradual process is not, however, of the kind that leads management to dramatic policy changes. A rapid shift in the numbers and quality of high school graduates could potentially have had such impact, but the percentage of seventeen-year-olds graduating from high school was virtually unchanged from 1965 to 1975. It stood at 76 percent in 1963–64 and actually fell below 75 percent in 1974–75 (Grant and Lind 1977:65). If anything, concern was being registered about a decline in the quality of American high school graduates. In sum, upward shifts in educational quality were not as apparent in the United States as in Japan and Sweden, nor did such changes as occurred combine with a shifting labor supply situation to produce a major management concern.

Female labor-force participation did rise significantly in the period between 1965 and 1975, from 39.3 to 46.3 percent. This was not, however, a response to labor shortages, and certainly not a well-articulated employer and government strategy, as was the case in Sweden.

For all practical purposes, small-group activities did not represent a choice for American managers during the 1960s and 1970s. The problems they recognized, the available solutions, and the focus of key policy makers combined to make small-group activities a non-issue. There were occasional managers and companies who for one reason or another took the initiative in establishing participative management practices, sometimes involving small-group activities. Companies like Donnelly Mirrors, Lincoln Electric, and Harman International Industries come to mind. These tended to be isolated examples, however, without much interest being shown in them by other corporations or the media. They were seen as mavericks rather than as trendsetters.

To be sure, some American managers faced problems of labor turnover, absenteeism, and rising educational levels similar to those in Sweden and Japan. In the case of automobiles, Gyllenhammar of Volvo was apparently unaware that there were key U.S. managers concerned about the impact of turnover and absenteeism on quality. In the 1973 letter of understanding between the UAW and GM establishing joint QWL efforts, GM specifically gave reduced employee absenteeism and turnover as the benefits to be achieved by the corporation. In turn, the consumer was to benefit by improved quality.

This letter of understanding established the first national joint labor-management committee on QWL in a major corporation. While the initiative came very much from Irving Bluestone, the then vice president of the UAW, the corporation had already been exploring "organizational development." Kanter (1983:331–47) describes the internal momentum building for participative management within GM in the late 1960s. What is striking in comparison to Japan and Sweden, however, is how long such discussions were confined to the corporate level. Despite a long developmental period, the degree of diffusion to GM plants, notwithstanding such showcase factories as Tarrytown, was extremely slow during the 1970s.

The 1970s were a decade in which internal and especially external pressures for change in the way American firms organized and managed themselves were building. Relatively few firms responded to these pressures; most continued patterns of behavior built up in the post–World War II environment of economic growth and expansion of world markets. Among business leaders generally, there was little sense of urgency, no conclusion that dramatic changes might be called for in how employees were organized and managed. Those who were concerned often had little support in the power centers of their corporations and had to move slowly to build a constituency. The environment that made such lackadaisical responses possible was changing rapidly, however, as one American industry after another became subject to intense international competition.

The pressure finally broke through and forced American firms into a decade of turmoil, experimentation, and testing of new approaches. Ernest Savoie, director of the Labor Relations Planning and Employment Office at Ford, reflecting on the experiences of Ford's eighty-six large facilities, made a statement that might have been echoed at other major corporations such as GM, General Electric, and Westinghouse. At a 1985 University of Michigan workshop, Savoie said that more had happened with respect to small-group activities and other forms of participation at Ford in the early 1980s than at all U.S. companies combined in the 1970s!

As American markets were being internationalized, the role of the United States as a leader in manufacturing was being eroded, with market share declining in industry after industry. With the growth in the strength of the dollar in the early 1980s, incentives increased for American producers to move toward offshore facilities and suppliers. To use the words of Jim Baker, executive vice president of General Electric, in a widely quoted speech of May 1981, the choice was seen increasingly as one of "automate, emigrate, or evaporate."

With automation came increasing recognition of the need to use the new technology in the most effective fashion, and many companies concluded that this involved greater reliance on an intelligent labor force. Small-group activities were part of this effort. At the same time, firms instituted strong cost-cutting measures, including especially measures to trim domestic labor costs. Notwithstanding Baker's colorful depiction of the hard choices facing management, these choices were not necessarily mutually exclusive. Companies like Ford that were investing heavily in new technology and small-group activities were the very same firms that were actively exploring offshore facilities and suppliers. This is one reason why workers often mistrusted management's commitment to employee involvement. Even General Electric, so prominent in selling its automation services to other U.S. manufacturing firms, was actively encouraging its purchasing department to explore offshore suppliers.

Ironically, it was only with the remarkable success of the Japanese in competing in American export and domestic markets that a more general reevaluation of small-group activities began. Suddenly in the early 1980s managers and the media were looking for the key to Japanese success, and participatory work practices based on small-group activities were identified as part of the package. Consider the following statement, which appeared in a friend of the court brief filed with the National Labor Relations Board by the International Association of Quality Circles (IAQC), the major organizational exponent of quality circles in the United States:

Faced with . . . challenge from Japan, American businessmen began to examine the situation and study the phenomenon of Japan's rapid economic expansion. They quickly became aware of the fact that Japan's success was largely attributable to its national concern for, and an almost single-minded dedication toward, achieving superior *quality* and high levels of *productivity* in the workplace. Moreover, American businessmen learned that the approach most extensively utilized by the Japanese to achieve these goals had its roots in the United States, to wit, "Quality Circles"—a specific and unique type of formally structured system involving employee participation.

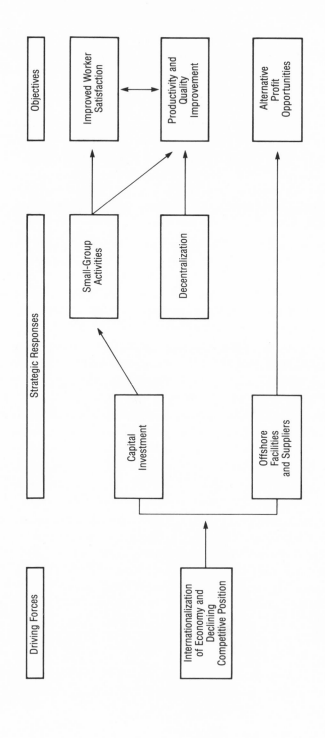

FIG. 4. Managerial Motivations for Introducing Small-Group Activities in the United States, 1975–85.

Ignoring the question of the correctness of these statements on the origin of circles and the specific causes of Japanese success, such views came to be widely disseminated in the popular management literature during the early 1980s. Management's objective in introducing participatory work practices was to provide for greater commitment of workers to their jobs in ways that would improve quality and productivity. The belief that the Japanese were making better use of their human resources through such practices as small-group activities was widely shared. Japanese managers were also seen as having developed more constructive relationships with their unions, and this also served to spur various participatory practices in the United States.

Decentralization as an approach to increased productivity and quality arrived in full force on the American scene in the early 1980s (see Kanter 1983). The rallying call was for fewer layers of management and more line responsibility at lower levels. This was rather later than in Sweden and almost two decades later than in Japan. Moreover, the American approach to decentralization had a peculiarly American quality, with stress being placed on "uncorking entrepreneurial talents" within the firm, or "intrapreneurial behavior," as it came to be called in management jargon. While some scholars such as Rosabeth Kanter tied this focus to small-group activities, for others the linkage was weak or nonexistent.

Figure 4 summarizes my analysis of the forces driving U.S. small-group initiatives. There is a certain "compactness" about the process in the United States that is lacking in Japan and Sweden, where the driving forces and strategic responses were more varied. Labor shortage in all its various manifestations was not a driving force in the United States, and the strategic responses to reduced competitiveness in an internationalized economy were thus more focused. Also notable are the differences in emphasis on "people-building." Whereas Swedish managers were likely to talk about changing the social and physical environment of the workshop in keeping with the sociotechnical system, and the Japanese about the need to build teamwork and communication among work group members, Americans were more likely simply to stress worker satisfaction. Moreover, the link between "people-building" objectives and increased productivity and quality improvement tends to be less well developed in the United States than in Japan and Sweden (Cole and Byosiere 1986:25–30). In conclusion, despite expectations based on cultural differences, my analysis of managerial objectives shows a good deal more similarity in this respect between Japan and Sweden than between Sweden and the United States.

Chapter Five

Bandwagons versus Dominoes

> Although all fashion looks mobile and rebellious at times, its roots are surprisingly constant: to think or act for reasons of fashion in any given field is to support that field's established centers of power.
>
> Kennedy Fraser,
> *The Fashionable Mind*

Thus far I have talked about a diffusion of small-group activities that is not wildly at variance with the rational model of decision making. That is, notwithstanding public rationalizations and reliance on the current visible and available solutions, the process is one in which managers identify problems of high turnover and absenteeism and resultant problems of quality and productivity. This, in turn, gives rise to a search for solutions and adoption of small-group activities. Moreover, the search for solutions is greatest in industries suffering the greatest problems.

This process may be characteristic of the early adopters in each country, but does it apply to all adopters? Early adopters account for only a small number of total adoptions. In any innovation process, some organizations or parts of organizations take the lead and others lag behind. Social scientists have documented the characteristic patterns associated with these developments (Griliches 1957).

A bandwagon effect typically develops as the process of diffusing new technology acquires momentum. This is well documented in terms of decisions within industries in which prominent firms adopt QC circles and are quickly followed by major competitors who fear a loss of competitive advantage. In Japan, for example, quality-control circles achieved rapid growth in the mid 1980s in the brewery and construction industries. In each case, a pioneering firm (Suntory and Takenaka Komuten respectively) adopted QC circles and the other firms in the industry responded in rapid succession. Both are highly competitive oligopolistic industries in which any management innovation that promises competitive advantage is likely to be picked up quickly by peer firms.[1] If the enthusiasm for the new ideas cannot be sustained, they will be labeled a fad. Those hostile to the innovation may anticipate such an outcome, possibly generating a self-fulfilling prophecy.

In Sweden a 1969 "hallelujah" conference featuring the noted advocate of semi-autonomous work groups Einar Thorsrud kicked off the bandwagon phase. In Japan it occurred somewhat earlier, and in the United States we seem to have entered this phase in the early 1980s, as testified by the treatment of the subject in business journals.[2] The participative programs of well-known large manufacturing firms like General Motors, Westinghouse, and General Electric were written up widely in the business press, and seminars and workshops on small-group activities were conducted by and for many major firms. The emotional character of such publicity, the promotion effort, and often the sheer power of the promoters tend to push careful evaluation of results by potential adopters into the background. At this point, companies begin adopting participatory work practices because it is the "thing to do." The public message is that your ability to compete successfully will be impaired unless you adopt this magic new formula. Prestige accrues to the early adopters (cf. Meyer and Rowan 1977). They are held up in the media as models to emulate and large-scale visits from other companies take place. The more skillful, like Volvo, Saab, the Buick Motor Division of General Motors, Hewlett-Packard, Sony, and Toyota, will convert this into a public relations success, increasing their legitimacy both internally and externally. Edward Lawler (1986:230–31) comes to similar conclusions, pointing out that such publicity often precedes any firm evidence of success.

---

1. The particular examples used here are documented in Lillrank 1988:197.
2. See, e.g., "The New Industrial Relations," *Business Week*, 11 May 1981, pp. 84–98.

NASA: Getting In on the Action

To more fully understand the extent to which the choice of small-group activities is separated from systematic search and evaluation procedures as the movement gains momentum, let us consider the experience of NASA. This is of interest because it allows us to investigate whether NASA's rationale for adopting participatory activity and the mode of diffusion differ from those of the mass-production blue-collar industries. Some 85 percent of the NASA budget goes to contractors (mostly in the private sector), and the impact of NASA policies on them is instructive.

As a government agency with a mission that is very much in the public eye, NASA has a strong interest in maintaining a good reputation for quality. Every failure or delay of a widely promoted space mission owing to quality defects is a source of national embarrassment, a demoralizing experience for NASA employees and suppliers, a threat to budget appropriations, and an invitation to political meddling, as well as a source of fear that the agency may lose launch customers (satellite owners) to NASA's European competitor, Arianespace. Last, but not least, failures or delays are a threat to individual careers, jobs, and contracts.[3] The 1986 shuttle disaster brought many of these very factors into play.

It is thus not surprising that quality circles came to the attention of NASA, which is continually looking for ways to raise quality and reliability levels. The agency recognizes that its quality problems have many causes, and that there is therefore a good chance any particular quality-related solution will address at least one of them. Consequently, NASA scans the environment for solutions rather than problems and seeks to match any quality-related solution it finds with some relevant quality problem.[4]

At the same time, NASA regards itself as an elite government agency performing a "sacred" national mission. At least until the Challenger accident, it also saw itself as practicing state-of-the-art management. There is a certain hubris associated with this world

---

3. See Arlen Large, "Shuttle to Try Satellite Rescue in Display Aimed at Customers," *Wall Street Journal*, 6 November 1984, p. 2.

4. James March (1981 : 569) arrives at these same conclusions from a theoretical perspective.

view that leads to a resistance to innovation. The mentality is, "If it's good, we must already be doing it."[5]

Around 1978 some key NASA officials who had been exposed to quality-circle ideas encouraged Martin Marietta Aerospace, one of NASA's prime contractors for the manned shuttle program, to initiate circle activities. Concerned about morale problems in their own operations and not oblivious to the political benefits to be derived from cooperating with new initiatives from a major customer, officials at Martin Marietta agreed, and activities were begun at Martin Marietta's Michoud Division in 1979. There was considerable trial-and-error experimentation over the next four years. Michoud personnel developed a set of measures that indicated that the circles were making significant quality and productivity contributions, and it proved a clever political stroke to create "integrated teams" of on-site NASA officials and Martin Marietta middle managers. The participating NASA officials sent back positive reports on their experiences.

NASA hung back despite repeated urging by Martin Marietta that nothing would come of the effort unless the agency took the lead. You have to "practice what you preach" was the argument used. Independent of NASA headquarters, the Huntsville NASA facility began experimenting in this area as well. At the same time, officials from NASA headquarters began visiting private sector firms such as Westinghouse to examine their productivity and quality-improvement efforts. Circles were identified as a key element in these efforts. By 1983 NASA began advocating employee participation through quality circles.

First, NASA pushed its own operations to adopt circles, known as NETS (NASA Employee Teams). Headquarter briefings were held to get the message across. The NETS were to be part of the NASA Productivity Improvement and Quality Enhancement Program (PIQE) adopted in 1983. The agency funded Martin Marietta's Michoud Division to provide the training for personnel at its various installations. In April 1983 Michoud held a facilitator training course for personnel at NASA installations. A 1983 summary report was written up and distributed widely within NASA and

5. Kanter (1983:347–51) identified a similar world view at General Motors, with an added dose of belief in organizational immortality.

among suppliers detailing the achievements of the employee-participation efforts at its headquarter operations and at each of its installations (NASA 1984a). Such reports are "show and tell operations" designed to put pressure on each installation to have some solid material to report that will make it look good next time around. The manager of a unit with a weak report would be on the spot. To give the reader a feel for such statements, here is the published report given by NASA headquarters Code M:

Code M established a NET in the Resources and Institutions Office, with participants ranging from GS 11–15, both supervisory and non-supervisory personnel. Two NET members were trained by Martin Marietta's Michoud Division's System Refinement Team (SRT). They, in turn, have trained the other team members in NET techniques. SRT training resource materials have been made available. A sizable list of problems have been generated. From the list, the consensus is that the top two problems are POP/budget techniques and staff communications. A second "unofficial" NET has been established and is comprised of the OSF secretarial and clerical work force. A secretarial retreat has been scheduled for early January that should encourage more team spirit, establish better communications, and provide an opportunity for the secretaries to complete several current projects. These projects should result in more consistency within each OSF organization in handling correspondence and personnel-related items.

In the External Tank Program system, refinement teams [quality circles] at the contractor continue to produce cost savings, reduce attrition, and enhance productivity.

(NASA 1984b)

We see here a situation in which, contrary to the rational model of decision making, a scanning of the environment for quality-related solutions led NASA to identify circles as one such solution and to experiment with applying it to its problems. The heads of each of its installations were not all equally convinced of the merits of this new approach, and we have seen one way in which pressures were brought to bear on these installations for adoption.

The rational model of decision making, which links the prior identification of problems with the subsequent search for solutions, breaks down even further when we examine NASA's activities vis-à-vis its suppliers. As NASA officials became convinced of the utility of participative management through the Michoud experience, they began to encourage adoption of small problem-solving groups in meetings with their other prime shuttle contractors (for example, Rockwell International and Morton-Thiokol). Soon the word was out among suppliers that it was advisable to begin employee-participation activities through the adoption of quality circles.

The Michoud Division of Martin Marietta again became a major training center for NASA. This time an informal arrangement through a "technical directive" from NASA at the Marshall Space Flight Center at Huntsville provided the funds to teach suppliers how to organize quality circles. The technical directive from Huntsville was a strategy to avoid the inevitable delay that would have resulted if approval had been sought from the bureaucracy at the national level. Suppliers learned that funds could be inserted in their budgets to cover the costs of such training *without reducing their profits.* In the world of bureaucratic organizations, that is a very powerful message! Moreover, for those contractors working on a cost-plus-award-fee basis, a strong favorable evaluation of their circle efforts by NASA could lead to points being added to the overall evaluation that went into their award fee (that is, their profit). The message was very clear: NASA wanted its suppliers to adopt employee-participation activities. Moreover, with a large number of agency officials working on-site at the supplier firms themselves, NASA could make its views known quite clearly.

In September 1984 a two-day conference was held for all major NASA contractors on productivity and quality improvement; executives from 110 corporations attended. Employee-participation workshops were a prominent feature of the two-day activities, again a clear message as to what NASA expected of its suppliers. When one of the participants asked the NASA administrator at the public forum if quality circles were going to be mandated in the future, he said no. My conversations with a number of the participants afterwards made clear that such a disclaimer was to be taken with a grain of salt. While it would be "bad form" to publicly impose circles on contractors, there was little doubt among most participants as to the direction NASA expected them to take. The signal was there for all who could read it. Customers are continually sending out signals to their suppliers in all realms about appropriate business behavior. The more adept among the suppliers are skillful in getting an early reading and turning it into a competitive advantage.

The Auto Industry: The Word Is Out

The kind of process described above is neither unique to NASA nor confined to the public sector. We see the same two-step process in the case of the U.S. automotive industry. The first step involved leaders of the auto firms issuing a strong message to their various installations in the late 1970s that employee-participation activities were strategies that had been identified as effective in dealing with various problems relating to productivity, quality, and worker satisfaction. At Ford this came in the form of a direct letter from the president of the company on 5 November 1979 announcing the new policy of employee involvement. The policy letter was accompanied by a directive to all general managers and above informing them in unequivocal terms that they were expected to develop employee-involvement practices (see appendixes A and B). Management was informed that it would be expected to operate within a set of guidelines, one of which stated: "Methods of managing should encourage employe participation in identifying and solving work-related problems."[6] In short, though it was not entirely clear to plant managers what form their employee-involvement program should take, it was clear that they had better "get cracking." Clearly, "circle-like activities" were high on the list of appropriate responses. The only option managers had was in choosing the particular form of employee involvement, and even that was subject to approval by the personnel and organization and labor relations departments.

General Motors made the same decision in 1979, with President Elliott Estes and James McDonald, then executive vice president for North American Operations, providing the sponsorship (Kanter 1983:340). GM took NASA's more gentlemanly approach. Every GM plant was "strongly encouraged" to launch a QWL program.

---

6. As if to illustrate the power of directives at Ford, the company still insists on spelling *employee* with one final *e*, a practice begun by a directive from John Bugas in the mid 1940s! Bugas, an ex-FBI man, was brought into the company by Harry Bennett in 1944 and became a confidant of Henry Ford II's. As vice president of industrial relations, and the man in charge of plant newspapers and news releases, he is said to have insisted that the spelling of *employee* conform to current newspaper style. Still another story that Ford managers have told me is that an efficiency expert sold the idea to Bugas, claiming that it would save a lot of money in typing and paper costs. I am indebted to David Lewis of the University of Michigan School of Business Administration for much of this background.

The message, however, was no less clear than at Ford. QWL programs, including small-group activities, were now mandatory.

The second step, taken in the early 1980s, was the strong initiative by the automotive companies to begin working with their suppliers to improve quality and productivity. Suppliers were made to understand that quality improvement was a precondition for maintaining their customer's business and some version of small-group problem-solving activity was clearly part of the quality-improvement package. With the widely anticipated reduction in U.S. automotive suppliers gradually taking shape in the mid 1980s, it behooved every supplier to take such messages seriously. Those who could move rapidly saw themselves as developing a competitive edge.

It should not be thought that the processes described above are unique to the United States. In the mid 1960s Toyota, with its well-developed communication links with suppliers, became one of the first large Japanese companies to make the decision to introduce its quality-circle program to its suppliers. We can be quite sure that these highly dependent suppliers responded with great alacrity, alert to the political implications rather than out of any profound understanding of the intrinsic benefits to be derived from circle activity. As one student of Japanese QC circles puts it, referring to the Japanese manufacturing sector generally: "If the parent company executives believe in QC circles, the subcontractors believe too" (Lillrank 1988:127).

Summary

We can see the bandwagon effect in both the diffusion of small-group activities to specific units within large firms and their spread to "captive" suppliers and contractors. But the popular image of the bandwagon effect as a kind of spontaneous combustion does not capture the full range of the process. Such spontaneity can apply among "peer" organizations, but is far less relevant when inter-organizational relationships are hierarchically structured. The popular imagery of the bandwagon has its counterpart in the social sciences, where some scholars see the process of diffusion as one of contagion. Borrowing from the epidemiological model, the new behavior spreads in response to contact among organizations and the attractiveness of the behavior or beliefs being imitated.[7] In contrast, the spread of small-group activities from customers to suppliers involves the exercise of power on the part of customers. Power creates the opportunities for streams of problems, solutions, and actors to come together at a given time and place. For Williamson's transaction cost economizing to have any meaning in this situation, the role of power in influencing future income streams (for suppliers) must be given center stage in any trade-off analysis.

We see here less a "bandwagon effect" than a "domino effect." Each successive adoption adds pressure for subsequent adoptions. Recalcitrant parties or "slow learners" are brought into line by sanctions if necessary. Internal diagnosis of work-related problems and a search for solutions is replaced by the adoption of "the solution" for quite unrelated, though nevertheless powerful, reasons. The approach outlined here is quite consistent with what has been labeled the "emergent norm" approach to the spread of fads (Turner and Killian 1972:21–25). Adapting this perspective to the organizational level, I would say that organizations are recruited to fads through preexisting networks of interaction, structured by power relationships. These networks account for the selective clustering of adopters. Fads are accompanied by strong informal pressures (emergent norms) to participate and penalties for those reluctant to do so (see Miller 1985:152). Whether these fads evolve into incipient or lasting social movements is a matter still to be addressed.

One consequence of this kind of process is that adopting units may have relatively little commitment to small-group activities per se. Many managers tend to see employee participation as just one more productivity program along the road—little more than a new set of acronyms. They respond to the political pressure to adopt quality circles with inflated reports of their achievements and hope that by the time it is obvious that not much has happened, their customer will be onto a new program. While this is not necessarily the case, the tendency to such attitudes is strong in situations where the innovation in question implies a delegation of power, thereby

7. See James March's discussion of this tradition (March 1981).

threatening existing authority relationships, and when the parent company or agency has a history of short-term programs that produce no lasting effects.

Over time there is a decoupling of motivation and search from solutions. Instead of problems chasing solutions, as posited in the rational model of decision making, solutions begin to chase problems. The solution is publicly dangled before companies with the promise that it will address a wide range of problems. Or, as we saw in the preceding examples, it is forcefully presented to specific operations and suppliers, who recognize that it is politically expedient for them to adopt the new practice if they expect to have successful careers in the company or to maintain their contracts. The presumption, whether true or not, is that the proponents have searched and found the most suitable alternative. Contrary to the standard model of diffusion, we see that in the "bandwagon" or "domino effect" phases, discovery and transmission clearly precede the search.

Chapter Six

Search, Discovery, Transmission

To learn, one must be humble.

James Joyce, *Ulysses*

In this chapter I examine the sources of the ideas that formed the basis for small-group activities in Japan, Sweden, and the United States and discuss some of the transformations that took place in the course of their transmission. When I began investigating small-group activities in the three countries, I was soon struck by the importance of the flow of ideas across national borders. How this operated and its significance became the subject of further investigation. The chapter also examines the nature of the search process at different phases of the diffusion of small-group activities, which sheds further light on the various decision-making models in use.

Swedish Developments: The Paradox of Success

The ideas adopted by Swedish employers during the early 1970s can be traced to a small degree to the contributions of American behavioral science and particularly the work of Abraham Maslow, Douglas McGregor, and Rensis Likert (Swedish Employers' Confederation 1971). The central line of influence, however, derives from developments at the Tavistock Institute in England (Emery and Trist 1969). The Tavistock researchers were strongly influenced by theories of group dynamics and particularly by the work of Kurt Lewin, a German Jew who came to the United States in 1932. Lewin did pioneering research into the determinants of group decision making, the productivity of groups, and the influence on individual behavior of participation in group discussions and decisions (Homans 1968:259).

The first social science experiments directly ancestral to the early 1970 Swedish efforts to adopt self-steering groups were conducted by Tavistock researchers in the early 1950s. These efforts began in a study of English coal mines and involved systematic comparisons of different kinds of work organization and wage systems and their impact on work performance. They led the researchers to conclude that "composite" forms of work organization with a holistic approach that stressed group work and responsibility were superior to conventional approaches. The new work methods involved integration of tasks rather than the differentiation of tasks characteristic of conventional mining methods.

These Tavistock ideas emphasized the development of the organization as an open sociotechnical system, with work organization based on the interaction of social and technical factors (that is, behavioral and physical events). Work was to be seen as a sociotechnical whole. At the group level, this means that the whole work group and the entire activity cycle must be taken into consideration in the design of work.[1] In coordinating the social and technical factors, the Tavistock researchers made the assumption that there are several degrees of freedom on the technical side, so that the form of technical organization that fits best with the social factors should be selected. This is in contrast to the traditional view that the technical side always determines the parameters for the social organization of work. The aim is to develop small work groups that maintain a high level of independence and autonomy. This involves highly group-oriented work processes and group decision making. It is expected that as a consequence jobs and learning possibilities will be enriched and individual responsibility increased. All this is to be achieved without any loss in productivity compared to conventional work organization.

1. See Sandberg 1982 for a fuller discussion of the development of ideas on work organization at the Tavistock Institute from a Swedish perspective.

English employers were slow to adopt these ideas, but they were carried to Scandinavia—especially to Norway—by the charismatic and visionary Norwegian scholar Einar Thorsrud (see Cherns 1979). The ideas came to Sweden indirectly through Norway and directly through the work of scholars like Eric Rhenman (1964), a researcher associated with the Swedish Employers' Confederation, and Reine Hansson, who conducted studies of how work motivation is influenced by organization and wage systems in 1967–69 (see Sandberg 1982:146–50).

Three of the key events that served as a transmission belt from Norway to Sweden were a visit to Norway in 1966 by a Swedish union and management team led by Reine Hansson, who was close to Thorsrud's research; the translation of Thorsrud's research into Swedish in 1969 under the auspices of a joint labor-management publication company (Thorsrud and Emery 1969); and the "hallelujah conference" held at the Museum of Modern Art in Stockholm in 1969 with Thorsrud as the featured speaker. The conference was sponsored by the technical department of the Swedish Employers' Confederation (SAF) and attended by officials of major companies, as well as by selected union officials. The original plan did not include inviting union representatives, but Thorsrud protested, and at the last minute some were invited.

As discussed earlier, Thorsrud's ideas were not as well accepted in Norway as they were in Sweden. This is commonly explained by the lack of relevant mass-production industries in Norway, middle-management opposition, too heavy a reliance on academic consultants, and the hostility of organized labor. The unions saw many of Thorsrud's ideas on direct shop floor participation as a threat to the centralized decision-making power of the labor movement (cf. Jenkins 1974). Swedish scholars often say that the ideas developed in England, were tried out in Norway, and achieved their widest diffusion in Sweden.

The sociotechnical approach is a package with far-reaching implications for a firm's organization, but has a diffuse quality, deriving from ambiguous operational goals and technology, that undoubtedly slowed the diffusion process. It was not a calibrated solution with known costs and outcomes of the kind management would have preferred. As Pehr Gyllenhammar, the president of Volvo, remarked in a 1984 speech at a Volvo workshop on production technology and quality of working life: "Management wants balanced change where you know what will happen—where you can manage change, and therefore it is good."[2]

As noted earlier, in addition to its diffuseness, the sociotechnical package has strong democratizing overtones. The books of Thorsrud and his collaborators typically focus on the themes of industrial democracy and democratizing the workplace. So important were these themes to the authors that the terms often appear in the titles of their works, which strongly challenged the traditional hierarchical control structure. The notion of autonomous work structures was explicitly linked to the freedom of workers from oppressive, arbitrary management. In the early days of the movement, Thorsrud was known in Sweden as "the foreman killer." We can see this challenge in the "psychosocial job design criteria" laid down by Thorsrud and his collaborators in the early 1960s (which assume that acceptable levels of income and job security have already been achieved). These criteria were expressed somewhat differently from publication to publication, but they typically included the following:

1. Freedom on the part of workers to make decisions about how to do their work
2. A meaningful set of tasks, offering some variety and some free space to develop the job over time
3. Opportunity for learning on the job and to continue learning on the basis of feedback of results and future needs
4. Freedom to give and receive help on the job and to establish mutual respect between people at work
5. Recognition and social respect outside the workplace for doing a useful job
6. Some form of desirable future at work, not only in the form of promotion

While a number of these criteria, seen in isolation from the others, could be supplied by management action, the first—freedom on the part of workers to make decisions about how to do their work— sets the tone for an approach to work design diametrically opposed

2. From author's notes made at the time.

to the control system of traditional bureaucracy. These criteria were widely discussed in Sweden during the late 1960s and early 1970s (Swedish Employers' Confederation 1971; Törner 1976).

This initial discussion in Sweden was, however, followed by a gradual diminution of the democratic theme as the concept was applied by management. That is, there was a sanitizing of the originally radical concepts as management tailored the implementation process to its own needs. In the late 1960s and early 1970s the term *democratization of the workplace* was much in vogue, particularly among trade unionists and scholars and in the mass media. But as management took over control of the implementation process, the theme of democratization gradually diminished in importance, at least as applied to small-group activity on the shop and office floor. Nowhere is this seen more clearly than in the shift in the language describing what managers thought they were doing. The term *autonomous work groups* (literally "self-steering groups" in Swedish) fell rapidly into disuse among management in the early 1970s. Increasingly the term *production groups* came to be used. By 1974 the technical department of the Swedish Employers' Confederation could write in a summary report: "Autonomous groups became for a time somewhat of a fad—today this term is less common and one now speaks most often of production groups, which better describes what it deals with." By the late 1970s and early 1980s managers even replaced the term *production groups* and began to speak of "group work" or "group organization" as one part of the creation of "new factories" characterized by small independent production units, freeing employees from machine-pacing, jobs with more personal involvement, and fast and reliable production systems (Agurén and Edgren 1979).[3]

Consistent with my observations about goal succession in chapter 4, concerns about democratization of the workplace had been replaced by a strong focus on improving productivity and quality.

3. Interestingly, many Swedes continue to use the term *autonomous work groups* when writing or speaking to American audiences; if they used it in Sweden, however, they would be criticized by managers for being old-fashioned and out of step with the times. It is as if they find it too hard to explain the complicated events of the past decade to Americans and therefore look for an accepted shorthand that they know Americans will understand. This illustrates well the difficulties of cross-national communication, even with the best of intentions and language skills.

In 1984 a workshop was held for foreign and local experts at Volvo's Skövde engine plant to observe and discuss the current status of group work and new directions in work organization at the plant. At that workshop Rolf Lindholm, a major formulator of the Swedish Employers' Confederation's policy in the 1970s, commented to the plant staff: "When I talked with managers in the early 1970s, it was a concern to meet the needs of human beings that drove change forward, but today it has the smell of business."[4]

Much of the discussion in the late 1970s centered around the kind of understanding that labor and management would reach regarding the implementation of the new co-determination law. But by 1984 the *Dagens Nyheter*, the leading Swedish newspaper, reported that unionists and management were no longer talking about co-determination but rather about "development," which they defined as "local solutions for local problems." Furthermore, "the new slogans, 'change' and 'development' belong together with service, efficiency, and all that is now called 'management.'"[5]

What we see here is the conversion of a blossoming mass movement stressing democratic principles into a much narrower business tool. In the course of this transformation a good deal of the enthusiasm and motivation behind the original changes evaporated. The initial conversion of radical scholarly theories to practical management knowledge may well have been necessary to ensure managerial acceptance. But this narrowing seems, in dialectical fashion, to have limited the potential for more widespread diffusion and acceptance by employees and unions. When I met Thorsrud and Hansson in late 1984, not long before their deaths, they both expressed disappointment at the direction developments had taken. "Founders" often have a difficult time seeing their ideas evolve.

Japanese Developments: From Elitism to Mass Movement

In the case of Japan, there was initially a similar cross-national diffusion process, but the source of the ideas was primarily the United States. American behavioral scientists' research is well known in

4. From author's notes made at the time.
5. Anders Mellbourn, "MBL inte så dålig some sitt rykte" (MBL isn't as bad as its reputation), *Dagens Nyheter*, 29 April 1984, p. 16.

Japan as a result of the broad "management boom" of the postwar period in which, from the 1950s on, the ideas of American management in all fields, especially personnel administration, attained an exalted position in the eyes of Japanese management. It is not surprising that the Japanese were willing and eager to study American management techniques in the early postwar period, when the United States was unquestionably the world's most advanced industrial nation, in addition to being Japan's conqueror and occupying power. Generally, the Japanese were willing, independent of any objective confirmation, to make the assumption that American management techniques were the most advanced. Over time, however, they found that they had to adapt them to fit Japanese conditions.

In the area of small-group activities, as in Sweden, the research of McGregor, Maslow, and Likert, as well as of Chris Argyris and Frederick Herzberg, to name a few key individuals, is particularly well known in Japan. This is a function of the almost instantaneous translation of books and articles, the steady stream of Japanese students to the United States (many of them company employees doing graduate work), and invited lecture tours of American experts to Japan (cf. Kobayashi and Burke 1976). It would be rare to find the personnel head of a major Japanese firm who is not well versed in the various ideas of leading American scholars in this area. These ideas, combined with and adapted to indigenous values and practices, formed part of the foundation of Japanese small-group activities.

We can see these processes in the work and influence of Juji Misumi, a noted Japanese social psychologist who studied at the University of Michigan in the mid 1950s and came under the influence of a number of the students of Kurt Lewin (for example, Ronald Lippitt, Alvin Zander, and Dorwin Cartwright).[6] Based on their understandings of group decision-making processes, he conducted research in Japan upon his return that led him and his co-workers to stress the importance of small-group discussions conducted prior to individual decision as a basis for group decisions. In 1963 he began work with a large transportation company, stressing

6. Kurt Lewin may come about as close as anyone to being the intellectual godfather of industrial applications of small-group activities.

a series of small-group meetings to devise strategies for accident reduction.

These activities were quite successful and the company expanded them throughout the entire bus department in 1969. At the same time, it merged Misumi-derived programs with the zero-defect (ZD) program in vogue in Japan at that time (Misumi 1980). ZD was also a U.S.–originated program, begun as a motivational campaign for workers aiming at zero production defects by quality-control personnel at the Martin Company in connection with its contract for the U.S. Army's Pershing missile system in the early 1960s (Halpin 1966). The program was modified by the Japanese to stress small-group processes and in turn has subsequently merged with the quality-circle concept in the eyes of most Japanese managers. We see in microcosm here the process by which Japanese students of American social science and organizations incorporated their new ideas and modified them in the course of applying them to Japanese work organizations. We also see how they merged with the different streams of development arising from the technical quality-control discipline, as well as with traditional approaches to group activity in industry, as mentioned in chapter 4.

We can pursue the contribution of the quality-control discipline in Japan to the small-group-activities movement through an analysis of the evolution of quality circles. This will also give us a sense of the capacity of the Japanese to borrow and adapt Western organizational technology to their own needs. Quality-control circles are the essence of the Japanese approach to small-group activities, an example of the creative process of borrowing and adaptation in the personnel policies of large Japanese companies.

The Japanese Union of Scientists and Engineers (JUSE) was established in 1949 and became the focal point of efforts to introduce modern quality-control practices and, later, quality-control circles in Japan. An early postwar effort to improve quality was organized by U.S. occupation officials seeking to restore basic services such as telecommunications. They helped arrange for American statisticians to go to Japan and teach American wartime industrial standards to Japanese engineers and statisticians. Prominent in this early effort was a series of postwar lectures beginning in 1950 undertaken by William Edwards Deming to teach the Japanese statistical quality-control practices (for example, control charts and sampling inspection).

In 1954 the noted quality-control expert Joseph Juran arrived in Japan to give a series of lectures. He emphasized a newer orientation to quality control, stating that it must be an integral part of the management function and practiced throughout the firm. Armand Feigenbaum's book on quality control in 1960, with its emphasis on total quality control (TQC), was also influential (see Feigenbaum 1961).

These ideas spread rapidly in Japan from the mid 1950s through the early 1960s, but there were some critical innovations (adaptations) on the part of Japanese firms as they began to adopt them in their daily practice. In the Japanese reinterpretation, each and every person in the organizational hierarchy, from top management to rank-and-file employees, was to study quality-control concepts and take responsibility for their implementation. As Japanese managers began to teach foremen the concepts of quality control, the idea developed of creating workshop study groups composed of the foreman and his subordinates as a means of getting workers to take more responsibility for quality (JUSE 1971:9). In particular, these study groups were seen as a solution to the problem of how to make workers read the QC materials that were being prepared. Group activity would encourage those who were otherwise not so inclined to read.[7]

Such developments in turn evolved into the quality-control circles of today. An examination of the first issue of *The Workshop and QC*, published in April 1962 by JUSE, reveals a conception of workshop QC activity still at something of a remove from the actual operation of quality circles today. The focus was on training foremen how to work with employees to get the latter to accept and maintain work standards so that quality objectives would be met. Getting workers more involved in taking responsibility for setting and revising work standards was the strategy advocated (JUSE 1962). The circles developed as a rather spontaneous adaptive process when management began to extend the new ideas of quality control. Gradually, these ideas growing out of the quality move-

---

7. Interview with Ishikawa Kaoru in 1977.

ment merged with ideas of decentralization of authority and group decision making.

Not only were all employees from top to bottom to be involved in taking responsibility for quality, but all branches of the organization, from marketing and design and purchasing down through sales, were also to do so in the new Japanese reinterpretation. Unlike Feigenbaum's narrow concept of TQC, which still left responsibility with the quality-control department, the broadened Japanese concept of TQC stressed that all departments had to take responsibility for quality control through coordinated action.

What happened in Japan was exactly the opposite of what took place in Sweden, where the democratic ideas of the Tavistock researchers were sanitized to make them acceptable. Instead, in Japan, the elitist American approach evolved into a management-led mass social movement. This is not to say that the Japanese adopted a Tavistock or American perspective on democratization. For the Japanese, democratization in this context meant mass participation more than it did expanded autonomy for individuals and groups of employees at the expense of the hierarchical control system.

Many of the Japanese innovations arose in incremental and spontaneous fashion as managers and workers took Western ideas to their logical conclusions in ways totally unanticipated by either the American experts or, often, even the Japanese leaders. Such was the case with quality circles.

Taking Western management strategies developed for use with management personnel and applying them to blue-collar workers has been a characteristic practice in postwar Japanese corporations. The evolution of quality circles thus fitted in with a more general borrowing pattern, reflecting egalitarian trends in the postwar period that broke down the barriers between white- and blue-collar workers (Shirai 1983:117–43). The extension of monthly pay systems and bonuses to blue-collar workers under pressure from militant unionists in the early postwar period was one manifestation of this egalitarianism. Still another example is the transfer of American ideas on career development to Japanese firms. These ideas on the importance of developing careers for employees and associated policies were evolved in America and designed for application to managerial employees. Characteristically, the Japanese borrowed many of these ideas and extended their application to blue-collar employees (Cole 1979:41, 172–73; Koike 1983:29–61).

The Role of Scholars

It is of particular significance that scholarly theories and ideas provide much of the foundation for the small-group activity movement that developed in Japan and especially in Sweden. In the three countries, the industrial relations scholars who most consistently ignored small-group activities were the Japanese (with some exceptions), at least until Japanese efforts acquired a worldwide reputation by the mid-to-late 1970s. Prior to that period, in characteristic fashion, the Japanese managers found that they could directly consult Western scholarly output as well as draw upon their own historical legacy. Swedish scholars were most directly involved as advisors to the government, management, and the trade unions in the formulation of policy. This seems to fit with the oft-noted penchant the Swedes have for relying on technical experts and seeing social problems as ones to be resolved primarily through the exercise of technical expertise. To paraphrase the noted Swedish social scientist Hans Zetterberg, the debate over how to proceed with participation at the workplace in Sweden tended to take on the character of a debate among rational experts, each side with its scholarly advocates, and the solutions proposed had the appearance of applied social science (Zetterberg 1984:85). Moreover, the academic fraternity in Scandinavia has generally been more closely associated with national political and economic processes than has been the case in other advanced industrial nations (Mead 1984:12–13).

The United States provides a middle case, with scholars filtering some Western European ideas (semi-autonomous work groups become self-managing teams in the American context) and developing their own approaches to participation; the work of Rensis Likert and Edward Lawler comes immediately to mind as an example of the latter. At a 1985 workshop on participative work practices at the University of Michigan, I asked the some fifty members of the audience (mostly auto industry managers involved with participatory efforts) who among them had heard of, or read, the work of Emery, Trist, or Thorsrud on the sociotechnical approach. Not one member of the audience raised his hand! Yet, undoubtedly, they were familiar with many of the ideas of these writers through the filtering process described above (see, for example, Lawler 1986). By and large, however, U.S. scholars have played only a modest role in mediating the flow of information about Japanese quality circles. American managers found that they could obtain access to information from U.S. consultants and later from Japanese firms through "transplants" and joint ventures.

Limiting Factors in the United States

To appreciate the different trends in the United States at the very time when the Japanese and Swedes were moving rapidly toward adopting small-group activities, let us turn to a consideration of the contributions of Charles Kepner and Benjamin Tregoe. The comparisons take on added meaning in the light of the aforementioned propensity of the Japanese to extend Western ideas developed for management personnel to blue-collar workers.

Kepner and Tregoe's approach to problem solving and decision making for individual managers was quite influential in American management circles in the 1960s and 1970s. At the time that the Japanese were developing quality circles, these researchers were crystallizing their technique for teaching individual managers how to solve problems systematically. In *The Rational Manager,* they claimed to have put 15,000 American managers through their courses (Kepner and Tregoe 1965).

An examination of their text leads to a number of interesting observations. First, the techniques espoused for identifying, prioritizing, and solving problems, though on an individual level, were not fundamentally so different from those being taught to blue-collar workers in Japan. In some respects, the Japanese techniques came to be more sophisticated! For example, the Japanese took another American development, value engineering, developed for engineers and used for assuring that the essential functions are provided at minimum overall cost, and introduced it for use among QC circle members. Many American managers would be ill-prepared to handle this technique. It is also a minor irony that in the late

1970s and early 1980s a number of major U.S. corporations explicitly absorbed some of the features of Kepner-Tregoe training into their quality-circle training materials.

In discussing the research of Rensis Likert, Kepner and Tregoe criticized his advocacy of group action and participative management for lacking problem-solving and decision-making techniques. In retrospect, we can see that what was required for the equivalent of small problem-solving groups at the shop and office floor to have emerged at this time was, first, for American managers to have combined Likert's ideas on group action with Kepner and Tregoe's ideas and, second, for them to have had the imagination to recognize that these ideas could apply to employees at all levels of the firm. The proprietary nature of the Kepner-Tregoe materials limited even other individuals from exploring those opportunities. More important, these ideas and solutions simply were not in the repertoire of practitioners. It was not until 1987 that Kepner and Tregoe announced in a promotional brochure a "totally new approach to Statistical Process Control which permits this powerful tool to be used not only by managers but other key shop floor workers and specifically develops trouble-shooting skills enabling them to participate in quality improvement opportunities." Even then, it was being limited to "key" shop floor workers.

We can see that the emphasis on the individual and on the decision-making authority of the manager blinded American managers and researchers at this time to the advantages of group action at the shop and office floor level. This is ironic; one of the typical criticisms of the Kepner-Tregoe training voiced by managers has been that once it is completed and you go back to your firm, there are no structured incentives for using the new approaches. This, of course, is exactly what the group framework of circles would have provided.

In the history of technology transfer—and we may think of these ideas on small-group activities as a kind of organizational technology—it is common that the inventors of a technology are not necessarily the commercializers. The jet engine, for example, was invented in England but successfully commercialized in the United States (Miller and Sawers 1970). The causes of this disjuncture form the basis for an interesting intellectual inquiry.

Why has American management been so slow in adopting the

ideas of American scholars in contrast to the interest shown in their work by foreign scholars and managers? Some explanations are suggested by the preceding analysis of the Kepner and Tregoe contributions and why they took the form they did.

Beyond that, Japan and Sweden are oriented to the outside world to an extent that is hard for Americans to understand. They perceive themselves as relying heavily on export industries to sustain their standards of living. Some one-third of Sweden's GNP is accounted for by exports. The Japanese widely believe that they are able to secure their national survival only by adding value to imported raw materials and then exporting the product. Both Japanese and Swedes thus believe that their success—indeed, their very survival as nations—depends on their ability to search out and absorb ideas from abroad rapidly and efficiently. In both countries, if a solution to a problem is not immediately at hand, it is second nature to management to look for solutions outside their national borders. To succeed in foreign markets, they have learned to be open to different cultures. In Japan this stems in large part from the "catch-up" mentality that has dominated the thinking of industry and government officials over the past one hundred years. To catch up you had to be prepared to adopt the better ideas developed in the more advanced Western nations. Moreover, defeat by the United States in World War II and subsequent occupation by a foreign power for the first time in Japan's long, proud history had a profound humbling effect that is hard for foreigners to understand. In the case of Sweden, the humility necessary for strong receptivity to foreign ideas seems to derive more from being a relatively small nation. As one industry official explained to me: "Swedes believe that there is always something better somewhere else. It is inconceivable for them with only eight million people and such limited resources to think that they have arrived at the best solution to a given problem. Therefore, they are always looking for ideas from abroad." The net result is that for diverse reasons mapping their foreign environment in a systematic fashion is a well-institutionalized practice in both countries.

One must be careful not to overgeneralize these observations. For example, the Swedes have been decidedly slower than Americans in grasping the competitive implications of Japanese management practices as related to small-group activities. I would speculate that this is both because the Swedes have been more buffered from the strong winds of Japanese competition and because their ideas on democratization have prevented them from understanding what the Japanese have to offer.

Nothwithstanding, the situation of the United States is very different from the situations of Japan and Sweden. Until recently, Americans appeared confident of their own managerial abilities and technology and not very attuned to learning from abroad. Even in the area of hard technology, not to speak of organizational technology, American companies maintained few listening posts in Japan relative to the size of the Japanese effort in the United States. Indeed, even with all that has happened between 1970 and 1985, it can be said without the slightest fear of contradiction that U.S. monitoring of global developments in technology has been, and continues to be, woefully inadequate. Yet increasingly our firms operate in an environment where new developments in management and technology are occurring outside U.S. borders (cf. Rowand 1985:15). To take the example of organizational technology, we have seen how few American managers are directly aware of the contributions of Emery, Trist, and Thorsrud, and they are even less familiar with the Japanese gurus of small-group activity. With a vast domestic market, the United States cannot be said to be export-oriented to the extent of Japan or Sweden. American managers were accustomed to being on top, and until recently there was simply not the same incentive to learn from others.

Moreover, the ideas put forward by American behavioral scientists seemed to fit much better with existing organizational practices in Japan and with the prevailing Japanese managerial philosophy than they did in the United States. The Japanese scholar Takezawa Shin'ichi caught the flavor of this in the following remarks:

The behavioral science model of management, however, is not perceived as an antithesis of the organizational reality as it might be in the United States. Instead, Japanese managers tend to accept the model as an idealized goal which essentially lies in the same direction as their own behavioral orientation. Often, they are puzzled to find out that American management in practice fits the scientific management model far better than that of the behavioral sciences.

(Takezawa 1976:31)

This difference provides an explanation for why these ideas were so eagerly received in Japan and why, once combined with small-group activities, they led to a choice opportunity. Similar judgments could be made in comparing Swedish and American management responses.

In the United States these same ideas did not lead to a choice opportunity; rather, they were seen as threatening by many managers and union leaders. The prevailing adversary relationships between managers and workers and managers and unions constitute a formidable obstacle to the adoption of new ideas about organizing work in a cooperative fashion. The potential improvements in productivity obtainable through cultivation of worker's loyalty and cooperation have tended either to be seen as trivial or dismissed as unachievable. In short, the gap between existing practices in American industry and the new managerial philosophies has been so great as to make search for and adoption of innovative solutions problematic. In the unionized manufacturing sector, even when top management has pushed in new directions, it has often been unable to have its ideas implemented. The everyday routines of individual workers, middle managers, and union officials seem grounded in struggles for power and control in a way that often defeats promising initiatives.

The upshot of all this is that small-group activities were not a serious part of American management's agenda of solutions in the 1960s and 1970s. Nor was the issue the province of any particular managerial level or department. It is no wonder then that Japanese and Swedish managers acted more quickly than American management in searching out, adopting, and transmitting ideas about small-group activities.

Chapter Seven

Borrowing and Culture

The crow
imitating the cormorant
drowns in the water.

Japanese proverb

In the preceding chapter, I dealt with the centrality of foreign ideas in inspiring the introduction of small-group activities. I have yet to consider explicitly the role of culture in the transmission of ideas cross-nationally. It has often been argued that cultural differences inhibit the adoption of foreign modes of work organization, especially in the United States. In particular, some argue that the small-group activities developed in Japan are so closely wedded to their cultural origins as to be inapplicable to Western firms. We need to get a clear understanding of the ways in which culture is and is not a barrier to cross-national borrowing. My analysis leads me to the conclusion that culture is a barrier, but not necessarily in ways that are commonly recognized. The cross-national transmission of ideas and practices such as small-group activities is, in fact, a process of technology transfer, not fundamentally very different from the transmission of, say, steel-making technology.

In his pathbreaking study of industrialization *Modern Economic Growth* (1966), Simon Kuznets maintains that the increase in the stock of useful knowledge and the application of this knowledge are the essence of modern economic growth.[1] This increase, he argues,

---

1. This section draws on Cole 1980.

in turn rests on some combination of the growing application of science to problems of economic production and changes in individual attitudes and institutional arrangements that allow for the release of these technological innovations. As industrialization spread through the world, technological and social innovations cropped up in various centers of development. These innovations were the outcome of a cumulative testing process by which some forms emerged superior to others; each historical period gave rise to new methods and solutions. The economic growth of any given nation came to depend upon adoption of these innovations. Kuznets concludes by stressing the importance of the "worldwide validity and transmissibility of modern additions to knowledge, the transnational character of this stock of knowledge, and the dependence on it of any single nation in the course of its modern economic growth." Raymond Vernon has gone on to argue that the costs to nations of assimilating information from foreign countries have been greatly reduced. The propensity of technology to cross national boundaries is growing very fast, based on word of mouth, technical journals, patent applications, scientific meetings, licensing agreements, and communications among affiliates in multinational networks (Vernon 1986:100).

This book deals with the borrowing and adaptation of small-group activities, a social innovation. Although Kuznets speaks of both technological and social knowledge, his reasoning would appear at first glance to apply most forcefully to the realm of technological choice. It is here, one might think, that the selection of the most progressive technique will be made unambiguously in terms of cost-benefit analysis. For example, the blast furnace using a hot blast and a mineral fuel adopted in nineteenth-century America was clearly superior in terms of reducing costs and increasing productivity to its predecessor based on charcoal technology.

Yet even with "hard technology," uncertainty as to the benefits of new technology is typically a prominent feature of the innovation process. To pursue a more recent steel-making example, it took some time before the feasibility of the basic oxygen furnace, and therefore its relative advantages over blast furnace technology, became apparent (Lynn 1982). One can make a similar point with regard to the need to adapt a given technology to specific environmental conditions. Thus, the basic oxygen furnace, which was developed in Austria, depended in part for its success on the availability of special heat-resistant bricks used to line the converters. The raw materials for bricks with these qualities were not found outside Austria. It was not until comparable heat-resistant bricks were developed outside of Europe that the basic oxygen furnace became economically feasible in North America and Japan. I distill two points from these brief observations. The success of a technological transfer process depends on the adopter, first, having the appropriate "know-how" and, second, having the requisite resources.

Application to Social Technology

With social knowledge and institutional arrangements, the situation is similar. Again, under the right conditions certain institutional arrangements are fairly rapidly grasped as being essential to economic progress. Consider the spread of the joint stock company, double-entry bookkeeping, and multidivisional decentralized management structures.

Many other institutional innovations, however, are not easily compared and evaluated vis-à-vis existing arrangements. Social innovations often interact with other processes in a way that obscures their respective contributions to economic growth. This was apparent in the ambiguous results of assessing the Swedish experience with small-group activities relative to the original managerial objectives for instituting them. Furthermore, the output of social innovations is often not as easily quantified as it is in the case of hard technology. Social innovations like small-group activities may have multiple goals, of which contribution to economic success is only one. Some advocates of small-group activities, for example, focus on their contributions to industrial democracy and worker satisfaction as ends in themselves.

The complexity and the lack of clarity in these relationships and the abundance of unwarranted inferences both lead to an element of fad in the adoption of social innovations. As a result, arguments are often grounded more in ideology and power relationships than in tested generalizations. It should be pointed out that such situations are by no means absent from the circumstances surrounding the adoption of hard technology. In the course of evolving the concept of "satisficing," Herbert Simon and his colleagues studied the reasons companies bought computers in the mid 1950s. "The biggest argument for computers was because your competitor had one. . . . It was just pretty hard to show up at lunch without one."[2] The inference that Simon drew from these observations was that the forces that result in the acceptance of innovations are not necessarily economic ones. Rather, economic decisions based on rational evaluation of carefully sorted and weighted criteria were no match for the emotion and excitement triggered by a technical or business innovation. We can see similar processes at work today as vendors "hype" the advantages to be achieved by adopting the latest technology. In the General Electric advertisement in appendix C, there is the not so subtle suggestion that those not jumping on the bandwagon will be left on the scrap heap of failed enterprises.

Viewed in this light, it should hardly be surprising that rapid diffusion of a particular social innovation may reflect such social and political considerations more than the economic superiority of the innovation in question (as measured in expected profit or transaction costs). We saw good evidence of these same phenomena in our discussion of the domino effect among supplier firms adopting small-group activities. Sometimes the claims to superiority of one social arrangement over another are cloaked in the language of objective social science. The task, for example, of evaluating the applicability of Japanese management practices in the United States and judging what the needed adaptations are is a herculean one. Many claims are made, often by those with vested interests. How is one to separate the wheat from the chaff? Can one identify "best practice," and, if so, how can one most effectively diffuse it? I shall deal with these matters in subsequent sections of this chapter.

One final introductory note is in order. Despite the seemingly greater difficulty in evaluating the objective costs and benefits of a social innovation, there is every reason to believe that once a decision is made to borrow, know-how and resources are just as critical to successful transfer of social technology as with hard technology.

2. J. Williams, "A Life Spent on One Problem," *New York Times*, 26 November 1978, p. F5.

Culture as Obstacle

Kuznets's model of the transnational stock of technological knowledge provides a basis for recasting the way we think about the role of culture in cross-national borrowing. If his model holds for social innovations with an impact on economic growth as well—and I argue that it does—this suggests that culture is less a barrier than it has sometimes been portrayed. Rather, dealing with culture is part of the normal process of adapting an innovation that grew out of and was shaped by a particular environment to the conditions required for survival in a new environment. Sometimes this effort is relatively easy; at others it is complex, with a high risk of failure. Sometimes the know-how and resources are there to do the job; at others they are harder to obtain.

Notwithstanding, the view that cultural differences create impassable barriers, especially in the case of the borrowing of organizational practices, has a powerful hold. My initial task is not to suggest that this view is wrong in principle, but to understand why such views hold sway particularly in the United States. We can pursue the matter in the context of the discussions in the United States on the suitability of adopting small-group activities developed in other nations. We shall also have the opportunity to compare this response to the responses of the Swedes and the Japanese to similar ideas developed in other nations.

In the early 1970s there was modest interest on the part of American managers in the Swedish innovation of autonomous work groups. The general conclusion, however, was that they were not suitable for the United States. Economic factors, in particular the small scale of production in Sweden, were typically cited as factors making the transfer of such techniques difficult, if not impossible. A broader argument was that the cultural environment of Swedish managers was so different as to inhibit useful learning. Swedish managers were thought to be "soft" when it came to dealing with workers and unions—a common view was held by conservative American managers that in "socialistic Sweden they had given away the store." There was the further perception that profit and efficiency considerations were not as highly ranked as in the United States.

On a different level, in a Ford Foundation report, six UAW workers sent to Sweden as part of a work experiment reported that the workplace culture was not to their liking. They found the cultural environment inhibited "self-expression" and that it was harder to communicate with union representatives and superiors. (One cannot help but wonder how much language problems entered into these evaluations.) The reporter for the trip concluded: "Work reform in America can proceed only in the context of American life and culture. The study of work reform in other countries can broaden knowledge, but it does not supply a blueprint for replication" (Goldmann 1976:42). The overall tone of the report was quite negative.

With the benefit of hindsight, these observations are amusing. Not ten years later, the president of General Motors' Saturn project, William Hoglund, lauded Volvo, saying that it was the "industry innovator in humanistic production methods and worker relations" (Hamilton 1985:2). He might have added that in its attempt to leapfrog Japanese leadership in the industry, GM was using many approaches pioneered in Sweden, such as modular construction, automatic carriers, and self-managing teams. In Spring 1988 Volvo and Saab held a high level presentation for GM on its work practices. Apparently, as suggested by the loose-coupling model, "Timing is everything."

Similarly, there was an extensive debate in the United States in the early 1980s about the suitability of adopting Japanese work practices in the United States. Many have voiced the view that the unique group culture and strong work ethic of the Japanese make the adoption of such practices unlikely to succeed in our more individualistic culture. To take one expression of this view, Prakash Sethi, Nobuaki Namiki, and Carl Swanson conclude in their book *The False Promise of the Japanese Miracle* that "a group orientation based on coercion and perceived against individual self-interest, either as a social norm or as a corporate goal, has little prospect of succeeding in the United States" (1984:244). Strong words indeed.

A somewhat similar debate was taking place in Sweden in the mid 1980s. As the Japanese "wave" hit Europe after having rolled over the United States—and therefore having been partially reinterpreted through American experience—the question of the suitability of people-oriented management strategies such as quality circles to the Swedish environment was much debated. Opponents argued that Japan's authoritarian work culture was not consistent with Sweden's democratic institutions. The unions sometimes labeled new management ideas on work practices "Japanese-inspired" in order to discredit them.

Culture as "Non-Issue"

Working against this perspective of culture as an obstacle have been the reported experiences of Japanese firms operating in the United States with American workers. The U.S. mass media have seemingly delighted in showing how the Japanese managers have been able to transport their "more humane management methods" to the United States. Japanese and American managers of these plants have been quick to exploit and facilitate this interpretation. Marvin Runyan, the former head of Nissan in Smyrna, Tennessee, has been perhaps the most adept in this regard. Yet, the evidence of social science on the subject is quite sparse (most such companies are not eager to allow serious social science assessment of their practices and their effectiveness) and mixed at best. In a 1984 survey conducted by Columbia Business School and Coopers and Lybrand, a major consulting and accounting firm, only 10 percent of the 150 responding firms (a 20 percent response rate) reported that they were using quality circles (American Productivity Center 1984:6).

In these and other areas, the Japanese have, in fact, been quite cautious in applying their practices in the United States. This indicates that despite their own eclectic approach to borrowing from the United States, they were quite uncertain as to the applicability of their methods to the American situation. Japanese managers in Japan were generally puzzled by the seeming enthusiasm of their American counterparts for Japanese management practices; their own sense of the "uniqueness" of the Japanese experience made them doubt the transportability of their methods. Notwithstanding, it became typical in the late 1970s and early 1980s in the United States to rebut claims that we could not borrow from the Japanese because of cultural differences by citing the experiences of the Japanese in the United States. By the mid and late 1980s the Japanese had become more confident of their ability to export their techniques for use with an American labor force, and the idea that we could not borrow from the Japanese because of cultural differences weakened among both Japanese and American managers.

The Reaction Sets In

The initial enthusiasm for things Japanese in the late 1970s and early 1980s was based on the view that the Japanese had found a better way. Their methods were presented as a strategy of human-resource management for restoring productivity increases and quality, thereby reinvigorating our economy. William Ouchi's *Theory Z* and Richard Pascale and Anthony Athos's *The Art of Japanese Management* capitalized on and contributed to these views (Ouchi 1981; Pascale and Athos 1981). The 1979 NBC documentary *If Japan Can, Why Can't We?* received enormous circulation, with many companies renting the film to show it to their employees.

As these ideas moved down to the office and shop floor, however, it was found that American workers and managers had little tolerance for being told that the Japanese did everything better and that we ought to learn from them. During the height of the deep recession of the early 1980s, such talk tended to induce a sense of helplessness on the part of many managers ("We just can't compete with those guys") and anger on the part of many workers. In this sense, the issue of cultural differences as an inhibiting factor reappeared.

As a result, advocates of small-group activities quickly moved to purge these ideas of any connection with Japan. We were told that Americans, not the Japanese, had really invented quality circles (just as the Russians have had a chauvinistic need to claim that most important inventions emanated from Russia and not the West). One common version is that William Edwards Deming taught the Japanese quality circles. The facts of the matter are quite to the contrary (Cole 1987). To Deming's credit, he has never claimed otherwise.

In another claim, quality circles are equated with the Scanlon Plan, developed by Joe Scanlon in the 1930s (Cartin 1981:550–53). The fact that Scanlon Plans typically do not have a problem-solving mechanism such as lies at the heart of the QC circle process is conveniently ignored. Still others stress the checkered history of labor-management cooperation in the United States as evidence that "quality circles are a contemporary form of . . . recurring labor-management cooperation" (Mitchell 1987:56–66). Even if there were similar organizational inventions at some U.S. companies, and surely there have been such cases, the compulsion to stress these similarities is in itself revealing. One could just as well reflect on why these isolated examples did not crystallize into a broad pattern of institutionalized behavior.

Yet one seldom sees such analyses. Instead, often-belligerent declarations on the U.S. origins of Japanese organizational techniques testify to the strength of the view that foreign ideas rooted in different cultures are unsuited for use in the United States. One should see statements claiming a U.S. origin for QC circles in terms of the myth-building process required for American managers to be able to borrow the QC circle idea from Japan. It was easier for American managers to think in terms of "borrowing back" than it was for them directly to swallow borrowing from a foreign competitor. This was especially the case when the borrowing reflected so negatively on their past management style and when pride had been hurt by a former student who was suddenly "beating their pants off" in the marketplace.

Some leading U.S. quality-circle consultants have aggressively stated in public forums that we have nothing further to learn from the Japanese. The basic training manual of the International Association of Quality Circles (IAQC), the leading promoter of quality circles in the United States, does not mention Japan once. This was the result of a deliberate decision to eliminate any mention of the Japanese origins of circles (the materials were originally developed by General Electric for use in its facilities). Similarly, the standard information package used in 1984 by the IAQC does not once mention Japan. One of the brochures in the package does, however, include a list of companies in the Western world that have adopted circles.

Pragmatism and Borrowing

From a cultural point of view, it is important to note that while Japanese managers adapted foreign ideas to their own needs as they saw them, they felt little need to naturalize them for the sake of avoiding "foreign pollution." As we have seen, American management was held in high esteem, and any adaptation could thus proceed on relàtively pragmatic terms. The Japanese have, of course, a long history of borrowing ideas from foreigners, most notably from the Chinese in the premodern era and from the West over the past one hundred years as they sought to "catch up" with the advanced industrial nations. Based on these historical experiences, they have institutionalized a highly eclectic approach to learning.

My point is not the earlier one, that the Japanese (and Swedes) have a greater tendency to search out foreign ideas, but rather that, given equal response to a foreign idea, the Japanese and Swedes seem to have less need to naturalize it for reasons of national pride than do Americans.[3] In the case of their quality-control efforts, the Japanese have been only too happy to give credit to their foreign mentors, William Edwards Deming and J. M. Juran, and to deliberately downplay their own accomplishments. The use of the well-known Deming Prize in quality to further spur company improvement efforts provides a case in point.

In contrast to the materials of the IAQC, the widely distributed handbook of the Japanese Union of Scientists and Engineers, *QC sākuru kōryō* (General principles of the QC circle), makes immediate mention of the origin of quality circles in Western ideas of statistical quality control. It discusses how these ideas were then modified and adapted to the Japanese climate by the development of the concepts of "companywide quality control" and "total participation." The Japanese continue to send teams of quality-circle leaders and professionals to the United States to study American progress in this area. Similarly, the Swedes continue to study and send teams to research American approaches to sociotechnical design and participation, though an independent assessment would conclude that both the Japanese and the Swedes were well ahead of American efforts in these areas.

This pragmatic approach gives the Swedes and the Japanese an advantage over those whose foreign borrowing concentrates on pu-

---

3. I hypothesize that this distinction applies more to ideas affecting existing social and power relationships than to more economic and technical ideas. The latter are often seen, at least initially, as less threatening. Thus, there was less resistance to borrowing "just in time" delivery (a "pull" system of production and inventory control developed by the Toyota Motor Co.) from the Japanese than quality circles.

rifying foreign influences. It would be hard to imagine the Americans adopting an "Ishikawa Prize" named after Ishikawa Kaoru, considered the father of quality circles in Japan, to reward the U.S. company with the most effective QC circle activities. Indeed, the National Quality Award signed into law by President Reagan in August 1987 is dedicated to Malcolm Baldridge, a former U.S. secretary of commerce. Beyond the initial visits by American executives to see how circles worked in Japan, there has been relatively little serious sustained investigation by American firms and consultants of how circles operate in Japan, how they fit into broader organizational practices, and how the Japanese have coped with motivational problems and ritualism. The exceptions to this statement are to be found mostly when viable partnerships have existed between American and Japanese companies, such as between Ford and Mazda and Fuji and Xerox.

In summary, the Japanese experience has not been used very effectively as a learning laboratory. For example, one would be unlikely to conclude from the popular U.S. literature on participation in Japan that a well-institutionalized labor-management consultation system is central to its operation. Even companies that have borrowed directly from this approach, such as Ford, feel a need to go to some lengths to conceal its Japanese origins: Ford calls its labor-management consultation program "mutual growth forums." It is not without interest to speculate why it is that Americans have generally showed so much interest in quality circles and so little interest in formal labor-management consultation systems. Certainly, a major factor is that U.S. labor unions have generally been unwilling to take responsibility for business decisions and be accountable to the membership for their decisions, while management is not willing to give up control. Circles, by contrast, are seen to constitute nice, safe, clearly defined packages. In a similar vein, relatively few American companies have explored the link in Japan between participation in small-group activities and job security.

I do not need to belabor the point further. Clearly Americans feel a strong need to indigenize quality circles. In so doing, managers minimize, if not eliminate, the Japanese origins of the concept. The danger is that this reduces their opportunities of learning from the "available stock of transnational resources." This, in turn, becomes disadvantageous for competitive economic performance. Thus, contrary to the popular wisdom, a major cultural barrier to borrowing Japanese small-group-activities approaches is not their rootedness in group-oriented Japanese historical experience. Rather, it is our own reluctance to seriously examine foreign ideas and practices in the area of worker-manager relationships that inhibits the learning process.

The Importance of Local Invention

I have documented the way in which resistance to foreign ideas and practices has been a significant cultural barrier in the United States to the adoption of small-group activities based on the Swedish and Japanese models. This does not exhaust the cultural obstacles. Another major cultural barrier is the failure to recognize the critical need for participants to have a sense of "local invention" at the national, firm, plant or office, and workshop level. Here I deal primarily with the national level. This is a cultural issue because it rests on the degree of discretion those in authority are willing to give to subordinates to initiate policy. Ultimately such willingness rests on the degree of trust and confidence that those in authority have in their subordinates.

Why is local invention so important, and how are we to understand this term? For the responsible parties to be effectively motivated to adopt the innovation in question, they must have a sense of having contributed to its invention. This is especially the case where participation per se is the desired social arrangement. Pure copying of someone else's solutions does not contribute to a sense of ownership, which produces commitment to the new activity and is thus critical to the success of the borrowing. Moreover, local adaptation (that is, invention) is also central to success because each adopting unit is unique and has unique problems.

We would do well at this point to recall the earlier discussion of technology transfer. My stress on the importance of know-how and resources in securing technology transfer accords well with the way many social scientists have come to treat the concept of culture and tradition (cf. Eisenstadt 1973). That is, we may interpret the concepts of know-how and resources broadly to include symbols, ideology, and the generalized societal codes that provide a basis for social action. They would, for example, include the kinds of authority relations and the kinds of interpersonal skills necessary for small-group activities to succeed. Culture provides a map of understandings that serves as a guide to social behavior. This map shows us how to proceed by outlining the options and how to value alternatives. Viewed in this light, culture becomes an obstacle to the extent that the adopter lacks the necessary know-how and resources to make the social technology work in its new environment. Know-how and resources constitute "local knowledge." This is the heart of the cultural barrier to borrowing.

The significance of this point of view is that contrary to the simplistic use of the term by many economists, there is, in principle, no such thing as diffusion of best practice. At best, there is only diffusion of best practices, practices that evolve in the course of their diffusion. Contrary to popular wisdom, there are times when it pays to reinvent the wheel! My stress on the importance of local invention grounded in local knowledge may appear less strange if we keep in mind that organizations themselves are social inventions designed to capitalize on the advantages of cooperation. Not surprisingly, changing them through "borrowing" thus involves further social invention. In many companies, top managers of highly centralized corporate structures have prescribed the form of small-group activity in a way that inhibits local invention. Each unit is instructed to do things in the same way, thereby reducing local spontaneous adaptation.

Devendra Sahal (1981:4), a sharp observer of the diffusion process, shows how significant innovation through adaptation to local needs occurs in the course of diffusion. He stresses that one of the problems with the contemporary theorizing of economists on the diffusion of technology is that it assumes that characteristics of the initial "innovation" do not change in the course of adoption. Many students of organizational behavior have, on the other hand, been quite sensitive to the way in which innovations are transformed as they move from invention to adoption to implementation (March 1981:569). As discussed later in this chapter, changes take place in the characteristics of the innovation as it diffuses, thereby affecting the rate of adoption. These observations allow me to append an earlier conclusion. While cultural barriers in terms of the historical rootedness of social ideas and practices may be less of a problem in cross-national borrowing than commonly thought, the process of technology transfer is itself rather more problematic than commonly recognized.

Moreover, the additional innovation brought about by diffusion often creates new uses for the innovation. This, in turn, affects the extent of the adoption as well. In that context, I have mentioned both the development of the physical technology of heat-resistant bricks associated with the use of the basic oxygen blast furnace and the case of the social innovations involved in transforming Western ideas on quality control into the concept and practice of quality circles. By evolving into circles, formerly elitist quality-control ideas could be adopted by a whole sector of the labor force that had hitherto been excluded from involvement. By way of contrast, I have suggested how in Sweden managers saw the democratic ideas of the Tavistock researchers as threatening, and thus sought to purge them of their radical implications. While this facilitated initial acceptance by managers, thereby ensuring some significant diffusion, it also drained the movement of long-term, spontaneous support on the part of workers and the unions.

Some Examples of Adaptation in the United States

It is clear that adaptation is involved in fitting an innovation into the new environment in which it is expected to operate. This is true both of physical technology, where different factor endowments (different costs of land, capital, labor, etc.) press adopters to use the technology differently, and of social innovations. Perhaps the clearest example of this process in the material under consideration lies in the evolution of the name of this small-group activity in U.S. companies. In Japan *QC sākuru* (quality-control circle) is the standard term (though even in Japan companies may have their own terminology),[4] reflecting above all the strong linkage of Japanese circles to the total quality control (TQC) movement, which stresses all-employee and all-department involvement in quality im-

---

4. That they use Western terms for the activity is in itself quite extraordinary (though quite characteristic as well).

provement activities. In the United States many companies found that the name neither sat well with workers and unions nor conveyed sufficient breadth and importance. With regard to the former, the term *control* tended to have coercive connotations in the American context that were not what the promoters wanted to convey. As for the latter, quality-control departments often conveyed an image of narrow departmental and professional concerns in U.S. companies. Moreover, as noted earlier, they commonly had low status in the management pecking order. *Quality circles* thus came to replace *quality-control circles* as the preferred term. Moreover, as we have seen, companies adopted a wide variety of other names as well. In part, this was to avoid branding the technique as Japanese, but broadly speaking, it was part of the local invention process described above.

On a more substantive level, a variety of adaptations by U.S. firms can be noted. Whereas for the Japanese QC circles evolved in the course of quality-improvement efforts, in America they were introduced as part of the initial attempt to reinvigorate quality standards in many U.S. companies. QC circles also arrived in the context of an indigenous quality-of-work-life (QWL) movement in the United States, and the participation theme was thus quite naturally given high emphasis in many industries. American firms typically created the post of facilitator to apply human dynamics techniques. We have seen that the statistical component of the problem-solving skills has not been as prominent in U.S. efforts to date. Still another feature of U.S. methods relative to Japanese ones is the former's heavy reliance on consultants. For the moment, let us focus on yet another difference, the degree of voluntarism, to illustrate the tensions between different adaptive national responses and universal requirements.[5]

U.S. firms acted initially to adapt the "all employee participation in circles approach" of the Japanese to fit a more voluntaristic model. There was much greater opportunity for employees to choose whether or not they wanted to participate in circle activity

5. Wayne Rieker, the initiator of quality circles at Lockheed Air Missile and subsequently a leading consultant on quality circles, arrives at a rather similar list of adaptations (Rieker 1984).

(though not necessarily for managers) than was the case in Japan. The idea was that one would be working with truly motivated participants if participation was voluntary.[6]

This stands in significant contrast to Japanese practices, where as we have seen typically over 90 percent of employees participate in circle activities. The Japanese do, in fact, stress the importance of voluntarism in making circles work in their literature, but they simultaneously stress all-employee participation. JUSE's handling of the matter in its handbook makes clear that it saw the reconciling of the two principles to be a matter of some difficulty. Consider the following tortured language:

Voluntary Participation by Everyone

Is it not a violation of the rule of "initiative," if some people, who [have] indicated that they do not like to participate, are still urged to participate? If it is clear that those people are reluctant to participate just because they are lazy, egotistical or conservative, they should be rightly encouraged to participate in QC Circle activities.

There are some people, however, who are individualistic by nature, and like to do their job without interference from others. . . . [But] the trend in the manufacturing workshop is such that no single person, however well he can perform his job, can fully satisfy the requirements now imposed on the workshop. It is no longer enough to "mind one's own business." The gathering of skill, technology and knowledge is a prerequisite of doing a job successfully in the workshop. Individual voluntary actions can be displayed on top of that.

Those who prefer working in solitude can be attracted by QC Circle activities, and participate on [sic] their own will, if the circles can successfully create a magnetic atmosphere, and if those people are properly guided and persuaded to participate.

(JUSE 1970:55–56)

The different approaches taken by Japanese and American managers reflect differing norms and expectations, in part growing out of cultural differences. For the Japanese, *voluntarism* refers less to the individual employee's decision to participate in QC circle activity than to the relatively autonomous nature of peer decision making in circle activity, independent of normal line authority

---

6. One of the few U.S. companies in the late 1970s that made circle participation obligatory in some of its units was Honeywell Corporation.

relationships (Lillrank 1985:5). At still another level, American unions have strongly stressed the voluntary principle in determining whether to support circle activity. Without such guarantees, they would have been far more hostile. Japanese unions, on the other hand, have shown relatively little interest in such concerns, except for protecting workers against compulsory overtime.

While Japanese managers use the rhetoric of voluntarism, it is apparent that in many companies strong management pressures, and peer pressures manipulated by management, make it difficult for workers to refuse to join in QC circle activity. The proper guidance and persuasion called for in the last sentence of the quotation above often takes the form of quite heavy-handed management pressures on workers to participate. Moreover, the autonomous nature of circle activities is often sacrificed through management manipulation of circle theme selection.

A 1975 Japan Employers' Association survey reported, for example, that of those enterprises involved in various types of small-group activities such as quality circles, 43 percent used performance in these activities as a factor in personnel assessment (cited in Tokunaga 1983:324). What employee wanting to get ahead in the corporation and impress management would refuse to participate under such circumstances? Here we see a good example of my earlier point about the subtle interaction between competition among individual workers and group activities.

Statements about differences in pressure applied by different management systems are, of course, relative. A leading promoter of the Japanese movement responded to my observations on this by commenting: "If you want to see pressure on workers to join circles, you should see the Koreans!" Over time, as the process has become institutionalized, the Japanese have moved in some respects toward a more voluntaristic model, especially in the selection of themes, quota requirements for suggestions, and actual participation in circle activities. The process is far from complete, however, with other pressures of institutionalization pushing toward ritualism and enforced conformity.

Indeed, in recent years new adopters of circles have taken a much more heavy-handed approach to getting employees to join circles. One Japanese observer refers to it as the "carpet bombing approach," alluding to the tactic in which planes are lined up in tight formation and go back and forth over the target leaving no area uncovered. In a similar fashion, circles are targeted by top management and no employee is left with a choice. Typical is the case of the Sanwa Bank, which set off a wave of quality-circle activity in the banking industry in the early 1980s. The president, Akashi Toshio, was persuaded to attend a week-long JUSE seminar on QC circles in 1979. Ishikawa Kaoru was invited to give a series of lectures, and he stressed the importance of top management support. Akashi was so impressed that he put all his executive vice presidents through circle training. This process was repeated down the organization until no one was left unexposed. Within a year, there were 2,400 circles in the bank, with some 13,000 members. In my interview with bank officials at the time, they indicated that this constituted about 99.4 percent of eligible employees. All this stands in sharp contrast to the early days of the movement, which had much more of a bottom-up quality to it, with a strong emphasis on persuading workers to join of their own free will. In summary, we see a tension between the benefits resulting from ensuring that all employees in a workshop participate and the benefits resulting from spontaneous contributions.

In the light of this discussion, it is not surprising that by the mid 1980s many U.S. firms were beginning to reassess their voluntaristic approach.[7] As one manager reported to me: "I have 15 percent of all my hourly employees in circles, but we seem to have hit the ceiling for volunteers and now I am worried about a loss of momentum." If a major objective is to build teamwork and communication in the workshop, then the typical American approach of having mixed workshops, with some in circles and some not in circles, seems unlikely to produce the desired outcome. By the mid 1980s, partly as a consequence of such concerns, firms were increasingly pushing mandatory involvement. As experience with circles and other forms of team building grows in the United States, we can expect more companies to take the position that teams are a part of normal job design, and that workers are therefore required to participate.

It is unlikely that the U.S. and Japanese approaches will con-

7. See the "point-counterpoint" debate between Wayne Rieker and Harold Kay on this (Rieker and Kay 1985:6–7).

verge. Nevertheless, the pressures for differentiated responses to divergent organizational environments are balanced to some extent by pressures of a more universal nature. In both Japan and the United States, for example, we find managers struggling to balance the need to ensure exposure and teamwork against the need to develop and maintain spontaneity. Such universal imperatives will keep the two countries' efforts from diverging too sharply over the long run.

In conclusion, adaptation to local conditions, using local know-how and resources, is essential for successful technology transfer. By adapting to local conditions, one ensures the commitment and motivation necessary to drive the innovation forward. In the example of voluntarism, different cultural standards in Japan and the United States lead to different choices and opportunities as managers work with the resources available to them. At the same time, we see that attention must also be paid to certain universal factors, lest the borrowing process so bastardize the original innovation that its intrinsic benefits are lost.

The imperatives that derive from the universal aspects of a process have other implications for borrowing. This becomes clear when we examine the actual process of borrowing as it relates to quality circles in the United States and Japan. The experiences of Nissan in Smyrna, Tennessee, are a case in point. Prior to the initiation of QC circle activity in late 1983, the manager of organization development, Steve Neuman, was sent to Japan for training in the circle procedures and practices of the parent company. He came to realize that the activities in the parent company reflected a mature movement with some 4,000 circles and 99 percent participation in circle activities. Some circles had existed for as long as ten years, and it was not considered extraordinary for a circle to take a whole year to work out a solution to a complicated problem.

In one project the American manager observed, the circle was seeking to prevent wrong gaskets from being put on an engine. It turned out that this happened only three times a year (though with disastrous consequences for the operation of those three engines). He concluded that the problems the Japanese were working on were simply of a different nature than those that would be experienced by the Smyrna workers and managers for the first few years of QC circles. "They were working with a different part of the curve." In contrast, he was wrestling with problems that the Japanese had dealt with over ten years before. How do you elicit middle management support? What is the best way to teach employees quality-circle procedures? How do you get employees to apply their training skills?

We can see from this concrete example both the difficulty of direct copying and the fact that the difficulty lies not only with cultural differences but with the differing imperatives arising from different stages of experience. Most American companies adopting QC circles did not have this direct pipeline to a Japanese company. The typical short-term visits of American executives hardly gave them time to figure out the right questions to ask, much less to get the right answers. What they generally see when they take their quick tour of Japanese plants is the result of some ten to twenty years' experience. Witnessing current practices does not provide much guidance as to how the Japanese got there.

Conclusions

We may return now to some of the original questions raised in this chapter on the role of culture and borrowing. Social scientists tend to operate with a holistic model; the suggestion that borrowing of social practices can take place on a selective basis tends to do violence to their perspective. The following quote from the 1984 report of MIT's International Automobile Program captures this view:

> The impressive success of the Japanese has led many in the West to argue that their own industrial relations systems should be reshaped to imitate Japanese practices. The lifetime-employment system and the use of quality circles have been singled out for much praise and some emulation.
>
> The difficulty with adopting individual Japanese practices is that the various features of an industrial-relations system interact with one another and may not be separable from other features of the total system. For instance, the method of setting pay interacts with the union representation structure (enterprise-based bonuses are supported by the system of enterprise-based unions in Japan) and also the form of worker participation. Even if they chose to, it may not be possible for Western producers and unions to adopt Japanese industrial-relations practices in a piecemeal fashion.
>
> (Altshuler et al. 1984:215)

Underlying this argument is the view that if you borrow a discrete practice, you are pulling it out of a complicated and highly interdependent social nexus. In so doing, the further assumption is that the practice itself will not survive transplanting to the new environment. Interestingly, this viewpoint does not get applied to physical technology, which is assumed to be different from the transfer of social practices. Yet physical technology is ultimately made up of "know-how," and what is more social than that?

The thrust of the argument in this chapter is that the ability to borrow discrete bits of hard technology applies to social innovations as well. In both cases, the proper application of know-how and resources (local knowledge) can be brought to bear to adapt the practice or equipment in question to its new environment. The pattern of Japanese borrowing of American ideas of statistical quality control, leading eventually to circle activity, well demonstrates the possibility of borrowing highly discrete practices. It also reveals a process in which the original ideas or practices are literally ripped from their moorings to create something almost entirely different in the new environment. As paradoxical as it may seem to people accustomed to equating borrowing with imitative copying, *borrowing is, above all, an act of social invention.*

As if to demonstrate this process in the extreme, one Japanese scholar has spoken of "creative misunderstanding." What he has in mind is situations where because of language difficulties and cultural differences, the Japanese misunderstood what they saw, but found some way to borrow what they thought they were seeing and to make sense of the practice in their own environment. Lest this sound a bit too cute, we would do well to return to the insightful analysis of Thorstein Veblen, an astute observer of the process of German borrowing from England and Japanese borrowing from the West. Writing in 1915, this son of Norwegian immigrants stated:

The interposition of a linguistic frontier between the borrower and creditor communities would still farther lessen the chance of immaterial elements of culture being carried over in the transmission of technological knowledge. The borrowed elements of industrial efficiency would be stripped of their fringe of conventional inhibitions and waste, and the borrowing community would be in a position to use them with a freer hand and with a better chance of utilizing them to their full capacity, and also with a better chance of improving on their use, turning them to new uses, and carrying the principles (habits of thought) involved in the borrowed items out, with unhampered insight into farther ramifications of technological proficiency. The borrowers are in a position of advantage, intellectually, in that the new expedient comes into their hands more nearly in the shape of a theoretical principle applicable under given physical conditions; rather than in the shape of traditional use, personal, magical, conventional.

(Veblen 1915:38)

While the language is somewhat old-fashioned, the thoughts are modern and applicable to my discussion of contemporary processes. The key to this whole process is adaptation, and it applies, as we have seen, to physical technology as well as to social innovations. That is, for effective borrowing to take place, one must make the kinds of adaptations that meet local needs. As we saw in the case of the United States, this may involve some purging of the foreign origins of the innovation, and it commonly involves creative interventions that change the characteristics and effectiveness of the practices in a dramatic fashion. This can be a very complicated process, as was the case with the Japanese reconceptualization of American ideas on quality control.

Commenting on the interdependency of borrowed elements and the dangers of "cherry picking," my colleague Michael Flynn observes that American managers "have been trying to model trees and haven't stepped back to look at the whole forest" (Holden 1986: 276). Flynn refers, of course, to the need to think systemically, and at first glance, his statement seems at variance with my analysis; his metaphor of the "whole forest" suggests the holistic model referred to earlier. But the question is, whose forest should we be looking at? It obviously can add important information to know how the original use of an organizational practice relates to other elements in the system, though Veblen cautions us that the borrower should not be so thoroughly imbued with such understanding as to lose the capacity to develop creative uses of the innovation. What is absolutely critical, however, is for the borrower to know how the intended use of the new practice in its new environment will relate to other elements in that environment. In other words, we need to be modeling "our" forest not "their" forest.

It may be that the term *borrowing* carries too much baggage. Especially in cases of extensive adaptation, where the original ideas are barely noticeable in the new practices, though they may have inspired them, or where foreign practices have served as a "negative role model," we might do better to speak simply of *learning*. It is clear that borrowing in the sense of mere replication simply does not exist for any complex social technology. Rather, there is adaptation and the invention of new social practices.

Part Two

Chapter Eight

Contenders for Action: The U.S. Case

Quarreling sparrows do not fear man.
Japanese proverb

I pointed out in part 1 that in a number of areas the loose-coupling model applies to the decision-making processes associated with adoption of small-group activities. Perhaps the most dramatic example thus far is the faddish quality of adoptions among suppliers where solutions are typically chasing problems and where power, rather than strategies emphasizing economizing of transaction costs, seems to explain adoption. One of the issues before us in the remaining six chapters is whether commitment to small-group activities represents a short-term management interest or support of small-group activities is in the process of evolving into a significant social movement within industry. Sociologists commonly define social movements as collectivities acting with some continuity to promote or resist a change in the society or group to which they belong (Turner and Killian 1972). Typically the social movements studied by sociologists are driven by a sense of injustice. As we saw earlier, this was not a primary driving force for the evolving small-group-activities movement in the United States, but the Swedish movement had rather more of a populist cast to it. Even in the United States and Japan, however, there was a sense that something was wrong with the way firms were organized—that we were not using our human resources very well—and that this ought to be changed.

In Japan, as we shall see, managers did create a social movement, although it was based less on a sense of social injustice than on a sense of corporate citizenship and improvement.

One way that sociologists distinguish between fads and social movements is by asking whether and in what way the informal interest shown by disparate individuals comes to be coordinated through the development of formal organizational activities, which can be powerful factors in attracting resources, protecting innovators from hostile forces in the environment, and supplying assistance (that is, resources) to innovative individuals and organizations. These activities also make clear the specific interests of the major parties to the labor market.

The preceding analysis indicates that for the period under consideration, roughly 1960 to 1985, all parties to the labor market in Sweden became committed to the small-group-activities movement; in Japan, management became committed; and in the United States no major party to the labor market developed such a commitment. One would expect that these different degrees of commitment would be reflected in the nature of the emergent national infrastructures for diffusing small-group activities. Specifically, I predict that, all things being equal, where at least one of the major parties to the labor market becomes strongly committed to small-group activities as a solution, especially management, a well-organized national infrastructure will be created. The next six chapters allow us to examine the data supporting this prediction.

At the same time, this will give us a chance to examine the ways in which such a national infrastructure smoothes decision-making processes for firms as regards small-group activity, thereby reducing the "garbage can" quality of these processes and economizing on transaction costs. It will also enable us to examine the different natures of the emergent collaborative activities among firms in the three countries and to attempt to account for them. Significant differences in the national infrastructures that evolved tell us a great deal about the character of small-group activities in different settings and their potential for institutionalization at the level of firms. These differences are indeed dramatic.

It is my strong belief, based on the data, that this approach gives a decidedly new perspective on the issue of how and why new social forms like small-group activities become institutionalized. This is in sharp distinction to the usual social science strategy of examining the potential for institutionalization by trying to evaluate the success of specific programs directly.

Contenders for Leadership

The task in this chapter is to examine the range of contenders for national leadership in the small-group-activities movement in the United States in the 1970s. I ask what path was taken by already existing organizations and interest groups that had the potential to play a leadership role in this area. This chapter is devoted to those who chose not to play and is premised on the view that we can learn a great deal from what did not happen.

The approaches taken in this and subsequent chapters are in keeping with emergent research initiatives in organizational studies stressing the entrepreneurial, environmental, and behavioral aspects of the creation of new organizations. Such approaches provide a healthy corrective to the cross-sectional research methodologies that have dominated the research of American scholars on "mature" organizations (see Kimberly, Miles and Associates 1980).

I turn now to the array of organizations and the interest groups they represented to consider the possible contenders for a leadership role in the diffusion of small-group activities in the United States.[1] Since progress in moving toward shop floor participation of workers has been relatively slow in the United States, it is not surprising that the development of a comparable infrastructure has been modest.

In thinking about the range of probable actors in the creation of national infrastructures, I assess the involvement of participants from the following sets of institutional arenas: university, government, foundations, firms, business association, and unions. If we examine the mid 1970s first, two key players stand out with emergent investments in what in the United States are typically called

1. This section draws on a variety of written sources such as Dickson 1975 and Davis 1977, interviews with numerous organizational leaders and their staff, and examination of institutional records. It also benefits from my own personal experiences and access to data that resulted from being a member of the board of directors of the American Productivity Center and a member of the academic advisory committee of the Work in America Institute.

participative work practices or the quality of working life: (1) the government acting through the National Commission on Productivity (established in 1970), the Department of Commerce, and other organizational instruments that evolved over time; and (2) the Ford Foundation, with an involvement dating from 1970 through support for the American Center for Quality of Working Life and the Quality of Work Program established in 1974 at the University of Michigan, the Center for the Quality of Working Life at the University of California (also dating from 1974), and the Work in America Institute (1975). I describe their activities not for the sake of description but rather to understand the reasons for the kind of role they did or did not come to play in the small-group-activities movement.

The Federal Government

The involvement of the National Commission on Productivity is particularly interesting, since government sponsorship is well known to be an important factor accounting for patterns of organizational creation and growth; state support and protection and access to public funds can obviously constitute an overwhelming advantage vis-à-vis competitors and with regard to achieving organizational goals (Aldrich 1979).

President Nixon established the National Commission on Productivity by Executive Order on 17 June 1970. The commission was set up as an approach to containing inflation through productivity improvement and was based on the Swedish tripartite model of a forum for top-level people from government, industry, and labor, plus public representatives. George Shultz and Assistant Secretary of Labor Jerome Rosow were the early advocates in the administration. President Nixon was attracted to the idea because of the potential political benefits. Addressing the "pocketbook" issues of inflation and unemployment could win blue-collar votes.

The commission was given token funding, never exceeding $3 million a year, and did not receive a legislative mandate until President Ford signed Public Law 94-136 establishing a National Center for Productivity and Quality of Working Life in 1975. The revitalized commission had a broader—some staffers were to say seemingly endless—list of missions, which included improving the quality of the workplace in both the private and public sectors, making better use of the nation's human and technological resources, and increasing national productivity.

As part of its activities, the commission planned ten to twenty demonstration projects at work sites in manufacturing, service, and government. These were to involve employers, trade unions, and workers. The commission envisioned that it would "seed" these projects by getting the parties together and securing and funding consultants to advise them how to proceed. Finally, the commission anticipated that it would then disseminate the results of these experiments through conferences, articles, books, and films. All this was to take place by 1980, by which time, it was hoped, wide-scale adoption of these new ideas would have taken place.

Participative work structures were a significant element in the demonstration projects, and small-group activities were part of this conception. Indeed, Eric Trist of the Tavistock Institute was involved with the Rushton mine experiment (and later with experiments with community revitalization at Jamestown, New York). European thinking about small-group activities was thus known to the organizers, as were quality circles. In 1975 the assistant executive director of the commission met with officials from Lockheed's Air Missile Division, the most prominent early adopter of quality circles in the United States. He offered to work with Lockheed to measure and evaluate its program; Lockheed declined the invitation.

The commission's goals were not to be achieved. Congressional funding was erratic, and in 1978 President Carter disbanded the commission on grounds that "it hadn't been sufficiently productive." Basil Whiting, then deputy assistant secretary of labor, and a former Ford Foundation official dealing with these activities, recalls being told by the OMB official in charge: "Forget it. Just you and a few other romantics are interested in this. There simply is no political support. In fact, there is even opposition from the AFL-CIO."

Indeed, labor's attitude toward the commission had been ambivalent from the beginning, and strong business groups had also been ambivalent. The Business Roundtable, a major business lobby group that was created to stand up to big labor, supported the legislation to create the commission, but consistent with its opposition to government intervention, it pushed for a cap on funds, so that the commission was never in a position to carry out its mandate.

With these kinds of "friends," it is no wonder that the commission accomplished little. Underlying this lack of support was the fact that both labor and management lacked full trust in the government as a partner. One sharp observer of the scene at the time (who prefers to remain anonymous) summarizes commission activities as follows: "Conversations on the Commission often degenerated into finger pointing about the same old issues, with labor complaining that they were not accepted and management complaining that labor was not cooperating with efforts to hold down costs." In the final analysis, the commission failed because it lacked a politically powerful constituency. The results, such as they were, tended to be invisible, and this gave rise to continual congressional criticism. From the congressional point of view, the commission was not tackling the political agenda between management and labor.

Although the commission had established an active publications program and helped inaugurate some innovative projects, such as the Bolivar and Rushton mining projects (see Goodman 1979), it cannot be said that it went far along the road to achieving its ambitious goals. Most notable is the failure to establish the commission as a permanent resource for organizations contemplating innovation and as an effective diffusion agent. Some of the functions of the commission were relocated back to other government agencies, such as the Department of Labor, while its records were transferred to the Work in America Institute. This scattering of accumulated assets hardly seemed propitious for the future.

It would be an incomplete picture of the early days of government activities in this area if one were to leave out the key role of the Economic Development Administration (EDA) of the Department of Commerce. Lou Phillips of EDA was a key participant in funding innovative projects such as the early experiments at Rushton and Bolivar; the labor-management committee program at Jamestown, New York; and the University of Michigan Quality of Work Program, as well as in directly and indirectly funding some of the organizations to be discussed later in this chapter. Between 1973 and 1976, EDA spent almost $2 million in support of these activities. EDA often collaborated with the Ford Foundation and the National Commission in sponsoring such projects. But as we shall see, government funding for such activities gradually dried up.

Since this early period of support, government involvement has limped along in fits and starts, typically supported on shoestring budgets. In the early 1980s, in an attempt, in part, to preserve existing staff, a Department of Labor task force developed a new program, the Division of Cooperative Labor-Management Programs, "to assist employers and unions to undertake joint efforts to improve productivity and enhance the quality of working life." The idea, approved in 1982, was to create a central clearinghouse of resources on QWL, with particular focus on the successful operation of labor-management committees. While funding has been unpredictable, the unit has shown modest growth; in 1985 it employed some twenty professionals and was budgeted at around $500,000 a year. In a reorganization it has since been elevated to bureau status (as the Bureau of Labor Management Relations and Cooperative Programs), but limited by mandate to the unionized sector and focused on labor-management cooperation, it is not in a position to play a national leadership role in the small-group-activities movement.

Still another federal initiative developed in the late 1970s. Spurred by the success of the communitywide revitalization efforts at Jamestown, New York, Senator Jacob Javits and Representative Stanley N. Lundine spearheaded the passage of legislation in 1978 to involve the Federal Mediation and Conciliation Service (FMCS) in labor-management cooperation efforts (Public Law 95-524). The service, a reluctant partner in this new venture, currently represents the only legislatively mandated federal involvement in the quality of work life area in the United States. Although originally authorized at $10 million a year, it has never received more than $1 million.

The Reagan administration eliminated the program from its budget requests from 1980 to 1985, only to have congressional compromises arrive at budgets varying between $500,000 and $1 million a year. Ironically, a number of other federal agencies that had financially supported QWL, such as the Department of Commerce and the Office of Personnel Management, saw fit to discontinue their activities with the advent of FMCS involvement. Thus the net increment of investment to the field was even less than the modest budget of the FMCS would suggest.

As prescribed in the legislation, the bulk of FMCS funds have gone to support labor-management committees on a competitive-application basis. The FMCS's only involvement with small-group activities is indirect, in the sense that many of the proposals submitted to it for support include plans for small-group activities under the auspices of labor-management committees.

The Ford Foundation and Its Offspring

The Ford Foundation began its support for participative activities in 1970 and by 1978 had spent on the order of $3 million in organizational and individual grants. This included some overseas support for the International Council on QWL.

The initial issue for the foundation was where and how to invest these new resources. A debate took place within the foundation among those pushing for the foundation to lead a national movement for QWL directly and those critical of the whole idea of QWL, which they argued was an approach in which workers and managers were not interested. The former strategy was based on the models developed in the civil rights movement and poverty programs. Initially, it would have involved direct support for selected on-the-ground projects and support to intervening "activators." These latter organizations were to serve as third-party advisor/trainer organizations that would actively diffuse the QWL concept and be involved in stimulating networking among activists and providing technical support to innovators.

This was the time, however, when the foundation was reining in many of its activities in response to outside criticism of its alleged "excessive activism" in the 1960s. The message went out from high-level officials that "we are not going to run a movement here on this subject." This reflected the outside criticism, but also the clear ambivalence on the part of many foundation officials who were not convinced there was a constituency for such intervention. Officials were also responding to the foundation's major budget crunch of the mid seventies. To be sure, the foundation typically had a "seeding" policy, which meant that if there was a social need, the movement once started would pick up other support and/or become self-sustaining. But such participative activities could hardly be said to have established a firm foundation by the mid to late 1970s. Indeed, an internal memo to the foundation trustees in October 1976 called for expanded funding, arguing:

This field [workplace reform focused on improved quality of worklife] is still very underdeveloped in the United States and larger resources could not be applied effectively, yet. First a base must be laid: existing grantees need further support; some additional centers of competence seem called for in a nation this large; the cadre of professionals competent to aid labor and management is limited and needs buttressing; case studies and materials on successful and unsuccessful efforts are lacking; training programs for managers, union leaders, and workers are needed, reform of traditional university criteria in business and industrial design seems possible; and alternative forms of ownership could be probed and carefully developed.

With the decision to move out of funding in this area, the major opportunity for the foundation to assist in the creation of a national infrastructure of support for participative work practices was lost. Such a commitment could reasonably have been expected to encompass small-group activities were it to have been made.

Given the original ambivalence within the foundation about supporting QWL activities and the growing resistance to the idea over time, advocates within the foundation were forced to change their strategy and turned to a "scientific rationale" to get the money into the field. It was thus political expediency above all that led to the flowering of social science research in participation and QWL in the mid 1970s—certainly not the first time that scholars have been the unwitting beneficiaries, if not agents, of their organizational sponsors. Again we see a situation in which problems and solutions are rather loosely coupled. It is an accident of foundation politics and timing that large-scale support for academic research became identified as a solution to the problem of how to diffuse participatory work structures in the early 1970s.

Ford Foundation activists hoped that these research efforts would legitimate QWL and gradually evolve into more active support for the movement. Such was not to be the case. The major manifestation of this approach was a large multi-year grant in 1974 to the Quality of Work Program of the University of Michigan to evaluate the eight major demonstration projects being facilitated by the

American Center for Quality of Working Life. All of the projects were at unionized sites. As Basil Whiting, program officer for the Ford Foundation, explained in his 1974 Senate testimony:

Despite the fact that only a minority of the American labor force is unionized, this program should concentrate primarily on unionized workplaces. There is a serious danger that job enrichment and other changes in workplaces will be seen as union-busting, anti-labor devices or management gimmicks. . . . The best way to prevent these concerns from emerging is to ensure that unions are involved from the beginning in the experimental efforts.

(Whiting 1975)

The detailed measurement strategies involved in the eight evaluations focused on five dimensions: productivity and other economic results of redesigned jobs; changes in workers' attitudes; social organization and other aspects of QWL; labor-management relations; and changes in technology and other physical aspects of work.

A great deal of effort and resources were spent on the development and validation of observation and measurement methods. Of the almost $1 million available to the Quality of Work Program at Michigan in this period from various grants (including $130,000 passed on to the American Center for Quality of Working Life), about one-fifth was devoted to this measurement effort. When these evaluation activities ended at Michigan, the quality-of-work program gradually contracted. It cannot be said that the results were fed back and came to have a significant impact on private- and public-sector management; rather they primarily became the basis for academic books and articles that influenced scholarly discussion and, no doubt, the careers of those active in the field.[2] Publication in academic journals and in the language of social science tended to minimize the impact of these findings on practitioners.

An understanding of the Michigan QWL project was that the researchers not provide direct feedback to those involved in the change process, a policy exemplifying the emphasis on producing valid scientific results in these "natural experiments." This con-

2. A preliminary bibliography of publications emanating from the project as of 1985 included forty-seven articles (not including those by contracted change agents and various project reports) and six books. Five other books were in varying stages of completion.

trasts with a strategy that would have provided rapid feedback to those involved. Finally, the long delay between conduct of the research and actual publication made the demonstration projects less than ideal as a stimulus for diffusion. Indeed, although the researchers submitted a technical summary report to the sponsor, the planned public report summarizing and comparing the eight demonstration cases was never completed. Perhaps the greatest impact of this work in the diffusion process was that it trained a significant set of young scholars who were to become increasingly active as organizational consultants with the renewed interest in participatory work practices in the 1980s.

The American Center for Quality of Working Life

The American Center for Quality of Working Life was set up by Edwin ("Ted") Mills, formerly of the National Commission on Productivity and the Price Commission, and prior to that a television producer and advertising executive. The center was established as a nonprofit institute under grants from the Department of Commerce's Economic Development Administration (EDA) and the Ford Foundation (through the Institute of Social Research at the University of Michigan). Funding has been erratic and the center had a near demise in 1978.

Initially, the center acted as a broker bringing parties together, providing outside facilitators to work with internal labor-management committees. In its early years two major conditions of center activity were that the site be unionized and that the parties agree to have developments monitored by an external evaluation group from the Quality of Work Program at the University of Michigan. The evaluation process was carried out independently and involved detailed measurements. The center sponsored eight such arrangements, picking up the Bolivar and Rushton projects referred to earlier (Davis 1977). Mills saw the center as moving through periods of experimentation, detailed scientific measurement, and dissemination (Dickson 1975:352–53). Mills was later to lose his enthusiasm for these evaluation activities and their ability to contribute to dissemination. He moved the center toward operating more as a permanent technical assistance bureau serving a broad range of clients.

Mills retired in 1982, and Kevin Sweeney became chairman. Sweeney's previous experience was as personnel director for the National Association of Home Builders. Under his leadership, the center refocused its efforts. It placed primary stress on changing organizational culture to improve the quality of working life. As in the past, the center worked exclusively with unionized firms as its long-term clients and stressed building labor-management committees. It also came to conduct its own evaluation studies under contract with various government agencies and private-sector firms. By 1985 the center was operating with about twenty-four staff members, including twenty professionals, and had an annual budget of $650,000 to $750,000. It worked at any one time with perhaps twenty-five clients, from both public and private sectors, and continued to maintain its nonprofit status.

Promotion of small-group activities constitutes a modest, though increasing, proportion of the center's efforts. It tended to define its market niche as both broader and narrower. It was broader than small-group activities in the sense that for the center QWL involved a change in the culture of organizations and therefore required heavy investments in securing the commitment and understanding of top and middle management. This suggested a specific focus on management training. The market niche was narrower than small-group activities in the sense that the organization stressed improving labor-management relations in unionized firms through the use of steering committees. To be sure, these steering committees often establish small-group activities, and the center often works with companies in this phase as well. By concentrating primarily on union firms for its long-term clients, however, it in effect writes off 80 percent of the market. Center personnel were acutely aware of these limitations when I interviewed them in 1984 and indicated that this might change in the future.

More generally, once foundation support declined in the late 1970s, the organization increasingly faced the choice of whether to be a national center or a consulting organization. The need to find a source of regular revenue pushed it in the direction of individual organizational consulting at the expense of a diffusion role as a national clearing house. It tried to minimize this tension through agreeing to work on projects with substantial learning opportunities whose results could be widely disseminated. But it has been a continuing dilemma. In any case, at no time in its history have small-group activities been a focus of the center's operations.

The Center for the Quality of Working Life

In 1974 a second set of Ford Foundation grants established the Center for the Quality of Working Life at the Institute for Industrial Relations at the University of California (Los Angeles). The program was headed by Louis Davis, a specialist in the application of systems analysis to the design of new plants. The center concentrated on developing new techniques for restructuring work; conducting training conferences for labor, management, and professionals; and providing advice to unions and employers on demonstration projects. The intermediate goal was to establish action research programs in which new concepts were tested. The center hoped to attract sufficient grants, contracts, and fees to sustain its efforts. This did not occur, however, and it is no longer a significant factor on the national scene.

The Work in America Institute

A third grant, along with contributions from other organizations, established the Work in America Institute in 1975. The institute is headed by Jerome Rosow, a former Exxon executive and assistant secretary of labor who was active in the creation of the National Commission on Productivity. Funded by federal, corporate, and foundation sources, the private nonprofit institute was designed to serve as a clearing house for experimentation, research, dissemination of ideas, and discussion of issues concerning the quality of working life. Along with the Center for the Quality of Working Life at the University of California, the institute was intended by Ford to be the major instrument in building a national infrastructure for diffusing the QWL concept. The Ford Foundation provided the institute with some $1 million in seed money over five years, a sum less than originally intended for reasons discussed above. In the mid 1980s the annual budget was running at $2 million a year.

The institute places considerable emphasis on providing information through conferences, site visits, and publications as a means of building awareness and stimulating action among corporate and union leaders. These activities are typically based on the case method, drawing on the experiences of leading organizations in a particular content area. The institute has an active publications program, but one lesson it learned, says Rosow, is that information dissemination is costly. Much of this activity has to be subsidized.

The publications program, workshops, and conferences have periodically included small-group activities as one of the areas to be promoted. But the emphasis on small-group activities tends to be ancillary to the primary focus on building labor-management cooperation in the unionized sector. The institute has a tripartite board of directors, consisting of management, labor, and government members, and stresses this principle in its activities. In 1986 almost half of the members of the board were active or former union officials. As a matter of principle, the organization conducts little activity in the nonunionized sector. Furthermore, Rosow "didn't see a constituency for a populist movement around small-group activities [such] as existed in Sweden."

Originally, the institute sought to provide direct field support in the form of training and technical assistance. Over time, the costliness of such efforts shifted the institute to more policy-related activity. It actively conducts policy studies funded by corporate and private foundations.

To have concentrated on direct technical assistance would, moreover, have turned the institute into a consulting organization. As Rosow saw it, consultants would have had to be hired and he would have ended up trying to figure out how to raise funds to meet the payroll. Means would thus have turned into ends, and the institute would have lost sight of its original clearinghouse objectives. Moreover, he says, one problem with learning from consulting activities is that you cannot go public with much of the information. With these considerations in mind, the institute pushed for endowment, initiating policy studies and a "Productivity Forum," established in 1979. The forum is composed of forty corporate, government, and union members, who together employ or represent some twenty-two million people; representatives meet regularly to exchange information at site visits and workshops.

Productivity Improvement
and Employee Involvement

A later entry into this arena was the American Productivity Center (APC), established in 1977 and renamed the American Productivity and Quality Center in 1988. It was founded by C. Jackson Grayson, Jr., a former chairman of the Price Commission who had worked initially with Ted Mills to set up a unit within the commission to explore the potential of QWL in offsetting inflation through raising productivity.

The APC represented the first in a second wave of national and regional organizations dedicated to improving productivity. QWL and related participatory work practices were not the centerpiece of its program as in the earlier organizations; rather they were one facet—smaller or larger depending on the organization—in its overall strategy to improve productivity. Labor-management cooperation and employee involvement are listed among the principal areas in which the APC works. Small-group activity was one aspect of the QWL or participatory theme, but it assumed only modest proportions.

The APC was initiated with corporate grants from some seventy-five major corporations totaling $8.5 million spread over five years. In addition, a group of Texas businessmen erected a building for the organization in Houston. The board of directors has typically included high-level business executives, but after a while some union leaders and, more recently, a scattering of academics were added. The APC was modeled in part on the German and Japanese national productivity centers. Initially the center concentrated on raising consciousness about the productivity problem and productivity measurement. With the termination of its five-year start-up grants and the failure of contributions and fees for services to keep up with expenditures, there was a dramatic scaling down of operations. Annual expenditures fell from roughly $6 million a year in 1980 and 1981 to $3 million in the mid 1980s, and the professional staff was cut from ninety to fifty.

In commenting on the scaling down, Grayson hints at the dilemma I have referred to earlier in discussing the Work in America Institute and the American Center for Quality of Work Life—that of reconciling the provision of national leadership with the need to generate sufficient revenues to sustain the organization. "We tried to be too many things. To be self-sufficient, we would have had to become just another consulting firm. That might have endangered our non-profit status," Grayson said in announcing the scaling down of activities.[3] To have relied only on consulting would have required that the APC forfeit any claim to a national leadership role. By their nature, many public-interest activities cannot be self-supporting.

Notwithstanding such concerns, we can see a transformation reflected in the APC's changing sources of revenue. Whereas in 1979 consulting accounted for 5 percent of its revenue, this rose to 43 percent in 1983. The change reflects the absolute rise in consulting income combined with a falling off in contributions. A major crisis occurred in the mid 1980s, when those contributing the consulting income split off to begin their own, at least partially competitive, organization. This, as we shall see, is a common pattern and a major dilemma for nonprofit organizations of this nature. From the consultants' point of view, instead of using the profits of their activities to subsidize the rest of the organization, they can do better by going off on their own and enjoying those profits themselves.

One interesting feature of the APC's new strategy that bears on subsequent discussion is that it has been the most successful of the organizations in this area in developing a mass membership. It has built up a core of 350 annual corporate contributors who serve as members in one capacity or another. With contributions accounting for only some 40 percent of revenues, the center turned more to conducting activities on a fee-for-service basis, such as its study in the mid 1980s of strategies for raising white-collar productivity. Throughout its existence it has also been heavily involved in productivity measurement.

Unlike the Work in America Institute and the American Center for Quality of Working Life, the APC did not limit itself to helping unionized firms. This, combined with its support from conservative oil industry leaders, Grayson's participation in the Nixon administration, its focus on productivity improvement and measure-

---

3. Scott Clark, "Productivity Center Cuts Back Education, Emphasizes Practical," *Houston Chronicle*, 23 October 1983, pp. 2, 5.

ment, and the prominence of nonunion firms such as IBM among its early sponsors, led to charges that it was anti-union. The lack of union leaders among the early board members added to this image. The fact that the APC did not limit itself to unionized firms was also the basis for some animosity on the part of the national organizations focusing on the unionized sectors as they competed for corporate and foundation funds.

However effective the center has been, it clearly was not prepared to assume the national mantle of leadership in the small-group-activities movement. It was juggling a great many balls in the air. Employee involvement/labor-management cooperation formed only one of its five principal areas of concentration. The others were productivity management, white-collar productivity, productivity measurement, and national policy. The organization has not been prepared to allocate major resources to the labor-management cooperation and employee involvement area, and specifically to small-group activities, at the expense of the four other areas.

Board members and corporate sponsors, especially in the APC's early years, saw the path to productivity improvement in terms of traditional approaches like increasing availability of capital at favorable terms, technology investment, and taxation policy. These individuals were more at home negotiating and lobbying for solutions in Washington than in the factories and offices of America. Union leaders on the board were just as comfortable focusing on the "big issues" associated with traditional labor-management concerns. Yet, support for small-group activities in terms of their productivity and quality payoffs requires the acceptance of a view that many small changes, in the aggregate, yield big changes. Receptivity to such views was in short supply among board members.

Other New Wave Organizations

In the late 1970s and early 1980s, a large number of statewide productivity improvement and/or quality-of-work centers were begun. The initiatives for these organizations have typically come from universities. A November 1984 Department of Commerce report (U.S. Department of Commerce 1984) lists thirty-seven state or regionally based organizations, of which thirty-three are housed in universities. In an overlapping list of comparable organizations compiled by the American Productivity Center, of the twenty-two organizations listed, the largest number started in any one year was six in 1977 and the second highest year for start ups was 1978, with four (American Productivity Center 1985a). Those two years alone thus account for almost 50 percent of the new wave organizations.

These new wave organizations were a response to the heightened competition of the late 1970s and early 1980s. As such, compared to their earlier counterparts, they tended to stress productivity improvement to a greater extent than quality of working life. If we simply examine the names of the thirty-seven state or regional centers referred to above, sixteen contain the word *productivity*, whereas only four mention quality of working life and three include both terms.

Notwithstanding the productivity emphasis, many of these centers set up labor-management committees. While typically limited to the unionized sector, such committees hold some promise for diffusing ideas and practices relating to new work structures. Tying demonstration projects into a local network of labor and management seems a fruitful means of carrying out the diffusion effort. Yet such state committees as do exist are still struggling to survive and appear far from achieving a self-sustaining momentum. Some, like Michigan, have had to scale down their activities drastically when initial foundation funding ended. In the Michigan case, consulting supplied much of the financial support for diffusion and promotion until the major consultant decided to go off on his own. Some of the state committees have died; the attrition rate is high, and some survive in name only. The National Productivity Network links most of the productivity centers in the United States, and by 1988 it had shrunk somewhat to a membership of twenty-nine regional centers and nonprofit groups. In general, it can be said that networks through which users and potential users could learn from one another have yet to be created on the local level.

Business Organizations

During this whole period under investigation, there existed a variety of organizations representing business interests. Key among them are the National Association of Manufacturers, the Chamber of Commerce, the Business Roundtable, and the Conference Board.

While each of these organizations shows some peripheral interest in participative management and even in small-group activities, they show no inclination to leave their traditional role of lobbying for business interests (or research in the case of the Conference Board) in favor of leading the movement for small-group activities in the United States. The Business Roundtable, perhaps the most visible representative of corporate America in Washington, is primarily concerned with the "big picture," with its efforts focused on lobbying in Washington for measures in its members' interests. Leading the small-group-activities movement would be the furthest thing from the minds of its leaders.

The National Association of Manufacturers (NAM), which has a Human Resources Management Policy Group as one of its five major policy groups, also found leading a movement for small-group activities far from its primary mission, which involves lobbying for members' interests in Washington. Even when NAM journals and publications began giving more play to employee involvement in the 1980s, this grew out of its Council on Union Free Environment, initiated in 1977 and renamed somewhat more benignly the Organization for Positive Employee Relations in 1983. Presenting small-group activities in the context of union avoidance or union busting gave it a very special cast and fed the hostility of organized labor. It is all too easy for labor in this situation to stigmatize all employee-involvement activities as anti-union.

Conclusions

Among these possible contenders for a national leadership role, some organizations have indeed actively conceived of the diffusion of small-group activities throughout the nation as a potentially significant part of their agendas. Others simply have different agendas, ones that typically focus on the "big issues." In the case of the former, lack of management support is clearly the prime explanation for their failure to proceed.

There is in any case little evidence either of informal interests being coordinated formally on the national level or of any proactive pooling of corporate resources to get small-group activities moving. Rather, there has been an unsuccessful cajoling of managers to show an interest in small-group activities and other related work issues by organizations like the Ford Foundation. Clearly one cannot expect companies to pool resources to advance their common interest in small-group activities when managers are still at the stage requiring consciousness raising. Nor did I see much evidence of an effective local information network, despite some preliminary steps in that direction by the new wave organizations. Indeed, there is little evidence in this chapter for the emergence of a social movement focused on small-group activities; rather the data for the period under investigation indicate only modest management interest, suggesting a fad rather than an enduring social movement.

One dilemma reported by a number of the organizations was the perceived conflict between nationwide diffusion activities (seen as requiring heavy subsidies), and consultant activities. The organizations tended to see these as mutually exclusive. There was pressure to do consulting to bring in badly needed revenue once initial start-up grants ran out, but this was seen as requiring a large staff of full-time or part-time consultants, and soon "the tail was wagging the dog." As one interviewee expressed the matter: "To become self-sufficient, we would have to become simply a consulting organization and this would defeat the goal of assuming nationwide leadership for diffusion activities." That such a dilemma existed again reflects the unwillingness of private-sector firms to pool their resources to meet common interests in the small-group-activities area. In subsequent chapters, we shall examine some organizations that approached the matter very differently.

Organizations that had small-group activity as part of their agendas were often active exclusively in the unionized sector of the economy. As such, they found that doing something about the strong adversarial relationships between management and labor took priority over small-group activity per se. Consequently, they never "got to" making small-group activities a high priority.

The organizations pursuing small-group activities in the nonunion sector, such as the APC, left themselves open, especially early on, to the charge of encouraging employers to use small-group activities in order to avoid or decertify unions. With some notable exceptions, the unions typically took a passive to hostile view of small-group activity. Either it was seen as irrelevant to their situation, a threat to their prerogatives, or part of a union-busting strategy. There were sufficient cases of the latter to fuel these sentiments.

Viewed in this light, the failure of American employers generally to grant legitimacy to the union movement has been a major barrier to efforts to create small-group activities in the United States. Efforts to create a unified national infrastructure championing such activities were bound to founder on the shoals of labor-management distrust. In both Sweden and Japan during the period under investigation, the unions were not confronted with a major movement among employers to challenge their very existence. In the United States, however, the challenge was continuous. It was especially encouraged during the Reagan years by the breaking of the air controllers' union and the strong pro-management stance of the NLRB.

This mistrust operated both at the level of building a national infrastructure and at the level of individual firms. In reflecting on the difficulty of getting union support for shop level employee-involvement activities in the United States, one Swedish observer said to me: "It is much easier for strong unions to support employee involvement. Weak unions and union leaders fearing management efforts to unseat them and weaken the union are much more fearful of cooperative activities."

Lack of management support, other organizational agendas, inability to resolve organizational conflict between diffusion and consulting, inability to build local information networks, and labor-management conflict all combined to make the organizations examined in this chapter "non-starters" when it came to playing a major leadership role in collaborating to spread small-group activities.

Chapter Nine

The American Society for Quality Control: The Liability of Age

Learning can also put forth leaves without bearing fruit.

German saying

Chapter 8 considered entrepreneurs, such as Rosow and Grayson, who created new organizations to deal with the changing nature of work, but who did not see small-group activities as the focus of their operations. In this chapter I look at an organization within which there were strong advocates of assuming a national leadership role in small-group activities, but it was an established organization that proved incapable of taking action to achieve this. Precisely for this reason, we need to pursue this case more closely than those of the organizations discussed previously to better understand the dynamics involved.[1]

On the face of it, the American Society for Quality Control (ASQC) had a variety of resources that could be brought to bear on its assuming a leadership position in small-group activity. Quality-circle activity in Japan had been sponsored by the national quality-

1. The initial treatment of the ASQC relies on a variety of official historical accounts as well as selected interviews with key informants. The official accounts include Brumbaugh 1946:6–34; ASQC 1986:56–67; Wareham, McClure, Medlock, and Hurd 1986:47–51.

control organization as part of its quality-improvement efforts. This organization, the Japanese Union of Scientists and Engineers (JUSE), saw the ASQC as its natural partner and was prepared to cooperate with it to pursue QC circle activity in America. The ASQC thus had a special pipeline to Japanese expertise.

Generally speaking, using QC circle activities to solve quality problems is far less threatening to workers than small-group activities directly devoted to improving productivity would be, with their implications of job displacement. Quality is an issue the average worker believes in. This focus thus gave the ASQC a natural opportunity to tie in its expertise in bringing about quality improvement with the small-group-activities movement.

Indeed, many long-term ASQC members were among those most knowledgeable about QC circle activities as a result of their early exposure to visiting Japanese quality-circle teams. The result of these relationships was that some key ASQC members and leaders were acquainted with circle activity well before general industry leaders. Joe Juran, a recognized leader in quality control, had written about quality circles in the society's journal as early as 1967. These members and leaders were introduced to circles in the context of an overall quality-improvement effort and could therefore reasonably believe that such activities fell within ASQC's mission.[2]

Many of these individuals, as well as later converts, strongly favored a national leadership role for the ASQC in supporting the circle movement. The ASQC had a regional network of 167 local chapters in North America in 1979, which were available to any diffusion effort. As a long-standing organization, it had a variety of resources available to support such a commitment, including an established publication program and an annual congress.

Given the conditions favoring the ASQC's assumption of a national leadership role in support of quality circles, how is it that it failed to assume this role? This section is devoted to answering that question. In the process we shall learn much about the way in which organizational age and inertia powerfully constrain innovation.

2. Joe Juran was one of the first to bring circles to Western attention, but at the same time he focused on the obstacles to U.S. applications and predicted adoption on "some slow evolutionary basis" at best (Juran 1980: 18–22).

The Historical Experience

To understand the reaction of its leaders to the swelling interest in quality circles, we must first understand what kind of organization the ASQC has been and was in the late 1970s and early 1980s. My purpose is not to provide a detailed history of the organization, but to focus on some key aspects of its evolving mission, as well as on the structure and process that were to influence the organization's response to quality circles.

The American Society for Quality Control was founded in 1946 and grew out of the modest success of the wartime experience with applying statistical methods to production. This in turn rested on the pioneering work of Walter Shewhart in the 1920s and 1930s. Shewhart, recognized as the father of modern quality control, laid the foundation for statistical quality control with his creation of the first control chart at Western Electric.

The society was founded with 1,000 members, and the first president was George Edwards, director of quality assurance at Bell Telephone Laboratories. The ASQC was the first national quality society in the world. Membership grew slowly but steadily, reaching 9,000 in 1955. Along with the membership growth, the original 16 regional sections (chapters) expanded to 86 by 1955. With the establishment of sections, national meetings, a regular publication, industry and functional divisions, education and training activities, and certification programs, the organization increasingly took on the trappings of a typical professional association.[3] Membership continued to rise on an annual basis, with the notable exception of a period of membership loss in the early 1970s. Membership stood at 24,000 in 1970, at 32,000 in 1979, and had risen to some 57,000 by 1988. A large spurt in membership since 1982 came in response to the growing recognition by American management that continuous quality improvement is critical to competitive success. The total number of sections has also risen, totaling 196 in 1987.

Above all, the ASQC saw itself in its formative years as a professional engineering society. George Edwards, the first president,

3. *Society* is the term the ASQC uses itself. For my purposes the generic term is *association*.

formed the first quality-engineering department at a major American firm. The founders typically held university or advanced engineering degrees. The typical president for the first ten years had a bachelor of science degree. Many of the activities of the society during its early years were devoted to securing recognition from the "allied" engineering societies. This focus has left a strong mark even today on organizational goals, structure, and process. In 1971 the ASQC officially styled itself "The Society of professionals engaged in the management, engineering, and scientific aspects of quality and reliability."

In the early years of the society, continuing efforts were made to secure entrance to the Engineers' Joint Council (EJC) and the Engineers' Council for Professional Development (ECPD). Associate status in the EJC was achieved in 1963 and full status in 1970. However, the ASQC never achieved membership in the ECPD; ECPD was important because it determined accreditation of engineering curricula in universities. As such, the founding engineering societies jealously guarded its membership to limit the demands of the proliferating new societies for accredited curricula.

The EJC had an entrance rule that required applicant associations seeking full member status to have over 50 percent of their individual members be graduates in engineering, the natural sciences, or mathematics of colleges and universities of recognized standing (implied ECPD approval), or be professionally licensed as engineers. There was, as one account recalled, "constant pressure" in the ASQC "to elevate the professional status of our membership by adopting more restrictive qualifications." To be sure, there were counter pressures, but the drive for professionalism was strong.

The issue of whether to be an engineering or technical society or one more open to a general constituency has been a continuing problem for the ASQC. A 1967 official reference to the society asks: "In regarding itself as an Engineering Society, what sort of company does ASQC keep? Among the some 90 engineering societies, ASQC, although now a youthful 21, is the 13th largest" (Shearman 1967:551). In recent years the largest increase in membership has been in the categories of lower-level inspector and statistical process control supervisor, and this has been a source of embarrassment to some ASQC leaders. The minutes of one ASQC committee meeting in the early 1980s record the vice president for education and development as saying: "ASQC is not a 'professional' society, but rather a 'technical' society. Many quality practitioners and ASQC members are para-professionals. No professional 'certification' is required for ASQC membership as it is for professional societies." Notwithstanding this recent frankness, such statements have not been typical of the public rhetoric of the society, where the push toward professionalism has been strong.

The drive to professionalize was reflected in a variety of other ways as well. One was the great emphasis the ASQC put on certification programs for those already members. The professional certification programs for quality engineers were begun in 1966 and later expanded to cover five specialties. As one ASQC publication put it, "professional development has been at the heart of ASQC activities since its founding." ASQC surveys report the salary differences associated with the different levels of certification, the clear inference being that certification has its rewards. The society has also had some modest success pursuing state licensing. Finally, there is a ranking of members according to technical expertise and contributions to the organization. Of the 37,051 members in 1982, for example, 11 percent were associate members, 78 percent were full members, 10 percent were senior members, and only 1 percent were fellows.

A few observations on the concept of professionalism are in order. First, although the society's official objective is to spread modern methods of quality control, its major activities have always revolved around achieving professional recognition and self-improvement of members. A professional association typically stresses individual career development.

With regard to the role of the individual, one of the admission rules of the Engineers' Joint Council was that an association applying for membership must have no less than two-thirds of its members be individuals who could vote in their own right rather than being subject to corporate regulation. We see here a concept of professionalism that stresses individual autonomy and development, not corporate improvement per se. Indeed, this is one of the major distinctions between a trade association and a professional association (Shearman 1967:551). In this same connection, we note that it is individuals who join professional associations, not companies.[4] To be sure, in the private sector, companies typically subsidize individual membership fees and activities in the association, and that subsidy is critical to maintaining the level of associational activity, but it is the individual who volunteers to join and be active.

These characteristics are important in understanding ASQC reactions to quality circles and to my later comparisons with the evolving infrastructure in Japan and Sweden. The point to be emphasized here is that the ASQC, as a professional association, did not represent a conscious pooling of resources by companies to optimize approaches to common interests. Rather, it was an association of individuals engaged in quality control seeking self-improvement through group action.

One other related aspect needs to be mentioned. Throughout the ASQC's history, the quality discipline has had relatively low status relative to management specialties such as finance, manufacturing, and sales. Its members have been primarily at the middle-management level, and only in recent years have a few members begun to scale the corporate ladder to the top. Consequently the attempt to use the ASQC to achieve group mobility for those in the society—a common feature of professionalizing associations—is not surprising. Professionalism and the rhetoric of self-improvement must ultimately be understood as a form of occupational control (see Johnson 1972).

By the end of the 1970s, there were changes in the membership and leadership that made the ASQC more responsive to problems of quality in the consumer-goods industries and the need to match Japanese achievements. There was a willingness to at least flirt with small-group activity as one approach to quality improvement. Still, it was not exactly a vibrant organization that met these new opportunities. In 1979 the ratio of staff to members stood at 38 to 35,000, or 1.09 per 1,000. The director of technical services at the time reported that this was about half the ratio for comparable organizations. Similarly, the annual budget of the ASQC at this time was about $2 million, less than half that of a number of comparable professional organizations. This small size suggests that it was not

4. Many associations do have companies as sustaining members; the ASQC adopted such a system itself. These sustaining members, however, are nonvoting.

very innovative in serving members' interests. Furthermore, a financial crisis in 1982–83 crippled many new initiatives just at the time when national interest in quality was blossoming. However little the ASQC may have done for members, it has had even less impact on the outside world. As one official commented at a committee meeting in September 1980: "ASQC produces material for itself—for members to talk to each other at meetings—but it doesn't reach out. It hasn't been an influential mover in improving product and service quality." While perhaps too severe an indictment, this nevertheless captures some of the stagnation prior to the burst of interest in quality and in the ASQC in the first half of the 1980s.

What Happened?

By 1975 there had been four articles in the journal of the American Society for Quality Control and a variety of intermittent contacts by ASQC sections and individual members with visiting Japanese quality-circle teams (JUSE began sponsoring such visits annually beginning in 1968). Society attention was, however, finally focused on QC circles by the 1976 ASQC Technical Conference, at which a whole day's "track" was devoted to the subject.[5] The meeting was well attended, with the response being so encouraging that the proceedings were published (Amsden and Amsden 1976).

The ASQC's quality motivation technical committee (QMTC), established in 1965, represented a stream of thinking on the subject of quality assurance that had existed since the founding of the society. Control charts, which allowed workers to plot the extent to which production was staying within process-control limits, were originally introduced in the late 1940s in part to give workers an objective means of getting away from domination by foremen. The quality-motivation theme was, however, submerged for most of the history of the ASQC, with the central focus being on achieving professional status for members.

5. This section draws heavily on my own experiences as a member of the ASQC (since April 1979) and my past membership of the quality motivation technical committee, participation as an official observer on the quality circles steering committee, and membership of the research committee of the Human Resources Division. I am indebted to those with whom I associated in this capacity for their frank explanations and sharing of information. They are not responsible for the conclusion I have drawn from the data they supplied.

In 1976 the QMTC announced in its description of its specific objectives that it had assumed leadership of the ASQC's efforts in respect to QC circles. Its three-year program beginning that year set as its objective a variety of educational activities to raise national awareness about QC circles, as well as providing specific tools for conducting them. These activities included conferences, case study research, production of educational materials, training packages on QC circles, and a certification program—seemingly a reasonable agenda for an organization seeking to achieve national leadership in a new industry movement. Yet it did not accomplish much of anything.

In attempting to explain this failure, let us first consider some of the manifest problems seen in the discussions that took place during 1979–81. The QMTC had a membership of twenty-four in 1980 and a vague mandate for improving quality motivation. There were a variety of opinions among members as to how to proceed. These views were strongly expressed, often in quite combative fashions. Many strongly believed that it was not the QMTC's job to endorse any particular vehicle for improving quality motivation. This view had strong support among those who had been in the organization for some time and recalled the ASQC's experience with the zero-defect movement. The zero-defect motivational program was developed at Martin Marietta by Philip Crosby and his associates in the early 1960s. Through constant awareness, workers focusing on the zero-defect concept were to promote a constant conscious desire to do their jobs right the first time (Halpin 1966:5–6). Critics pointed out that it was a movement without any operational mechanism. It was also hostile in its original conception to small-group activity and worker participation.[6]

Despite strong support from some members at the time, the ASQC had resisted endorsing the zero-defect movement and opposed the movement to set up a separate society to promote ZD. When ZD initiatives collapsed in the early 1970s, many felt that they had just missed being "burned." More important, there had been tremendous conflict in the organization, with the threat of a split. The November 1966 issue of the society's journal reported all

6. For an elaboration of this theme, see Cole 1989. Ironically, the Japanese later adapted the idea of zero defects and combined it with quality-circle techniques to create ZD groups.

the reasons why the board of directors opposed the formation of any new society or group focused on quality motivation.

The QMTC had been heavily involved in these issues, insofar as it was the major unit within the society addressing quality-motivation issues. The lesson that many in the ASQC and on the committee in particular drew from this experience is that there are a lot of fads out there, commitment to any one of which can lead to painful internal conflict, and we ought not to be too quick to leap on any bandwagon. In short, the experience with ZD stigmatized specific quality-motivational techniques as fads. The burning question for ASQC leaders in the late 1970s and early 1980s was whether quality circles were just another motivational fad. Popular discussion focused on this same issue, thereby adding fuel to their concerns (see Lawler and Mohrman 1985:65–71).

A second source of division lay in the strong argument by some committee members that quality-circle endorsement be closely tied to the then-developing quality-of-work-life (QWL) movement and made part of a total systems approach to participation.[7] A number of QMTC committee members had little background and/or knowledge in this area, however, and were not comfortable on such new terrain.

A major source of difference lay in the differing positions that tended to get taken by the quality-circle consultants on the committee and practitioners (company employees). There were five consultants on the committee, and two of the company employees were soon to become consultants. A common view expressed by the consultants was that the society should not compete with its own members (the consultants). In practice this meant that the consultants tended to oppose the society developing training packages that would compete with their own. The view was also expressed that the ASQC should not perform in-plant training, but should rather limit itself to public training to upgrade members' qualifications. Consultants questioned the legitimacy of a membership organization training nonmembers for profit. The consultants' position was consistent with the existing informal policy of the ASQC not to engage in in-plant training (a policy generally adhered

7. For the concept statement developed by Sidney Rubinstein in this connection, see Rubinstein 1980:28–31.

to by professional associations, testifying to the strength of consultant members in many such organizations).

ASQC committees like the QMTC also became skirmishing grounds for consultants with different interests in the matter. Some consultants opposed ASQC's involvement with circles because they were associated with the new International Association of Quality Circles (IAQC) and saw business advantages to its success. Other consultants supported ASQC involvement, perhaps in part as a way of neutralizing the IAQC and their consultant competitors.

Still another issue that surfaced in QMTC discussions concerned the role of the committee in ensuring the sharing of information. For company people, professional associations were an ideal way to share information without violating antitrust regulations. This subject came up often. As one company person expressed the matter:

In the old days of the committee there was a general atmosphere of sharing experiences. We developed training manuals and strategies for motivation. Now there are a lot of consultants and they don't share as much, especially their "failures." They are more interested in making speeches and getting exposure for their products. They don't come to meetings unless it serves company business.

Despite an obvious romanticizing of the past, these statements do represent some common sentiments among company members.

The various differences discussed in the preceding paragraphs could easily have been enough to produce a paralysis of the committee and an inability to implement its quality-circle agenda. In fact, this divisiveness paled next to the problems inherent in the committee structure itself. The major problems arise from the voluntary nature of committee activities. Members are by and large self-selected or "tapped" by colleagues who think they have some interest and talent. But participation is strongly influenced by the presence or absence of company financial support.

Company support for membership dues and travel often appears and evaporates with little notice and makes continuity of program activities very difficult. Ups and downs of the business cycle often have the effect of dramatically reducing the numbers of individuals from a given industry who are able to participate in society activities. Beyond the annual meeting of the committee at the annual society convention (which typically was the minimum required by

ASQC rules), it is often extremely difficult to get company support for time for and travel to committee meetings.

Company support would be less of a problem if ASQC members had higher management status, but, as noted earlier, they are typically of low and middle-management levels. Additional meetings are thus either difficult to hold or poorly attended. In this situation, it is extremely difficult to conduct coherent, continuous initiatives. The incentive for unpaid volunteers to contribute their time and labor under these conditions is limited. It takes extraordinary situations such as the start up of new organizations to provide sufficient motivation to overcome such inertia. In a heavily bureaucratized organization such as the ASQC had become in the 1970s, however, such motivation simply was not there. Moreover, corporate members turned over rapidly, requiring much duplication of effort to reeducate new members; new chairpersons every two or three years also try to leave their mark, thereby often leaving earlier agendas unfinished. All this makes progress difficult.

An exception to what has just been said here is consultant participation. Consultants typically see society membership as a business investment and have control over their time. Consequently, they have strong incentives to participate, and they tend to have a high profile and stronger influence on decisions than their numbers alone would suggest. As we have seen, moreover, some of that thrust is to limit society activities that might interfere with their business opportunities. This is not to suggest that consultants' involvement is always instrumental in serving their business, but clearly there is a nonrandom direction to many of their contributions. In talking with "practitioner" members of the ASQC, it is clear that there often is a distrust of consultants' motives and resentment of their using the society to advance their interests. When two newly elected ASQC presidents became consultants, there was a great deal of criticism among members. As one member expressed it to me, "It became hard to distinguish normal society PR from that which was self-serving to the consulting firm."

This description of consultants in the society raises a more general analytic point. In chapter 3 I described the alternatives facing companies of going to the market to obtain consultant expertise or pooling their corporate resources in associations. The real world is a bit messier. There are association and associations; and not all represent a pooling of corporate resources. The behavior of consultants is intertwined with associational activity. This will become even clearer when we look at the IAQC in the next two chapters.

The Evolution of the Quality Circles
Technical Committee

Industry interest in QC circles was growing rapidly in the late 1970s, but the ASQC was not doing very much to take advantage of it. In response to this situation in early 1980 Charles Mills, the vice president for divisions and technical committees, arranged for Robert Amsden, a faculty member at Wright State University and long-term ASQC member, to head up a steering committee to prepare a report on circles. In his letter of request, Mills, an employee of Westinghouse Canada, indicated that he strongly believed that the ASQC "should be deeply involved" in circle activity, providing both technical and training support. There was thus high-level support for ASQC leadership in this activity at the outset.

There was, however, resentment on the part of some QMTC members at the creation of the QC circles steering committee. The outgoing chair made it clear to me that he opposed having his committee bypassed and putting so many consultants on the new steering committee (two out of the initial four members), and that he would work to keep a role for the QMTC.

The instructions of the General Technical Council (the key initiating and decision-making body within the ASQC that made recommendations to the board of directors) to the new steering committee were contained in a six-page document that covered charges, objectives, functions, organization, membership, finances, meetings, rules of procedure and records, areas of exclusion, areas of cooperative effort, and areas of responsibility.[8] Little was left to the imagination. It was the kind of document one would expect from a tightly organized association. The new steering committee was responsible for determining the need for participation by the ASQC in QC circles and, if there were such a need, for deciding what

---

8. The General Technical Council, made up of volunteers heading up the various divisions, reported to the vice president of divisions and technical committees, who in turn reported to the president.

kinds of participation and societal structures would be appropriate for meeting it. QWL and other quality-motivation techniques were excluded from consideration by the committee. This was to ensure separation from the QMTC's turf.

In addition to the initial suggestion from Vice President Mills that the chair put two consultants and two company people on the committee, the General Technical Council also recommended adding two additional company members, bringing membership to seven including the chairman. One of the company members, however, was soon to turn into a full-time consultant working for one of the other consultant members on the committee. The major attribute of this new committee as opposed to the QMTC is that it was focused exclusively on QC circles. Moreover, all the members of the committee were committed to circles and to expanding the ASQC's responsibilities in this area. There was little doubt from the start that they would put forward a positive recommendation. It is also clear that this was the intent of the General Technical Council when it established the committee—it wanted to get the ASQC moving on QC circles.

At the first meeting of the steering committee in May 1979, there was unanimous agreement that the ASQC should become involved in QC circles. Among the reasons given was the rapid growth of the International Association of Quality Circles (IAQC), many of whose members were quality professionals. The ASQC, and the steering committee in particular, felt a sense of urgency in preventing the void from being filled by a competitor organization. The IAQC was a threat to ASQC membership and it reminded many of the ZD movement, where splinter groups had threatened to break off to form separate organizations. Indeed, the Society for Non-Destructive Testing and the Reliability Engineering Society had done just that.

One ASQC member expressed his concerns on this matter in a letter to the editor of the society's journal in December 1979. He was worried that there would be increasing acceptance of quality circles without the active involvement of the society or its members. This would "weaken the efforts of our profession to increase its collective position/prestige/effectiveness within the managerial hierarchy." In other words, circles were a rising movement that the ASQC ought to be leading as a means of raising the members' collective status.

A major substantive reason for ASQC involvement concerned the technical contributions that quality-control techniques could bring to workshop problem-solving activities. In Japan, this had been well documented. The committee believed that the ASQC was in a unique position to focus on these technical aspects and diffuse their applications.

The initial recommendations developed at the steering committee's first meeting included:

appointing a full-time staff person at the ASQC's Milwaukee headquarters as director of QC circle activities in the United States;

developing an ongoing sub task force to survey QC circle activities in the United States;

developing liaison with professional and academic societies;

defining QC circles in contrast to other programs and defining the objectives/goals of QC circles;

developing certification of facilitators jointly with the IAQC;

evaluating and certifying training materials;

interfacing with the IAQC in sponsoring conferences, training, and publishing;

exploring development of QC circles in white-collar situations;

publishing case studies;

developing group problem-solving techniques;

determining where QC circles fit into the overall quality-control picture.

This was not an unreasonable agenda for a group trying to steer the society into a national leadership role in introducing QC circles.

In keeping with the dependence on volunteers, the second meeting of the steering committee on QC circles was held a year later at the next national conference in May 1980. No formal communication seems to have taken place between these two intervals other than circulating the minutes of the first meeting. No budget was provided to the committee to make possible any additional meetings; nor does one seem to have been requested.

The second meeting opened with a review of past events. The chair reassured committee members, based on his conversations with members of the General Technical Council, that members of the council were committed to taking firm action to embrace QC circles within the ASQC.

The major action taken at this meeting was the steering committee's approval of the motion that the ASQC form "a QC Circle Technical Committee." The following day, members of the General Technical Council assisted the committee by supplying the elaborate and detailed guidelines, content, and format required to request establishing a technical committee. It was like navigating a maze. Tasks were assigned to committee members and drafts mailed in. The committee chair mailed the 26-page report of the QC circle steering committee recommending technical committee status for circles within the ASQC. No time was allowed for a full-scale committee review of the report. One committee member registered his objections to the report, noting that the financial arrangements with regard to budget "appear to be an impediment to serving our membership and industry." He also noted that although the exclusion of areas such as QWL from consideration might serve some of the society's political objectives, it inhibited the real job to be done. Notwithstanding such objections, the General Technical Council formally approved the formation of the quality circles technical committee (note the Americanization of the original name, QC circles) in November 1980.

As indicated by the objections of one of the committee members just mentioned, the new arrangements left a lot to be desired. The key issue for the committee, although it was not appreciated at the time by most members, turned on the implications of technical committee status within the ASQC's highly bureaucratized structure. Briefly put, to meet the great industry interest in quality circles at the time, one needed a flexible organizational structure capable of responding quickly and taking many different kinds of initiatives. ASQC technical committees simply did not have the autonomy to act in this fashion. Above all, they did not have the ability to engage in income-generating activities without securing either divisional (if they were attached to a division) or headquarters approval. Typically, this involved long lead times to keep them in sync with the ASQC's annual budget process. Any proposed expenditures not included in the society's annual budget had to negotiate an even more complicated approval process. Technical committees did not have their own treasurers. Thus even a relatively simple operation like running a conference involved extensive negotiations with other units. Most important, the use of any surplus generated had to be negotiated with either a division or with headquarters. An analogous situation prevailed with regard to the ability of the technical committee to issue publications and training materials. In both cases elaborate bureaucratic approval was required.

Flexibility was further limited with the prohibition of working in areas such as QWL. While designed to avoid a confrontation with the QMTC, many felt that this was an artificial distinction that did not reflect needs in the real world. Finally, members of a technical committee and its chair are appointed by the division chairman if the committee is part of a division or by headquarters if it is a free-standing technical committee. This selection mechanism fundamentally limits the autonomy and incentives of any technical committee. In summary, these arrangements are not designed to enhance entrepreneurial activities; rather they speak of bureaucratic caution, maintenance of standards, and risk avoidance.

ASQC staff and General Technical Council members did not make these implications very clear to the QC circle steering committee, probably out of a desire to get things moving in the direction they wanted. What was made clear to the steering committee was that although divisional status would remove many of the limitations on it, "One can't get to be a division until you have served two years as a technical committee." There is a catch-22 quality to this. To get the job done, you need divisional status, but you can't get that until you have served two years as a technical committee, at which point the opportunity for successful initiatives may have passed. Faced with this choice, anxious to do something, and unaware for the most part of the limitations of technical committee status, the steering committee had nonetheless recommended technical committee status.

At the very first meeting of the new technical committee, held in Dayton, Ohio, in February 1981, seventeen people attended, with many new faces and—reflecting the realities of travel costs—heavy local representation. The most important information at the meeting came from the technical director, who reported that owing to budget problems, there was a hold on the hiring of any new staff personnel. He indicated that this would restrict his ability to provide services for the new committee. This in fact initiated a two-year period of austerity and crisis within the ASQC. Staff services were cut (nine professional staff employees were let go) and the committee was left primarily to its own devices. This meant that success was to be dependent on volunteer committee members, a poor recipe for success in a project of this magnitude.

The committee responded favorably to a report of one of its sub-committees that QC circle registration be initiated at the ASQC with a registration fee and a newsletter edited and published by the ASQC staff, two copies of which were to be sent to each circle. This was a model developed by the ASQC's Japanese "counter-part," JUSE. It was an activity that had also been under study by the International Association of Quality Circles, but no action had been taken. Thus it was seen as a chance for the ASQC to get a jump on the competition and make a name for itself in QC circles.[9]

In February 1982, in cooperation with the QMTC, now renamed the human resources technical committee, the quality circles technical committee submitted to the General Technical Council a detailed plan for QC circle registration, with the rationale outlined, including its income-generating potential, and a step-by-step procedure for implementation.

Despite the board of directors having indicated support for the idea in principle at an earlier date, this plan was never funded. It was the height of the ASQC's budget crisis and the figures did not add up in the eyes of the executive committee of the board of directors. In a letter to the chair of the quality circles technical committee dated 25 February 1982, the new vice president for divisions and technical committees, Mills's successor Dana Cound, currently of Gencorp Corporation, suggested that the plan was too ambitious, too risky financially, and unlikely to be accepted by the board. Cound proposed that the committee instead focus on joining with the human resources technical committee to attain divi-

9. One of the interesting issues that surfaced, apropos of my earlier discussion of professionalism, was broadening ASQC constituencies. Some saw circle registration as an ideal way to broaden ASQC membership. Others saw it as a way of avoiding giving membership to nonprofessional groups, while still having them associated through registration with the ASQC. As one member of the committee put it, "Registration of circles avoids problems with our professional engineering groups who object to our having members who are nonprofessional [i.e., nondegreed]."

sional status for the latter body.[10] He held out the hope that the resulting division would be able to do a lot of the things being asked for. The assumption was that the quality circles technical committee would report to it. This eliminated the old QMTC opposition to the supporters of quality circles receiving technical committee status. Yet if quality circles flopped, it would be only a committee that had failed, and the broader human-resource activity could go on. It was an organizationally "tidy" solution.

More important, this letter was a clear sign—even though the chair of the committee was not yet willing to recognize it—that the dream of making the ASQC the focus of QC circle activities in the United States was at an end. It was not just registration that was over, but all the activities that symbolized national leadership in a diffusion effort—education for all levels of employees, diffusion of best practices, conferences, publication of case studies, arranging for intercompany sharing of experiences, and a variety of publication vehicles. In retrospect, the end had been foretold long before when the "technical committee" structure was made the society's vehicle for QC circle activities.

Cound clearly had another agenda in mind. In particular, his priority was focusing top management's attention on quality. The ASQC had long suffered from a lack of top management support, and quality had long suffered from the lack of top management recognition of its importance. Cound's initiative had strong support among many long-term ASQC activists. While there can be no doubt as to the importance of top management's commitment to quality, it is interesting that the quality-circle initiative was seen as incompatible with it. The ASQC had also absorbed from the Japanese the idea that only 15 percent of quality improvement came from QC circles, the rest deriving from management and professional initiatives. The decision to focus on top management's involvement thus seemed a reasonable one. As president-elect of the ASQC in 1985–86 and president in 1986–87, Cound was in a strong position to push forward his agenda within the society.

As recommended by Cound, the quality-circle technical com-

10. There developed a consensus at this time that "quality motivation technical committee" did not reflect the issues of the time. Activists wanted to reach out to a broader constituency and the vehicle for this was to the new human resources technical committee.

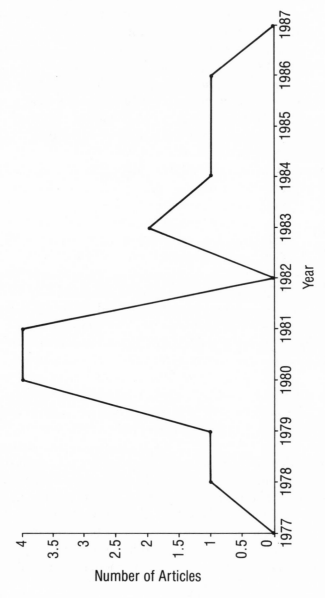

FIG. 5. Number of Quality-Circle Articles in the ASQC Journal *Quality Progress*, by Year.

mittee came increasingly to focus on the achievement of divisional status for the human resource technical committee. It was the kind of bureaucratic paper-shuffling activity and jumping through a series of organizational hoops that drained the enthusiasm of everyone but the most committed or unthinking. Participation in committee meetings in 1982 began a downhill slide over the course of the year. Interest declined as committed members looked elsewhere for ways to achieve their goals for quality circles. As one staff person, reflecting on past events, said to me in 1987, "I think those who were really committed to circles went over to IAQC." These kinds of people had not come to the ASQC to play musical chairs or climb the rungs of the ASQC organizational ladder. In a volunteer organization, member involvement dries up very quickly without motivation.

Divisional status was achieved for the human resources technical committee in November 1982. The quality circles technical committee was duly folded into the new division, eventually to lose its status as a separate technical committee and become just a standing committee. As such, it had even less significance than as a technical committee. For all practical purposes, it disappeared from sight.

The "neat" organizational solution at which the ASQC arrived was an empty victory for those who envisioned the society as the leader of a national quality-circle movement. Its structure did not allow for a national leadership role and, most important, the wave of national interest had subsided. The momentum was no longer there. There were no longer highly motivated volunteers available, and the response of industry was not as warm as it had been just a few years earlier. As we have seen from the discussion of the garbage can model, timing, if not everything, is a great deal. We can assess the wave of industry and ASQC interest by the number of quality-circle articles in the society's journal, *Quality Progress*. As shown in figure 5, the peak of interest as reflected in journal articles was in 1980–81. When the registration proposal finally reached the board of directors, a severe financial crisis was pushing it to reject all new budget initiatives. This, combined with its general conservatism and an alternative agenda, doomed the proposal.

Could a strong QC circle steering committee chairman have made a difference? Even if the chair had been a highly respected corporate quality engineer, well connected in industry circles and capable of exercising decisive leadership, it is still unlikely—we can never know for sure—that the outcome would have been fundamentally different. Inherent constraints made the technical committee structure inadequate to the task. Moreover, the political (the human resources technical committee had a stronger claim) and bureaucratic (you had to be a technical committee for two years before you could even apply) reasons that made divisional status unobtainable created an impossible situation. It simply wasn't in the cards for the ASQC to become the national agency for the diffusion of quality circles in America. Quality-circle supporters in the ASQC did not know it at the time, but they never had a chance. Only if the society had had the ability and vision to spin off some sort of subsidiary could it perhaps have played the role that so many of its enthusiastic circle supporters sought for it. But even that was not in ASQC's repertoire.

A Broader Perspective on Obstacles to Change

The thrust of my argument thus far is that the organizational vehicle the ASQC chose for its quality circle policies was inherently incapable of arriving at the destination sought by those who wanted to make the ASQC the premier institution for developing and diffusing quality circles in America. While I believe the evidence in this regard to be overwhelming, it is nevertheless useful to step back and take a broader perspective on the matter. Why was this choice of an inappropriate vehicle made? Was it lack of leadership, political intrigue, or simply poor planning?

The population ecologists' study of organizational change and survival provides a useful framework. Howard Aldrich and Ellen Auster (1986:168), from whom I draw the subsequent analytic framework, identify the following four internal conditions, associated primarily with the aging of organizations, that inhibit adaptation to change:

retention of control in the hands of the original founders;

pressures toward internal consistency as a basis of coordination and control;

the hardening of vested interests; and

homogeneity of members' perceptions.

When we talk about these conditions being associated with aging, we are really saying that the organization has a history. What the authors have done is select out of this history some characteristic processes occurring over time that they and others have identified in their research as inhibitors of change. The case study being discussed here provides a further opportunity to examine the fit between the empirical reality and the analytic perspective offered by Aldrich and Auster. By and large, the fit is pretty good, though some modest adjustments need to be made.

The first factor said to inhibit change is retention of control by the original founders. Strictly speaking, this was not that much of a problem for the ASQC. At worst, problems arose from the retention of many of the ideas of the original founders, especially as the organization moved into new areas. This broader view is consistent with the earlier observations of Arthur Stinchcombe (1965), who noted the tendency for a significant correlation to exist between the time in history when a particular type of organization was invented and the social structure of organizations of that type that exist at the present time. Such persistence can inhibit adaptation to change and even threaten organizational survival if environmental changes are significantly large and/or rapid.

The ideas at the ASQC that most fit this discussion are those concerning the drive toward professionalism. Professionalism as a goal developed in the early days of the society as it sought to win recognition from other professional associations. Having been formed at a time when there was a proliferation of new professional societies, the ASQC naturally tended to model itself on the five existing founder societies (the basic engineering societies, founded in the late 1800s).

I would speculate that had a quality-control society first been organized in 1980, it would have had quite different characteristics. By 1980 the idea of quality as a total management system had begun to take root. This way of thinking suggests the need for a more open kind of association. In addition, consultants are a far more pervasive influence on the organization of American society today than they were in 1946. Based on discussions earlier in the chapter, we can hypothesize that had the first quality association been organized in 1980, the consultants would have fought harder to limit professionalism. Moreover, there is some reason to think that consultants are more influential in the early stages of establishing organizations, when norms and practices are quite fluid. I provide related evidence for this proposition in the following chapters.

Professionalism has been built into the ASQC's structure and policies. Today, it is most associated with the orientation toward self-improvement of members and career enhancement of quality professionals. The very same ideas that contributed to the gradual upgrading of member credentials and status have, however, worked to limit the willingness of society leaders to open the organization to nonprofessionals. It made them less able to draw upon the tremendous power of applied statistics for involving production workers in the quality-improvement process.

The ASQC *is* changing and the hold of professionalism as a dominant organizational ideology *is* weakening.[11] The push toward involving top management in society activities in the mid 1980s may be viewed as evidence of this change. However, the pace has been slow. As one member put it to me, the ASQC may have to be dragged kicking and screaming into the twenty-first century. That is to say, its posture has been defensive and reactive rather than seeing the involvement of nonprofessionals as an opportunity to expand its focus. In this environment, it is hardly surprising that the ASQC greeted quality circles and all they stand for with a measure of caution and skepticism. My point here is not that professionalism per se blocked a positive reception to quality circles, but that in conjunction with other factors it served as an inhibiting force.

In this connection, there is another characteristic of the ASQC's organizational history that served to block a positive reaction to circles. It is sufficiently generalizable as to merit creating a fifth internal condition that serves to inhibit adaptation to change, though it is related to the hardening of vested interests and the growing homogeneity of members' perceptions. I would label this fifth factor *stigmatization of innovative behavior because of some past experience that resembles the new initiative.* I believe this is a rather

11. The number of members taking the certified quality-engineering exam is nonetheless increasing.

common situation that leads organizations to selectively perceive experience in such a way that new opportunities come to be seen as threats.

Here, the ASQC's experience with the zero-defect movement is instructive. The zero-defect movement served as a negative role model that made ASQC leaders extremely suspicious of quality circles. Some of those associated with the ASQC had been hurt professionally in their organizations by the demise of the zero-defect approach, and the society had flirted with endorsing it, engendering a good deal of internal conflict.

In common with the ZD movement, QC circles involved the commitment and motivation of production workers in the quality-improvement effort, and both innovations arrived with a great deal of fanfare. There was also an element of self-promotion as consultants and those in companies who had had a pioneering role used ZD to advance their personal careers. Sensing these similarities, many ASQC leaders feared that the QC circle movement would soon decline, just as the ZD movement had died. Creating the technical committee structure for QC circles was a "nice" way for the organization to try them out without overly committing itself.

Yet there were fundamental differences between QC circles and the ZD movement. First, the national mood was far more favorable to employee involvement and making better use of our human resources than had been the case almost two decades earlier. Competitive survival seemed to demand it. Second, the zero-defect movement as it developed in the United States lacked an engine to drive it. However, the Japanese had evolved a clearly defined problem-solving methodology to advance QC circles. They had proved the validity of this methodology over some twenty years, so that it hardly qualified as an organizational fad. QC circles as they developed in Japan were task-oriented. As many circle supporters within the ASQC argued, it was natural for the society to play a major role given the quality profession's[12] use of similar problem-solving methodologies and its identical goal of improving quality.

Aldrich and Auster list pressures toward internal consistency as a basis of coordination and control as a second factor inhibiting organizational change. As organizations age, patterns of behavior stabilize,

12. *Quality professionals* is a term in common use in industry to refer to specialists in quality assurance.

individuals settle into standardized roles, and standard operating procedures emerge and become institutionalized. The emphasis is increasingly on producing reliable and accountable outputs. Even when managers recognize problems and act to monitor them, they tend to create ritualized solutions, adding to the inertia they are publicly acting to combat (Aldrich and Auster 1986:169).

The ASQC's leaders' search for an existing organizational mechanism that would "handle" QC circles fits this description almost perfectly. Ideas like appointing a full-time staff member at headquarters to direct quality-circle activity for the society were anathema to the leaders because they did not fit anywhere on the organizational chart. They suggested disorder, not the neat organizational boxes to which ASQC officials were accustomed. How would they be funded? What kind of precedent would they set? Even though technical committee status was clearly inadequate for the national leadership role in circles that some ASQC officials talked about, there was no willingness or ability to think about creative organizational strategies that could make it happen. In routine fashion, the QC circle steering committee was created to come up with an organizational response to quality circles, but the ritualized treatment of its recommendations only resulted in further inaction.

The next inhibition of change associated with organizational age is that vested interests harden as organizations age and grow larger. People develop investments in given practices and solutions. Proposals for change are seen as mechanisms for gaining power, and alterations in organization are resisted because it is believed they will disturb the existing distribution of resources and privileges. Under these circumstances, organizations may add tasks or divisions to accommodate new groups rather than alter existing arrangements. This can be a costly strategy (Aldrich and Auster 1986:170).

In the case of quality-circle supporters and the ASQC, there was first the fear among QMTC members that a separate focus for quality circles in the organization threatened their interests; they felt that they had already staked out that territory. Only when it was made clear that they would achieve divisional status under the rubric of the human resources technical committee, and that the quality circle technical committee would report to them, were they prepared to drop their opposition and support the "package deal."

Here we see a variant on Aldrich and Auster's position. The separate existence of a quality-circle organization was seen as a greater threat than the alternative of having the new unit report directly to the new Human Resources Division. This is, of course, hardly surprising. The best way to control potentially dissident units is to have them report to you. This is not the best way, however, to bring about change in an organization! To be sure, there was a logic about this decision that made sense to society leaders. In the private-sector organizations they dealt with, quality-circle coordinators were typically slotted into human-resource departments, so it made "sense" to replicate that model in the society.

More generally, there was also the issue raised by the possible entry into the organization of large numbers of nonprofessionals. Some ASQC constituencies feared that the registration of circles or a merger with the IAQC might lead to a large influx of members without degrees. Implicit here is a possible shift in the ASQC's power base and potentially lower status for the organization as a whole.

Finally, the homogeneity of members' perceptions makes organizational transformation difficult. Indeed, such homogeneity may threaten organizational survival by reason of the obstacles it poses to adjusting to environmental change. Such homogeneity can have various causes. Recruitment efforts focus consciously or unconsciously on particular categories of individuals. One tends to recruit those who are most similar to those already members and to be most successful with the recruitment of these very same categories. Socialization, training, and common experience all contribute to the homogenization of members' outlooks (Aldrich and Auster 1986: 170). This homogenization inhibits change by sapping organizational confidence in the ability of the leadership to deal with new constituencies and situations.

Expressed more generally, homogeneity of members' outlooks and perceptions inhibits change by reducing variety. This is probably the central principle of the population ecology approach to organizations. Limiting variety reduces an organization's ability to map its external environment and respond to new challenges effectively. Lack of internal diversity thus makes an organization vulnerable to external challenges. Professional associations which by definition draw their membership from those possessing specialized characteristics, seem particularly vulnerable to this threat.

If I were to identify which of the five factors I judged most critical to the failure of the ASQC to move more positively toward QC circles, it would be the homogeneity of members' perceptions. It is difficult to quantify these relationships, but we can make a plausible case. The narrowness of the ASQC's constituency—all quality-control practitioners—limited the variety of skills and knowledge in the organization and made it difficult to respond forcefully and intelligently to the challenges posed by quality circles. As traditionally conceived of in the United States, quality control was seen as the responsibility of quality-control departments at the plant level. There was thus no full-scale involvement of all departments and their skills in quality improvement in interaction with quality-control personnel. This meant that ASQC members were likely to lack human-resource-development skills and familiarity with the associated behavioral theory.

The term *quality control* is misleading. The association had over the years expanded its mission in response to specialization that had taken place at the firm level. Many companies began to have specialized functions for quality assurance separate from quality control. Quality-assurance activities came to focus on broader defect-prevention activities to be achieved through quality control's primary contribution to the firm's business planning and business implementation. Quality assurance also focuses on quality control's total system responsibilities. By contrast, quality-control responsibilities focus on the discipline's traditional functions of detection associated with inspection and testing activities (see Feigenbaum 1983:160, 190). We can see from this description that, independent of other considerations, quality assurance involves quality personnel in higher-status activities with more power, while quality-control activities typically involve working with low-status personnel. Understandably, then, the ASQC was eager to expand the quality mission in the direction of quality-assurance activities. By contrast, taking a leadership role in circle activities would have involved working with an entirely new low-status constituency in ways that challenged conventional norms and practices. This was a much bigger leap than the ASQC was capable of making.

This history made it extremely difficult for the ASQC to evaluate QC circles. There was a feeling among the leadership of the ASQC that none of the people pushing circles understood the behavioral science aspects. As one former president of the society told me,

"There was a feeling that we should stay away [from circles] because we don't have people of sufficient stature leading the way." Charles Mills, the chairman of the General Technical Council at the time of the initial push for QC circles, was a strong advocate of doing something. But he was viewed by many as an amateur in this area. There was also a concern among leaders about infighting among the consultants and that the society could end up being used. There was, in short, a lack of confidence in the organization that this was something that it could manage and bring off in a credible way.

As we have seen, the society has been moving away from its earlier narrow view of professionalism toward a broader systems view of quality, with a recognition that continuous quality improvement requires involvement by all levels and parts of a firm. This, however, has been a slow evolutionary process, and QC circles represented a big jump over a large gap in knowledge. Under these circumstances, it is hardly surprising that conservatism came to rule the society's response. Moreover, if it was going to reach out, it was going to be after top managers who would bring status and recognition to the organization, not lower-level quality-circle coordinators and blue-collar circle members.

The disjunction that saw quality-circle activities assigned to human-resource departments in many companies rather than to quality-control departments also made ASQC leaders uneasy. While they knew they had something to contribute, it was still a big step to try to assume national leadership of a movement that contained dimensions they did not have a total grasp of. In particular, for many of the technical people, there was a sense that the body of knowledge associated with QC circles was too soft and not certifiable. This was an organization comfortable with hard numbers and certification!

In summary, all five factors, but especially the homogeneity of members' perceptions, operated to limit the ASQC's ability to take positive and innovative action with regard to quality circles. Organizational history had a profoundly conservative impact on the society's response to opportunities for change.

Chapter Ten

The International Association of Quality Circles: The Liability of Newness, Part 1

With an annual original budget of less than $100,000, the IAQC has grown to an organization of 1.5 million dollars in just 9 years. This accomplishment is surpassed only by the amount of mismanagement, theft, and political mismatch that has plagued the financial resources of IAQC.

The passage quoted above appears at the beginning of "The IAQC Chronology: A Financial Perspective," an internal document developed by the IAQC staff (Tarter et al. 1987).[1] It captures well the themes developed in this and the subsequent chapter, both the significant accomplishments of this organization and its miscues and failure to capitalize on a variety of opportunities.

1. While I was involved with the ASQC as a member of the QMTC and as an official observer on the quality circle steering committee, my experience with the IAQC was far more extensive. I was a member of the board of directors from 1980 to 1983 and again in 1985 and chair of the strategic planning committee in 1984–85. As such, I shared in the successes and failures of the organization.

Typically participant observation research is done in anonymous organizations, often with lower-status individuals. In this research, there can be no concealing of the organization's name. The norm among social scientists is that the researcher plays a passive role so as not to influence any outcomes. In keeping with the Heisenberg principle, the premise is that mere observation affects social processes. I chose an explicitly activist role, however, which included participation

Research shows the central issue facing small new organizations, once founded, is survival (Aldrich and Auster 1986:186). By this measure the IAQC, founded in 1978, would appear to be quite successful. Its tenth anniversary was celebrated in 1988 under a new name: the Association for Quality and Participation (AQP). Yet its existence has been problematic throughout its life. It has lurched from one crisis to another.

At first glance the organization would seem to have a lot going for it. It came into being as the promoter of a new set of organizational practices. As a consequence, it had no existing domestic competitors. Moreover, as we have seen, none of the most closely associated organizations chose to make a major entry into this market. All this occurred in a period in which Japanese management practices were all the rage. In the late 1970s and early 1980s, talk of quality circles was on the lips of many American managers as they sought ways to solve competitive problems of quality and productivity. Circles were a much-discussed solution in the business press and at management conferences.

Thus, the association had little difficulty getting attention for its product and the solutions it offered. Marketing costs were modest. With a seemingly simple package of organizational technology, the association's entry into the market was rather easily carried out with only modest capital costs. All these advantages are typically problems for small new organizations (Aldrich and Auster 1986: 177–83). Clearly, the IAQC had a lot in its favor. As a new organization, moreover, it was not burdened by a history of precedents, bureaucratic inertia, pressures for internal consistency, and stigmatization of failed past initiatives; in short, it was not burdened by

---

on the board of directors and the chairmanship of the strategic planning committee. I believe the trade-offs in information and insight more than compensated for any possible impact I may have had on the organization. I was both a researcher and someone who cared about the success of this organization in achieving its lofty goals. It will be for the reader to judge whether the latter role compromised the former. Finally, in terms of the ethical issues involved, the board of directors was informed periodically (necessary because of turnover on the board) that my major objective was to conduct research. So people knew when they were talking to me that writing about the IAQC was part of my agenda.

I do not want my analysis to be construed as an attack on any individual in the organization or the organization itself. As I expect this chapter to make clear, the resultant outcomes do not reflect the actions or personality of any one individual, but rather the institutional forces in our society.

many of the factors that limited the ASQC's action. Yet the IAQC has hardly been an unqualified success, and one might seriously question whether it has been even a qualified success.

While the IAQC is the major national group promoting quality circles, its acceptance by private and public-sector management has been limited, and its development and spread of best practices have been decidedly weak. Diffusing best practice involves monitoring what is going on in firms at the "cutting edge," digesting and feeding it back to the field in generalizable form. The process involves getting firms to share experiences and synthesizing these experiences in the form of effective training materials. It involves stimulating local organizations to work together.

Based on this criterion, IAQC contributions have been modest at best. Central to the story is the role consultants played in the organization. In chapter 3 I discussed the alternatives available to firms seeking the information they need to adopt and practice small-group activities: (1) obtaining information from the market via consultants or (2) building associations to pool corporate resources to collectively pursue common interests. In the discussion of the ASQC, we learned that in the real world associational activity and consultant activity are intertwined in a variety of ways. In this and the subsequent chapters, this relationship gets carried to the logical extension where the associational governance structure gets taken over *in effect* (not formally) by consultant interests. The choices posited in chapter 3 are thus reduced to a single possibility. It was not, however, a matter of the venality of opportunistic consultants producing this outcome. Rather, it was the absence of a commitment from corporate America to small-group activities that created a vacuum. Consultants simply pursued their economic interests in a reasonably rational fashion. My account of events turns on the process by which this was played out in the IAQC and its consequences.

Overview of the IAQC

The most useful overview of the organization would be to provide some comparisons over time. This task is made difficult by the exceedingly poor record keeping that has plagued the IAQC throughout most of its history, itself a telling point. Some of the data will

TABLE 1.   *IAQC Membership Growth*

Fiscal Year	Total Members	Individual	Organi-zational	Circle
1978	110	N/A	N/A	N/A
1979	400	N/A	N/A	N/A
1980	607	303	304	N/A
1981	1,433	715	718	N/A
1982	3,875	1,932	1,943	N/A
1983	4,215	2,101	2,114	N/A
1984	5,751	3,417	2,242	N/A
1985	5,422	3,010	2,207	205
1986	5,350	3,119	1,929	302
1987	5,534	3,399	1,911	260
1988 (March)	5,605	3,384	1,989	232

SOURCE. Tarter et al. 1987. Supplemented by the author's research materials.

therefore start from 1982 rather than 1978 when the organization began. Table 1 provides a breakdown of membership as best the organization has been able to reconstruct it and based on my own research notes. We see that by 1988 the organization recorded a total of 5,605 members, breaking down to 3,384 individual members, 1,989 organizational members, and 232 circle members. Organizational membership entitles the participating company to five persons receiving membership status (one voting and four nonvoting) so the organizational membership total (1,989) can be divided by five to give the actual number of company registrations (398). Conversely, circle membership (begun in 1983) can be multiplied by ten (assuming that to be the average circle size) to reflect the total number of persons involved (2,320).

From the data reported in table 1, we can see that membership in the individual and organizational categories peaked in 1984. In 1985 the organization was reporting a nonrenewal rate of 37 percent. A more recent membership survey revealed that of the total of 5,605 members in early 1988, new members joining in 1987 and early 1988 accounted for 53.5 percent of the total. These rates are notably high when compared to professional associations like the

ASQC (20 percent nonrenewal rate); the norm for professional associations seen as doing quite well runs about 15 percent. One partial explanation for the high nonrenewal rate of the IAQC is that many companies treat quality-circle facilitator and coordinator jobs as "pass through positions." Thus they rotate staff through them, with each new staff member in the job replacing the existing IAQC member.

Data from table 2 report the growth in regional chapters. Again we see rapid growth followed by a marked slowing of growth after 1984. There has also been a growth in inactive chapters, so that by 1988, of the 107 chapters, only 76 were officially regarded as active. Informal staff estimates put the number even lower, somewhere around 65.

Table 3 provides a breakdown of revenue sources for fiscal years 1982 and 1987. We can see that conferences accounted for 58 percent of revenues by 1987, as against 25 percent in 1982, with a drastic fall off in the percentage of income accounted for by education (training courses) and material sales. This occurred at a time when total revenues rose from approximately $1 million in 1982 to $1.6 million in 1987. Notwithstanding that increase, in absolute

TABLE 2.   *Growth in IAQC Chapters*

Date	Number of Chapters
November 1979	0
May 1980	2
November 1981	30
November 1982	50
November 1983	75
November 1984	90
November 1985	94
April 1986	97
April 1987	104
April 1988	107

SOURCE. Tarter et al. 1987. Supplemented by the author's research materials.

TABLE 3. *IAQC Revenue Sources
for Fiscal Years 1982 and 1987 (U.S. $)*

	1982	%	1987	%
Membership	135,578	13	267,159	17
Education	362,213	34	235,722	15
Spring conference	262,227	25	727,580	46
Fall conference			195,634	12
Publications			23,880	1
Material	285,077	27	114,104	7
Interest and other	11,222	1	33,283	2
Total	1,056,317	100	1,597,362	100

SOURCE. Association for Quality and Participation, Six Year Trend Analysis, 30 January 1988.

terms revenues derived from education and material sales fell 35 percent and 60 percent respectively during this period. We see, in short, that over this five-year period, the IAQC increasingly became a conference-driven organization.

Table 4 shows the industry composition by the Standard Industrial Classification Category (SIC). Manufacturing represents 52 percent of IAQC membership despite its accounting for only 20 percent of the nonagricultural labor force nationally. What is remarkable notwithstanding is the large size of the nonmanufacturing component. It should be remembered that in Japan in the late 1970s quality circles occurred almost exclusively in the manufacturing sector (that is less true today) and initial adoption in the United States was also heavily weighted toward the manufacturing sector. A 1981 survey of "early adopters" of quality circles found that only 9 percent were nonmanufacturing firms (Cole and Tachiki 1983:10).

We can also examine the distribution of members by job title. A 1986 IAQC-commissioned survey of 2,047 IAQC members (response rate 28 percent) revealed that quality-circle facilitators and quality-circle coordinators accounted for 55 percent of those surveyed; these positions are rather low-ranking ones created to manage quality-circle activities. An additional 18 percent listed them-

TABLE 4.   *Distribution of IAQC Members by Industry Classification (SIC Code)*

Industrial Sector	%
Manufacturing	52
Transportation and public utilities	10
Wholesale trade	1
Finance, insurance, and real estate	5
Service industries	17
Public administration	11
Military	3
Total	99

SOURCE. Tarter et al. 1987.

NOTE. Total does not add to 100 because of rounding error. Data are derived from responses of 60% of the membership.

selves as managers, but my experience suggests that they hold relatively low-ranking managerial positions. One way to further examine this is to look at the departments to which IAQC members belong. The top-ranked departments were human resources and personnel (46 percent of IAQC members), production (14 percent), and quality assurance (14 percent) according to the same survey (University of Cincinnati 1987). Again, I note that these are not the high-status departments where organizational control is typically lodged. Finally, one way to evaluate the members' level in the management hierarchy is to look at salaries. The 1986 survey revealed that those earning more than $51,000 a year totaled only 13.9 percent of the membership.

In summary, the corporate political clout of the IAQC membership is quite low. In this connection, it is also the case that women, typically in low-ranking management positions, make up 35 percent of the membership (43 percent of the quality-circle coordinators).

Another membership characteristic relevant to my subsequent discussion is the number of consultants. Four percent of IAQC members designate themselves as consultants. On the face of it, this does not seem to pose a threat to organizational independence, but motivated individuals in key positions can have a decisive impact.

Some additional facts to round out this overview are that the average (median) size of employing organizations of IAQC members is somewhat below 1,000 employees. Forty-seven percent of IAQC members report having a union at their location (18 percent of the nonagricultural labor force is organized). In 1986 only 10 percent of IAQC respondents reported having less than one year's experience in an employee-involvement program, with 38.5 percent reporting from one to three years' experience and 51.5 percent more than three years' experience. That distribution suggests a decline in the growth rate as the movement ages (University of Cincinnati 1987).

"In the Beginning . . ."

The history of the IAQC begins with the development of quality circles at the Missiles System Division of the Lockheed Missiles & Space Company in 1974. Wayne Rieker was the MSD manufacturing manager responsible for introducing the program; Donald Dewar was the QC circle coordinator, and Jeff Beardsley was the QC circle training coordinator. Based on a study trip to Japan and contacts with JUSE, Lockheed translated and adopted JUSE's training materials with only modest changes.

While not the first quality-circle program in the United States, it was the most highly publicized of the early attempts. By 1977 savings were reported to be $3 million, the ratio of cost savings to the cost of operating was reported to be six to one, and thirty circles were operating. Visitors flocked to the plant for further investigation. The early quality-circle successes at Lockheed and other firms were widely written up in various business journals, including the *Wall Street Journal, Time,* and *Across the Board,* in 1979 and 1980 (see Cole 1979). The NBC television program "If Japan Can, Why Can't We?" further heightened interest. (Ironically, the program also was shown on Japanese TV and contributed to increasing interest in circles in Japan as well.)

Rieker, Dewar, and Beardsley discussed the possibility of leaving Lockheed and forming a consulting firm. Unable to agree, they departed one by one to start their own businesses.[2] Rieker left first,

---

2. The year 1977 was the high point for circle activity at Lockheed. By 1979 only eight circles were operational there, and not long afterwards circles disappeared. In typical fashion, the publicity given to the demise of circles at Lockheed

purchasing the rights to the training materials developed at Lockheed. He carried out his first assignment as a consultant in the fall of 1977. Beardsley followed, setting up Beardsley & Associates and building on the Lockheed program and his own experience to create his own training materials. Dewar joined Beardsley in mid 1978, but their association lasted only a short time owing to differences, and in late 1978 Dewar started his own consulting firm.

Having acquired some expertise by virtue of their employment, these managers saw an opportunity to market these skills and set up their own consulting firms. This turned out to be a pervasive pattern that was repeated again and again in the early years of the quality-circle movement. It seems so natural to Americans that it would hardly be worth commenting on if it were not for the fact that the pattern is almost nonexistent in Japan and is relatively muted even in Sweden. We shall have occasion to discuss the significance of these differences in later chapters.

Once on their own, Beardsley and Dewar saw that no one seemed prepared to build a national organization that would focus on quality circles. So in spring 1978 they set about establishing a national organization—the International Association of Quality Circles. Dewar became president; Beardsley, vice president.

The first visible manifestation of the new association was the appearance of the *Quality Circle Quarterly*. In the first issue (second quarter 1978), the founders promulgated their objectives. I reproduce this statement in appendix D. The first issue contained mostly background information about quality circles, including a couple of company testimonials, as well as an advertisement for the association's first product: an audiovisual package for introducing circles. The issue also announced the first annual IAQC international conference, to be held in San Francisco in February 1979. The journal was a modest effort, and it continued in that fashion, with lots of "boilerplate" content, until 1981. Notwithstanding the modesty of this initial effort, we can see that the first two elements of the association's activity had been set in motion. A journal had

---

was tiny compared to the earlier massive publicity. When pressed, management said it had built on circles to create additional team activities. It was generally understood, however, that with Rieker's departure, the program had lost its champion, and it died soon afterwards.

been launched and planning had begun for an annual conference, two of the three core services of the association to date.

The second issue of the journal, which appeared in the third quarter of 1978, placed greater emphasis on company experiences as that data started to become more available. Other features included the first discussion of what was required of a quality-circle facilitator, a function and term developed at Lockheed that adapted the Japanese approach, with the facilitator taking responsibility for promoting the program on the shop floor, training leaders, identifying and removing roadblocks, and providing overall guidance to the program.

By the first quarter of 1979, the association announced a certification program for quality-circle facilitators. The first one-week course was held in spring 1979 and enrolled seven individuals. The association solved the problem of training materials for this course by buying copyrighted materials from Beardsley at cost. Completion of the course and the passing of a certification exam entitled the enrollee to be certified as a quality-circle facilitator. The course fee was $1,800. Its content was modeled closely on the program developed at Lockheed. Apart from the annual conference, this course was to be the IAQC's bread and butter in its early years.

The IAQC plunged headlong into facilitator training and certification, a decision that gave rise to considerable controversy over the next few years as the IAQC came to compete with consultant-offered facilitator training. Consider the following letter to the editor of the IAQC journal in February 1982 from Ed Yager, a well-known organizational consultant. Yager opposed IAQC facilitator certification on grounds of the unstructured character of quality-circle facilitation and its un-American regulatory character. He closed with the following argument:

Who is the IAQC, and what gives this organization, which is heavily chaired, influenced and managed by purveyors of materials and consulting services (and which soon may be marketing its own materials) the right to make such judgments? This is not to condemn the IAQC, indeed it has the potential to provide a major service to the organization development and quality circle community. However, it is certainly in no position to become a certifying agency in any context other than offering its own most professional training and advice. Membership in the IAQC may at some point become a sign of prestige and professional association. It seems to me that the goal, like that of ASTD, the OD network, ASQC, etc. will be to reach such a point of professionalism that one would want to be a member in order to point out their own professionalism.

Clearly, this was a contentious issue, pitting the association against consultants and consultants providing materials to the IAQC against those on the outside.

In February 1979 the IAQC held its first "international" conference in San Francisco. It was a modest affair, with sixteen presentations, including a report on a problem-solving effort by the members of one quality circle at Hughes Aircraft. There was tremendous energy and excitement at the meeting. Some two hundred individuals attended this first conference (co-sponsored by a local ASQC chapter).

A few months later, the IAQC took its next major step toward becoming a national organization. It announced the policy of chartering local chapters. The first chapter was formed in April 1980 in Louisville, Kentucky. This was the third core activity that was to characterize IAQC services.

At the second annual conference in February 1980, paid attendance doubled, and there was a growing sense among the participants that something special was happening. A special meeting was called to "open up IAQC," with some forty conference participants attending. The agenda proposed by the two consultant co-founders, still president and vice president, was that a new steering committee be set up, composed primarily of users, to review bylaws, elect additional directors, complete incorporation, plan the following year's conference and decide what kinds of education the IAQC should be doing. A long discussion followed, in which great enthusiasm for the reorganization was apparent. It was agreed that a meeting be held in May by those interested in forming the new steering committee. Forty people volunteered to work on the steering committee and/or other committee assignments.

The unstated driving force of the meeting was the need to "professionalize" IAQC activities and to take the association out of the hands of consultants and put it into the hands of users. The co-founders seem comfortable with—and, indeed, proposed—this direction. The evidence suggests that they were finding association activities increasingly burdensome in the light of accelerating requests for information and the various obligations connected with the annual conference, conference transactions, chapter registrations, and quarterly publications. At the same time, their own consulting businesses were starting to take off. Thus, it is not surprising that they were willing to share responsibilities.

On May 16, 1980, twenty-three of the forty volunteers arrived in Saint Louis for a two-day "reorganization meeting." The two consultant co-founders, nineteen company employees, and two academics were involved from early morning to late evening with plenary sessions, special committee meetings, and socializing. By and large, the company employees were people in middle- to low-level management positions who were in charge of implementing and running quality circle activities in their own firms. They were attending this meeting on their own initiative, having gotten their companies to sponsor the trip. Of them seven became full-time consultants within the next two years—such was the growth of circle activities nationally and the demand for outside expertise. Given the importance of this first meeting to the future direction of IAQC, a detailed account is in order.

The meeting began with a financial report showing that the organization had a net worth of $58,838 (including an inventory valued at $26,000). The participants discussed again whether there should be an IAQC. Robert Amsden, the academic who chaired the ASQC Quality-Circle Steering Committee, reported that ASQC had not yet taken a stand on quality circles. A suggestion was made that the IAQC merge with ASQC. In response, the following objections were raised: the ASQC was too limited—oriented toward statistical methods, not people development; the IAQC had to develop itself first, or it would get lost in the merger; and it would take forever to accomplish anything. Whether there should be an IAQC was never really in question. This was a fired-up group that wanted to do something. In short order, it was moved and passed that there should be a formal IAQC organization. Clearly the participants were excited about creating something new.

The objectives of the organization were identified and turned out to be identical to those promulgated in the first issue of the *Quality Circle Quarterly* (see appendix D). The functions of the IAQC were designated as:

issuing the *Quality Circle Quarterly;*

publishing educational materials on the subject of quality circles;

encouraging the development of local chapters;

sponsoring seminars;

sponsoring conferences;

conducting the IAQC certification program.

Facilitator training and conferences were seen as the major sources of income to pay the association's staff. Jeff Beardsley, one of the co-founders, argued against the association continuing with certification, even though he had initiated it at the IAQC. He now argued that it was hard to set standards. At one point in the discussion he said that "training by IAQC takes bread out of the consultant's mouth." On the other hand, Dewar argued for the IAQC tightening up the standards for certification, but continuing it. Still others argued that the IAQC should continue to provide training but abandon certification.

Next, discussion shifted to what educational materials the IAQC was to use to provide its facilitator training. Only two consultant packages, those by Beardsley and Rieker, were available at this time in addition to company-developed materials. Beardsley stated that he was no longer willing to make his materials available to the IAQC. His materials were still available through the IAQC, however, since the original arrangement involved the IAQC mass-producing the training materials and selling them back to Beardsley and Dewar at cost plus 10 percent. With large-scale production, this reduced the costs of publishing and thus was one way in which the IAQC subsidized the business activities of the two co-founders.

A continuing issue for the organization has been whether it should engage in training or leave it to the consultants. The argument for training is that it is a basic service to members and a focal point for professional activity. The alternative view is that it competes with consultant members. Practically speaking, training was a major income generator for the organization at a time when its organizational survival was in question. This, perhaps more than anything else, carried the day, and it was agreed that the facilitator training courses be continued with the next session, to be coordinated by Dewar, who still had access to the Beardsley materials through the IAQC.

One member proposed using chapters as a focal point for membership growth and income, based on the national organization providing service to the chapters. There was, however, little response or follow up. There was considerable discussion of what definition of *quality circle* the organization ought to use. Various committees were set up, with individuals volunteering for those in which they were interested. It was agreed to elect a board of directors pro tem to serve until the next annual meeting.

After a long discussion, twenty-one of the twenty-three who attended the meeting volunteered to be on the pro tem board (including the two co-founders); five additional individuals not at the meeting were also invited to join. The newly constituted board acknowledged Don Dewar's and Jeff Beardsley's contributions to quality circles and for organizing the IAQC, and in recognition of this achievement made them both lifetime members. A second decision authorized Dewar to select an executive secretary to staff the IAQC office.

In the 1980 second quarter issue of the *Quality Circle Quarterly,* Dewar reported to the membership on the recent developments. He noted the accomplishments of the IAQC to date: two "international" quality-circles conferences and publication of the proceedings, one facilitator conference, completion of four facilitator training courses, establishment of a facilitator certification program, creation of an 80-slide audiovisual program to introduce the uninitiated to QC circles, and publication of a quarterly magazine. These were, as Dewar noted, not trivial achievements. He also pointed out that all this had occurred without benefit of a single full-time paid staff employee. This same issue also reported that the newly "elected" members of the expanded IAQC board of directors numbered twenty-four and would serve until the 1981 annual conference and business meeting.

Evaluation

What observations can we make about this organizational meeting? First, one cannot help but be impressed by the energy and enthusiasm of those involved. For two days they met from early morning to late at night. Moreover, they not merely committed themselves to three annual board meetings over the next eight months; many of them, such as the publications committee members, also took on further meetings (typically by phone or mail) and a great deal of additional work. For some, this was to continue for the next three years.

Clearly, in the right environment, volunteers are prepared to give a great deal. The contrast with the ASQC treatment of circles is overwhelming. The ASQC potentially had this same energy at its disposal, but strangled it by forcing the volunteers to work on creating the "right" organizational structure. The IAQC, however, possessed a major motivator not available to the ASQC. The "pioneers" at the first IAQC reorganization meeting felt they were building a new organization. This gave them a sense of ownership not possible within the ASQC. At the outset of the May 1980 meeting, the participants had referred to the "IAQC" as an object to be acted on, but before long they were using *we*. Finally, the IAQC allowed the volunteers to work on building a national organization with relatively little concern for precedent and conformance to regulations.

It was an exhilarating experience for these mid- and low-level managers; most had never been on a board of directors before. That also meant that they were amateurs in respect to a variety of critical matters facing the organization and were thus bound to make some serious mistakes.

The immediate dilemma that underlay the first meeting, and one that was to foreshadow subsequent problems, was that the organization needed access to the training materials and expertise of the consultants—in particular, Dewar and Beardsley, and Rieker. At the same time it needed to divorce itself from the consultants in order to achieve legitimacy in the eyes of the outside business world. This was enormously complicated because of the strong competitive and personal rivalry between Rieker and the two cofounders, but also because the two co-founders had had a falling out as well. Then there were the other consultants, who were in varying degrees dependent on, and in competition with, the "Big Three." These rivalries had a strong impact on the consultants' view of the association and the ways in which they tried to move it.

To complicate matters still further, each of the consultants had a number of former clients, company employees, on the pro tem board. These former business ties formed the basis of cliques. Indeed, some of the pro tem members were eventually to go to work for their former consultants. As one astute board member put the matter to me:

Not only are Jeff and Don dependent on IAQC but many pro tem members are former clients and students of Jeff and Don so they still have a personal tie of dependency on them. That tie needs to be broken if the organization is to professionalize and not make decisions constrained by the impact of consultants. Not only do consultants have to be weaned from the organization but also board members have to be weaned from them. That will take time.

Board members with such insight were in short supply. Many felt that consultants brought skills and energy that such a weak young organization could ill afford to lose. This was the heart of the dilemma facing the IAQC. The reference to "political mismatch" in the quotation opening this chapter refers precisely to the ongoing struggle between consultant and business user interests and its negative impact on the use of IAQC resources.

All this brings us back to a point noted in the previous chapter. Aldrich and Auster (1986:168) suggest that one of the internal conditions associated with aging that inhibits adaptation to change is the retention of control in the hands of the original founders or members of their families. For "members of their families," we might substitute the term *clique* to reflect the consultant-client ties referred to above. It is noteworthy that whereas Aldrich and Auster discuss this factor in the context of the problems faced by aging organizations, we see it emerging here very early in the life of a new organization (the IAQC was only two years old when it became a major area of contention).

One of the founders of IAQC, Don Dewar, seemed quite relieved at the prospect of letting go, as his subsequent failure to attend many board meetings demonstrated. The second co-founder, Jeff Beardsley, was more ambivalent. "This is your association; it ain't mine," he had announced at the special meeting during the February 1980 conference. But his actions belied these statements. At the May meeting he was an active presence trying to shape the association. He volunteered to be on the committee to define quality circles, the certification committee, the finance committee, the education committee, and the pro tem board. Moreover, in a later interview Beardsley made it clear that he would someday like to be president of the organization, and indeed he allowed his name to be put into nomination on more than one occasion. So we have a clear case here of a founder saying he was turning the organization over to the users, but not really being willing to let go. Yet for many of those in industry and elsewhere who cared about the development of quality circles, Beardsley symbolized the inability of the organization to leave its consultant origins and move toward professional status. This was to prove to be a continuing problem for the IAQC.

The IAQC Moves On

A major problem for the association, as Dewar quickly moved to reduce his role, was to find a staff. At a meeting in August 1980 attended by twenty-one of the twenty-four board members, one of the pro tem members, R. D. Diener, volunteered to take the job of executive director temporarily on a half-time basis. He was known as someone who had helped coordinate the 1980 conference and who had guided the growth of quality circles at Tinker Air Force Base.

While the board discussed various alternatives to Diener, no one had any specific names to suggest. Time was seen as critical, and meeting only once every three months was not sufficient to allow members to identify alternatives, compare them with Diener, and make a decision. Thus it was with a great sense of relief that the board accepted Diener's offer. It kept the IAQC alive and gave the members a sense that they were turning a corner. In a volunteer organization where willingness to commit time is often at a premium, it is extremely hard to turn down volunteers even if officials or fellow board members know that the volunteer is not the best person for the job. Time and budgetary pressures often preclude more thorough searches. It was not the last time that the IAQC was to have this problem. To be sure, unlike the ASQC, the IAQC could innovate freely without being tied up in rules and precedent, but it was also free to make mistakes without firm standards to guide it.

New by-laws were adopted that included provision for a 21-member board of directors. The board also set up a nominating committee for the first election of a board by the membership. The education committee reported on its plans to staff facilitator courses. The committee discussed ways to deal with the problem of relying on the training material of Beardsley or other consultants for its training activities. IAQC members in companies with their own

QC circle materials were encouraged to have their companies share them with the association. With Beardsley unwilling to continue to provide his materials to the IAQC and no other immediately available alternative open to it besides disbanding its training activity, the IAQC turned to the training materials developed by Don Dewar.

The year 1980 ended with the association seemingly moving forward. Income for the calendar year was reported to be roughly $200,000, with some $135,000 in expenses, leaving a modest balance of $62,000. Membership had grown by 50 percent over the preceding year. More important, industry interest in QC circles was exploding, and the association seemed poised to grow with it. A variety of fundamental problems still remained to be solved, however, and still new dangers were to appear.

At the January 1981 board meeting, the issue of hiring a full-time executive director dominated early discussion. After a long debate, in which it was agreed that the board should employ a full-time executive director, the acting director volunteered for the job. There was tremendous pressure for immediate action, as demands on the office staff were increasing exponentially. No one had any other definite candidate to suggest. Nor was the board inclined to begin a national search.

The board therefore empowered the executive officers to negotiate a contract with the acting director, setting only the salary limits and the length of the contract (two years). Thus, the acting director became the full-time executive director (ED 1). Some accommodation was made for his wish to conduct outside seminars, with agreement reached that fees for such engagements be split with the IAQC. No limit on the amount of such income was set. Some members opposed this on the grounds that if he did too much consulting, "We would be right back in the box of being a consultant front."

The nominations committee developed criteria for candidates and voting procedures. A persistent theme in its discussions was how to limit overrepresentation of consultants on the board. Given the consultants' high name recognition nationally and their ability to mobilize past clients, the committee was fearful that candidates who were company employees would be swamped. Various measures were taken to limit this possibility, including a rule that no more than one consultant per consulting firm would be selected as a candidate and that a mail ballot of the whole association would be conducted. It was feared that voting at the annual business meeting would allow consultants to stack the meeting with their own supporters. Special voting procedures were instituted to minimize any loading in favor of consultants; they included specifying a minimum number of candidates on the ballot for whom votes had to be cast.

The board approved the overall design proposed by the committee. Subsequent to the board decision, Vice President Beardsley lashed out at the board in the February 1981 issue of the association's journal for placing "limits upon which members may be eligible for national offices." He compared his relationship to the IAQC to that of a parent enjoying his child's freedom but reluctant to let the child make mistakes.

The education committee continued to run facilitator training courses, but put certification on hold as the IAQC wrestled with the implications. For all practical purposes, IAQC certification was a dead issue. There was continued pressure to find alternatives to buying training materials from consultants. The switch from the Beardsley materials to the newly developed Dewar materials did not solve the problem. No matter whose material the IAQC used, it seemed to aggravate the other consultants. And the board members sensed that their claim to professional status was on thin ice when they had to rely on consultant material. Ideas that were discussed again and again were to develop the IAQC's own materials (which seemed beyond the budget capability of the organization), to obtain access to "state-of-the-art" company-developed materials, or to come up with some combination of the two.

The consultants, who so often disagreed among themselves, generally tended to be united in their opposition to the IAQC doing any training, although at this time a consultant who favored the association developing its own "professional materials" headed the education committee. Eventually, however, he came to support the idea that professionalism could include the education committee screening and choosing the best consultant-developed materials (education committee chair, memo to the president, 2 November 1981). During this period, the education committee operated on the explicit assumption that all it would take to develop the IAQC's own facilitator training materials was time and money.

At the January meeting there were indications of growing tensions resulting from pressure by the executive director and other executive officers to centralize activities in headquarters and opposing pressure to locate decision making and resources in the committees and at local chapters. The latter position had a strong constituency among many board members and among chapter leaders. In particular, committee chairpersons complained they were being bypassed in the decision-making process by the executive director.

These are typical tensions faced by any national volunteer association as it seeks to develop the right balance for organizational development. Central administrators are concerned about quality control and the enormous discretionary power available to volunteers in the field. Chapter and committee members are suspicious of central administrators for not making decisions based on proper information, criteria, and membership views. This tension began to produce considerable conflict and suspicions among board members. Over the next few years, efforts to support chapters with rebates from national dues were repeatedly made, but administrative incompetence and the roller coaster quality of IAQC financing made this impossible to implement. As later became apparent, however, these tensions over the centralizing tendencies of the organization were made more severe in the IAQC by the self-serving activities of the new executive director.

There were also periodic discussions of how to better serve circle members. Some board members developed plans for circle registration, but they were repeatedly postponed. It was not until August 1982 that a small publication for circle members was made available, and not until 1984 that a circle membership program was developed. The whole effort, however, proved very costly to administer and was not very successful. Generally speaking, the national organization made only modest efforts to reach circle members, in sharp contrast, as we shall see, to the Japanese approach.

The March 1981 annual conference, held at Louisville, was an outstanding success. Paid attendance was 1,100, up from the previous year's figure of 400. Facilities were inadequate, panels insufficient, and conference administration poor. Some questions were raised about irregularities in the handling of cash and checks for the on-site registrations. The inadequate facilities relative to the demand again created an excitement and electricity; participants felt the explosive growth in circle activity taking place around the country. There was a "true believer" quality to many discussions and a sense of being on the cutting edge of a major social movement. One of the circle coordinators from the South described in her talk how she had convinced top management that individual employees could be "transformed" by participation in circles. The presentation had a fundamentalist born-again quality that was to be seen on a number of occasions.

The editor of the *Quality Circles Journal*[3] captured this enthusiasm and both the promise and dangers it posed in the following editorial remarks in its May 1981 issue:

An event occurred in Louisville Kentucky that should lay to rest any doubts about the interest of American business in the quality circle movement.

The event was the Third Annual Conference of the International Association of Quality Circles, and I cannot recall another time when I witnessed such enthusiasm and excitement by a group of people. This enthusiasm was evidenced by the extraordinary conference attendance. The "Standing-Room-Only" workshops and the burgeoning chapter and national membership roles were also indications that the quality circle idea had come of age. The overwhelming interest by the conferees in all facets of the quality circle process is a clear sign that this concept is sweeping through the American business consciousness. It is at this point in our association's evolution that a clear and sober evaluation of the long-term impact of quality circles management and its effect upon the structure of organizations must be made.

It becomes incumbent upon our association to clarify and impress on the prospective practitioners exactly what the adoption of the quality circle process implies. That is simply, that all individuals within an organization who participate in a quality circle have the right to contribute and participate in the management of the organization. There should be no doubt on the part of management that once the circle process is started, then any aspect of the day-to-day operations is subject matter for circle evaluation. To implement quality circles based on a superficial, short-term return on investment, which in most cases will appeal to management, would be an erroneous application of the concept. Management should, therefore, study the long-term implications. Upon this examination, management may not be ready to embrace the distinctly participative style that the quality circle process creates. It is for this reason that our collective enthusiasm to "spread the word" should be tempered by cautious, managed growth.

Let us proceed as an association, and as disciples of the quality circle concept slowly, albeit deliberatively, towards a solid foundation of mutual understanding with American management.

3. The name was changed from *Quality Circle Quarterly* early in 1981.

This sober assessment points up the growing professionalism reflected in the journal under the new volunteer editorial staff. The journal proved a bright spot of professional endeavor during these years, some would say the only one.

Suddenly the IAQC was transformed. Instead of scraping along from one facilitator training course to another to pay outstanding bills, instead of being in the position of hiring an executive director without the funds to pay a full year's salary, the organization now seemed to have the problem of how it was going to spend its new revenues. It cost some $20,000 to put on the Louisville conference, and it generated over $100,000. This was the situation that confronted the newly elected board of directors.

What were the characteristics of the new board? First, there was a very high overlap between the new board membership and the pro tem board it replaced. Second, there is the question of the level of management skills represented on the board. The full-time jobs held by the new board members were as follows:

academic

president, consulting firm

academic

company circle administrator

president, consulting firm

divisional manager, quality-of-work-life program

president, consulting firm

industrial relations department member

training instructor

manager, employee and community relationships

head, personnel training and development

manager, reliability engineering

quality-control manager

quality-control manager and product manager

president, consulting firm

product assurance manager and quality-circle coordinator

division quality-circle program coordinator

industrial engineer and program coordinator for quality circles quality-compliance manager

program development coordinator for quality circles

There are three observations that can be made about this list: (1) there was a significant representation of quality-control personnel on the new board; (2) those in charge of circle programs were typically talented young staff people, not very high in the management hierarchy, who management had decided had the energy and brains to lead circle introduction; and (3) while there were four consultants among the twenty-one elected members, two other members were to become consultants before long, making the consultant presence more significant than the nominations committee had expected.

It is clear that we are not dealing with a high-level management group. This has two implications. First, one might predict that the new board would have trouble managing a national organization of rapidly growing complexity because of a shortage of management skills. Second, the relatively low status of the board members would make obtaining outside resources and acquiring legitimacy in the eyes of the outside world difficult. The IAQC was not created by companies delegating staff members to pool corporate resources; it was rather an organization of middle- and lower-level management volunteers in a weak position to obtain access to company resources. This difference will be critical to our comparison with emergent national organizations in Sweden and Japan.

The first issue facing the new board at the March 1981 meeting was the election of officers. All but two members of the new board were present. Fred Riley, a middle-rank manager with Hewlett-Packard, was elected president. Jeff Beardsley was elected one of the two vice presidents, based on an informal understanding that he would withdraw his candidacy for president. Throughout the discussions, there was talk about the role of consultants. Two members took the position that there was no problem with having a consultant as head of the organization, but majority sentiment was clearly opposed. Rather, the view predominated that the IAQC was moving toward becoming a user organization and should not give the impression to the outside world that it was still a consultant-run body.

Although this was the third time this group had met, the conducting of business was still quite clumsy. There was heavy reliance on *Robert's Rules of Order*, to the point where the group often tied itself in knots. For a group who did not yet know one another very well, this was not surprising. Reflecting the modest level of management skills, however, this pattern continued for some time. The focus on quality circles often created confusion as to the role of circle problem-solving techniques and procedures in the conduct of the board meeting itself. At regular intervals, someone complained that the board was not proceeding or making decisions in a way consistent with quality-circle decision-making processes (for example, cutting off debate or not using a cause-and-effect diagram to diagnose a problem). Just as often some member would then argue that this was a board of directors', not quality-circle, meeting. Gradually such discussions disappeared from the board meetings as the latter sentiment came to prevail. After each new election, however, there would be some new board member who would return to the theme and have to be "educated."

The June board meeting, attended by all but three of the board members, confronted what had started to be the "usual" list of issues to be discussed: conference preparation, chapter relations, problems of getting rebates to the chapters, and the financial status of the association. With an anticipated $235,000 in revenue and $187,000 in costs, the budget looked tighter than had been expected. This served to limit new initiatives. Jeff Beardsley volunteered to chair the conference committee, and since no one objected or offered to do it, he got the job. At a subsequent meeting of the conference committee (at which Beardsley was not present) in October, it was agreed to limit Beardsley's role in the conference because of concern that he would use his participation to advance his business interests.

The conference chair was a nice position for a consultant to have. At a minimum, the conference chair had the opportunity to address the opening and closing of the conference and thus received considerable exposure and status. For an organization looking to shed its consultant background, selecting a consultant was hardly the ideal decision, but once again it was hard to turn down a volunteer, especially for a demanding job. Consultants simply have more discretionary time than company employees. A mid-level company manager would immediately have to consider whether his or her boss would tolerate one or two more trips a year and/or whatever other time was involved in addition to the four board meetings a year. Self-employed consultants could, however, make the decision on the spot. If they believed that a commitment to association activity would serve their business interests, they were only too willing to volunteer.

The question of whether the association should be conducting facilitator training once again became a major topic of discussion. The association's economic incentives for doing so continued to outweigh thoughtful evaluation of whether facilitators themselves were necessary for the quality-circle process, much less the question of whether the association should be competing with consultants in offering it.

The board developed a plan to make company training materials available to an academic research team that was to conduct a survey of those who have gone through IAQC facilitator training. Based on the results of this survey, the research team would then construct the new IAQC training materials. Subsequent to the meeting, however, it was found that legal constraints made it impossible for most board members to deliver on their initial commitments to provide company training materials.

Had there been a strong corporate commitment to IAQC activities by a large number of firms, one suspects, companies would have found a way to cooperate with the IAQC request. In November, lacking this option, the board began to consider purchasing training materials on the market, including both company and consultant materials. This was the beginning of the end of the idea that the association should develop its own materials.

Chapter Eleven

The International Association of Quality Circles: The Liability of Newness, Part 2

Got a fox in the henhouse.
Charley Chavis, IAQC president

The October 1981 meeting of the IAQC board was to be a momentous one for the association. Amid a swirl of rumors that the executive director had been engaging in improper behavior, President Fred Riley announced to the board that the executive director had resigned. The immediate event triggering the resignation was the discovery by the executive committee that the organization hired to run the annual conference had been misrepresented by the executive director. He had concealed the fact that one of the principals in that firm was his wife. Moreover, evidence accumulated that significant embezzlement was involved as well. Criminal charges were filed against the executive director, which eventually led to a felony conviction. He pleaded *nolo contendere* and received a three-year suspended sentence. In addition, the association filed civil charges and eventually a judgment was rendered in its favor. In March 1984 the following item appeared in the association's journal:

During the fiscal year ending August 31, 1983, a judgment was rendered in favor of the Association against R. D. Diener, a former executive director, and related parties to Mr. Diener. The Association was awarded approximately $80,000 plus legal and court fees of approximately $64,000. As of August 31, 1983, a garnishment bond of $18,000 has been received by the Association and has been recognized as additional income in the financial statements. However, no provision has been made concerning the remainder of the judgment because of the uncertainty of the collectibility of the remaining amount due.

Fortunately, the association was bonded, though it took until mid 1984 to receive the reimbursement of $75,000. The fraud associated with the conference arrangements was, however, the tip of the iceberg. Association officers believed that the extent of embezzlement may have been as much as $200,000. However, the paper trail was inadequate to document this amount.

An Organization in Crisis

How did this happen, and what were the organizational consequences? How it happened is in fact neither difficult to explain nor unique. I have already discussed the pressures that led the association to accept Diener's offer to become executive director. Volunteer associations are vulnerable to opportunistic behavior, a tendency greatly heightened in young, rapidly growing organizations. Such organizations typically have very weak financial control systems, and fraud is not uncommon. In the case of the IAQC, the voluntary board met only four times a year; the executive officers met more often, but ultimately they were also volunteers holding down full-time jobs. In this situation, the executive director, in a geographically isolated location, had a great deal of freedom to devise ways of circumventing the weak controls that did exist. The relative lack of financial and managerial experience on the board (though the treasurer was a bank official) certainly facilitated the outcome.

It would be hard to overestimate the organizational consequences of these events for the IAQC. Over the roughly sixteen months that Diener had served as part-time and then full-time executive director, the level of mistrust on the board had risen dramatically. The executive director's policy of centralization had been very divisive, and those who had supported it for honorable reasons were nevertheless subject to implicit criticism. The sense of camaraderie that had been part of organizing the association had gradually been undone, and in its place suspicion and anger had grown. There was a "post-Watergate" mentality in board discussions, with lots of recriminations. The board was caught between trying to inspire trust in one another to bind the wounds and move on for the good of the movement and a sense that past accusations and rumors had been found to have a basis in fact. Anything and anyone was now suspect of having colluded with the former executive director. This attitude was encouraged inadvertently by the association's lawyer, who asked all board members to be detectives and unearth leads and clues—the paper trail—for the law firm to build its case for a civil suit. Everyone felt stained by the scandal, but the board nonetheless had an association to run.

The initial dream of collectively creating something new as part of a national social movement had been shattered. Suddenly the board was in a swamp, struggling to extract itself. Directors worried about their own liability and were mistrustful of many of their colleagues. Moreover, if timing is everything, as the loose-coupling model of organizations suggests, then the IAQC was missing the wave. With the QC circle movement taking off around the country, the organization was knee-deep in embezzlement and unable to take the initiatives that might have made it a major force. The embezzled money could have funded the IAQC's creation of its own training materials. Instead, that goal had to be abandoned. It was not just the loss of the embezzled funds that limited the IAQC financially; it also had to pay lawyers' fees in advance of any settlement.

This is not to suggest that all IAQC activities ground to a halt. There were monthly facilitator training courses to be staffed and administered, a conference to be planned for March 1982, a board of directors election to be run (to fill seven vacancies left by those elected to the initial one-year term) and committee work to be done. Moreover, membership was doubling every twelve months, and chapter formation was proceeding at a rapid clip. Most of this activity at the local level took place without much involvement of the national organization. The staff were too busy meeting board directives to have time for members' needs. This lack of involvement was a major irritation for chapter leaders, who believed they were not getting enough from the national organization. Not only were they not getting their promised dues rebates, they did not feel they were getting much else besides an annual conference and a journal. It was not until 1982 that the rebates started to be paid, and even then only partial rebates were made because of continuing financial problems. Throughout the first half of the 1980s, the board was constantly refiguring the basis and arrangements for the rebates, and that uncertainty did not sit well with those in the chapters.

One additional point with regard to the chapters is important for the discussion that follows. The chapters were typically organized by enthusiastic low- and middle-level management volunteers, who typically joined with volunteers from other companies and met once a month, with invited speakers, typically from among their own membership, to share experiences, problems, and solutions to QC circle development. With the exception of a few large chapters with good corporate support, most local chapters suffered from many of the same problems as the national board. Local chapter members had little association experience and were unable to operate chapters in a way that would promote QC circles over the long term, much less sustain their chapters. Because the chapters typically depended on individual enthusiasm, and especially the leadership of two or three individuals, when that enthusiasm evaporated, so did chapter activity. This created a volatility in chapter activities; there was no stabilizing corporate commitment or shared professional ethos to provide additional incentives for leaders to keep the chapters moving forward. In the place of such incentives, the IAQC did impose a requirement in September 1983 that chapters meet at least six times a year to be considered active, but enforcement was difficult at best. Such bureaucratic requirements were a poor substitute for real incentives. In late 1981, however, all this was not yet much of a problem, as there was still a powerful momentum pushing the movement forward, with high levels of enthusiasm prevailing.

In responding to the crisis, many board members did rally round and make additional time available to the association. Yet the crisis clearly drained the energy of the executive committee. The president noted in a November 1981 memo to the board that some committees needed to become more active. More important, all new initiatives had to be put on hold as the organization struggled just to do the minimum, to hold things together in the face of unprecedented demands by a rapidly growing membership.

One of the immediate tasks of the organization was to begin the search for a new executive director. On this there was quick action. Yet the board was determined to avoid the past mistake of hiring the first live volunteer who came through the door. A committee of the senior members of the association was established to conduct the search. A detailed job description was drawn up and circulated. Telephone interviews were conducted with prospective candidates, local board members were asked to meet with and evaluate candidates from their regions, and finally seven candidates, including two internal candidates (two board members and the treasurer), were brought to the January 1982 board meeting.

An offer was made to one of the outside candidates, pending reference checks, and he accepted. He was long on QC circle experience but short on management skills relating to this kind of national organization. For the first time, some of the candidates had strong management skills in related human-resource areas, but had little or no quality circle background. It was clear that majority sentiment on the board still favored hiring someone with strong circle experience. Yet most of all at this time the association needed a strong and effective manager; instead, it limited the field of candidates by making circle experience a primary factor in selection. Put differently, the association was not yet able to make professional decisions. A high-level management board with strong corporate backing would have been much more likely to understand the importance of choosing the best manager for the job regardless of circle background.

Many of the board members had arrived on the board and in their current company positions as circle administrators after only a year or so of experience with circles, and many had had "on the job training." There was no reason why an executive director could not do the same. The failure of the board to look for the best manager reflected its commitment to the social aspect of circle development and failure to understand the managerial complexity of operating a national volunteer organization. The new executive director (ED 2) did in fact lack leadership abilities and lasted only thirteen months on the job.

The remainder of the January meeting and much of the special meeting held in March were devoted to various aspects of the Diener matter. These were grueling meetings, each of them lasting two and one-half days. What is remarkable is the attendance at these and prior meetings. One board member was absent from the January meeting and one from the March meeting. The willingness of these volunteers to contribute time and effort to the association was extraordinary.

Attendance at board meetings was surprisingly high up to this point, testifying to the commitment and excitement that QC circles and the IAQC had generated. If we examine the total number of meeting days available for board attendance from its inception in 1980 through 3 December 1982 (a total of twenty-one days times the number of members on the board for each year) and divide that by the number of meetings attended during the time each of them was on the board, we find an attendance rate of 80 percent. These were not people who simply walked away from the association at the first sign of serious trouble. One clear indication of this occurred with the Spring 1982 board election, when six of the seven incumbents up for reelection choose to run again (they all won). Yet one began to wonder how long these efforts could be sustained. The continued stressful events clearly were taking their toll.

One of the first efforts of the new executive director (ED 2) was in the field of association training and training materials. In a series of memos to the board, he outlined some ideas for moving ahead. While not all of them materialized, they nicely point up some of the ways members were thinking about the key issues relating to professionalism and the role of consultants. I have summarized some of his key points in these memos over a few weeks' time as follows:

2/4/82

What follows are some preliminary thoughts about revisions of our training course offerings. It is also an attempt to take a first small step toward moving the IAQC away from its current status of being a quasi-consulting organization "in many ways in a somewhat conflict-of-interest status with many of its own members."[1] For the short run, this proposal will generate

1. In what may be seen as a confirmation of that status, the association was notified by the Internal Revenue Service on 18 June 1982 that it was not eligible for non-tax status. The basic reason given was the IRS felt that "IAQC is the same as a for-profit business, and, to give it a non-profit status would confer an unfair competitive advantage on IAQC." The IAQC appealed and in September 1982 received 501(C) (3) status, which exempted it from paying federal income taxes.

additional income. For the long term, it will set the stage for the IAQC to move away from a consultant role into being more of a professional society.

The executive director then went on to suggest that given the high cost of generating the necessary training materials and keeping them up to date, the IAQC should serve as a coordinating agency for interested parties to oversee the development of a new generation of training materials. He also proposed the development of an advanced facilitator course going beyond the introductory offerings that had hitherto characterized association training and the offering of an executive briefing for top management.

2/20/82

It is becoming clear to me that we must rapidly step up the pace of change to alternative sources of revenue for the IAQC. The quality circle training business is literally exploding, and I feel it will soon pass us by. Not only is our course and its materials no longer the best in the business [the association was still using the training materials of one of its consultant co-founders at this time] but there are so many alternatives available that those who stay in business must be among the very best to survive. There are already scores of sources for low-priced training. With the entry of major groups, such as big corporations who already have training programs, the whole nature of the training business is changing. We could compete, but I feel it would take a great investment, and I believe that would be a mistake.

Our future is to become a truly professional society sustained by its individual and organization members in return for the valuable service they receive. I'd like to move rapidly and get out of controversial and competitive areas.

Our enrollments in the facilitator training course, which has been our bread and butter, are already starting to decline. We need to move rapidly.

2/26/82

One more matter, in phone conversations with several of you over the past two weeks, I received strong encouragement to bid on the Defense Logistics Agency quote for teaching twenty-five facilitator classes. It would of course be a lifesaver financially. But thanks to sound counsel from the president, I am comfortable with the decision not to go ahead since it would be a significant step toward "in-company" consulting, which is the direction opposite to the way we want to go.

The executive director's ideas for joint development of materials never did get off the drawing board, though his plans for introducing an advanced facilitator course and executive briefings were adopted. The latter were never very successful, despite repeated efforts. Small morning breakfast meetings were organized in different cities, with the IAQC organizing a short program introducing circles to which local CEOs were invited. Despite the absence of a fee, they typically did not come or sent some staff person.

We see from the executive director's remarks how the issue of training materials inextricably tied together the issues of professionalism and competing with consultant members. His idea on joint development of materials with those companies and/or consultants who were interested was in fact a rather clever effort to reconcile his ideas on professionalism and service with the presence of consultants. His ideas on joint development of materials were shaped by the belief that managers of company circle programs and consulting organizations faced a heavy cost in developing and updating circle training materials (as did the IAQC), with the risk that they might not recover their costs. In other words, when these organizations could not "make a market," the IAQC's role was to help them achieve that end; that was the executive director's idea of providing service to its constituency.

In the executive director's version, this meant that the consultants' organizations in particular become the "drivers" for what constituted professionalism; professionalism became a residual category of services where consultants could not make a market. Note the contrast with the initial model presented in chapter 3. There the idea was that companies would pool resources when the high transaction costs made it difficult for them to make a satisfactory market. A strong corporate commitment by firms to the IAQC's success would have resulted in corporate representatives on the board who would have pushed this position. Instead, with relatively ineffective middle-level managers on the board acting on their own initiative, it was difficult to resist the emphasis being put on solving consultants' problems. As a consequence, it was the consultants' difficulties in making a satisfactory market that drove developments.

What was in this residual category? The executive director said that he had received some thoughtful suggestions from one of the consultant board members as to where the IAQC would have an "almost exclusive territory": fostering and supporting local chapters; sponsoring conferences, widespread publication of circle successes and innovations, sponsoring of demonstrations of circle success, and providing executives with authoritative information on quality circles at the corporate level.

This is by no means a trivial list. It was, however, a much narrower role for a professional organization than had traditionally been the case. Professional organizations have routinely been involved not only in identifying best practices but in codifying these practices in training materials, school curricula, and certification procedures. In the March 1984 *Quality Circles Journal* a letter writer defending association involvement in training wrote: "Most societies consider themselves as a source of (professionally prepared) materials for their members. The review (and presumably sponsorship) by people with the stature and experience of a board of directors or appointed professional committee is a time-honored practice in our voluntary standards organizations." By contrast, the overall tenor of the executive director's remarks makes it clear that his ideas on professionalism were fundamentally shaped by the need to avoid competing with consultants.

The executive director correctly identified the rapidly growing number of competitors in the training business and rightly predicted the association's growing loss of competitiveness in the market. We see in table 3 that the combined percentage of IAQC revenues derived from training and material sales dropped from 61 percent in 1982 to 22 percent by 1987. The average class size for the basic facilitator training course was seven in 1979, thirteen in 1980, and forty-three in 1981. After this dramatic growth, however, there was a precipitous decline to thirteen in 1982, twelve in 1983, eight in 1984, ten in 1985, and eight in 1986.

The Emergent Consulting Industry for Quality Circles

To fully appreciate the growth of competitive forces in the market, we need to describe what happened from 1978 to 1983. I have talked a lot about consultants in the previous two chapters, but to more fully understand the IAQC's successes and failures, we need to know more about the nature of the market for consultants in quality-circle services.

When the association was founded in 1978, there were only two, then three, firms with independent training materials exclusively oriented toward quality circles (the "Big Three" that sprang from Lockheed). There were some additional team-building materials from various sources, but by and large the IAQC's entry into the training business was relatively uncontested. Indeed, it was initiated by the consultant co-founders of the association. By 1983 it was quite another matter. First, the initial "Big Three" had grown substantially. In December 1981 two of the Big Three were quoted as reporting that each of their businesses had tripled in the past year to sales of about $1.5 million annually. One of the firms, Rieker's, had nine full-time consultants on the payroll and was operating with a three-month backlog of customers.[2] The extraordinary demand brought a large number of competitors into the field.

An important point here that bears on entry costs concerns copyright protection. Such "organizational software" is often copyrighted, but the protection is slight. Consequently, potential new entrants found it quite easy to rewrite materials; with only a modestly different slant, they had their own materials. A typical rewrite in the early days was to shift from the original Japanese emphasis on statistical problem-solving techniques contained in the Lockheed materials to various behavioral science emphases on team building, communication, and small-group dynamics. I looked at many versions of quality-circle training materials in the early 1980s and was struck by just how similar most of them were to each other. On a number of occasions I met consultants and, especially, company managers who freely admitted they had simply given one of the training manuals on the market a quick rewrite, just enough to avoid the charge of plagiarism. Furthermore, copying machines allowed companies to reproduce training materials in violation of

2. "Two California Firms Find That Attention to Quality Pays Off," *New York Times*, 8 December 1981, p. D4. By 1984, a peak year, Rieker had twenty-five employees (clerical staff and consultants) on the payroll. By then, however, he was expanding more strongly into the quality field and away from exclusive reliance on circles. By 1987 he reported that only one-third of his business was in circles, with most of the rest in the quality field, including statistical process control. A number of other consultants reported similar, if not equally dramatic, trends.

the author's copyright protection. In summary, the need for training materials, one of the potentially high entry costs associated with servicing quality-circle clientele, was in fact not a very significant deterrent to entry. This was to have major implications for the IAQC.[3]

It was not just the weakness of copyright protection that facilitated market entry, however, since some consultants entered by either becoming licensees of one of the Big Three or simply buying IAQC materials (which were produced by the third member of the Big Three) and attending one of the IAQC's public seminars on facilitator/leader training. With a little intelligence and talent, they could then soon be in business for themselves. To be sure, word of mouth is the most important advertising in this business, so those who were "winging it" had some credibility problems. Many of those entering the consulting market, however, had either prior company experience with QC circles or prior management consulting experience. Either of these served to mask some of their deficiencies or at least buy them enough time to learn on the job.

In my own survey of the consulting field in December 1983 I recorded roughly seventy firms that were offering services in quality circles. These ranged from the production of a single video to a full package of services, including in-house training packages, implementation, and follow-up. Since much depends on one's definition of circles, it is in fact difficult to make an accurate estimate of the total number of firms offering quality-circle consulting services. The only publicized marketing survey of quality-circle consulting, conducted in 1980–81, estimated there to be 150 such firms (Morris 1981).[4] There were probably a large number of local firms serving local markets that did not enter into my data base. My listings were based mostly on tallying those with representatives attending the annual conventions and those advertising in various national journals.

In addition to the typical consultant firms, a number of large firms that had adopted quality circles set up departments to market

---

3. Recall that a professionally *developed* set of original materials could easily cost $250,000 at that time.

4. The information from that survey reported below typically was based on the responses of between twenty-five and thirty-one respondents.

that expertise. This can be seen as an attempt to cover the large start-up and operating costs. The services typically included the conducting of public and in-house facilitator/leader training. Prominent among such entries in the early 1980s were General Motors, Westinghouse, and Sperry. Moreover, a few firms, such as Georgia Power Co., launched QC circles at dozens of companies without charge as a public service.

In her 1981 survey of the quality-circle consulting industry, Rosemary Morris characterizes it as oligopolistic (the Big Three had a dominant role, with many others imitating their offerings) with very narrow boundaries, many part-time sellers (only a small part of whose total business was circles), significant product differentiation, surprisingly low barriers to entry, little buyer concentration, relatively low fixed costs, and very high demand. She also reports that 75 percent of respondent firms had entered the field less than two years earlier, with the number entering having doubled annually for the previous few years. Sixty percent of the respondents said that less than 50 percent of their total business was derived from circles. Finally, 26 percent reported licensing other firms.

It is clear from these data that in a rapidly growing industry, the IAQC was increasingly hard put to maintain its earlier dominant position. Price competition became stronger, and the quality of services being demanded increased. It is difficult to know precisely how many firms were actually offering public facilitator/leader training in competition in the early 1980s. Based on various sources, I think the number could easily have totaled twenty. I do know, based on response to an IAQC request for bids on training materials, that a minimum of seventeen firms had basic facilitator training materials for sale in early 1983.

The rest of 1982 saw a continuing decline in the IAQC's facilitator course enrollments and flat or declining materials sales. There was increasing recognition that the days of the free lunch were over and that the association would have to start seriously marketing its products.

Education committee members and the executive director agreed that it would be a good idea to create bidding procedures and communicate to all firms with quality-circle training materials that the IAQC was interested in securing a training package. The bidding procedure, which involved a formal selection committee, was designed to avoid charges of favoritism by consultants whose materials were not selected. The wheels ground slowly, and it was not until the December 1982 board meeting that it was resolved that an advertisement be placed in the association's journal requesting bids for the supply of facilitator training materials. The notice itself did not appear until March 1983.

A Leadership Crisis

The May 1982 board meeting was another critical turning point in the development of the association. The continuing pressures and strains associated with participation on the board were starting to show. Notwithstanding that this was the meeting at which the following year's association officers were to be selected, attendance fell off for the first time, with only fifteen of the twenty-one members present. In a secret ballot, nine individuals were nominated for the presidency (eight board members and one outsider). Seven of the internal candidates declined, leaving the outside write-in candidate and Jeff Beardsley, co-founder of the organization. The outside candidate was Charley Chavis, vice president of the Dover Corporation. Reached by telephone, he agreed to fly in to meet with the board the following day.

Chavis had a strong appeal for many board members simply because he was a vice president of manufacturing and as such had the kind of status that had hitherto been totally lacking on the board. Moreover, one of his subordinates who was a board member testified to Chavis's commitment to quality circles. Finally, he brought with him the support of his company, a company known for its strong quality-circle program. Chavis was an unknown quantity as a person, but he looked good to many of the "users," at least one of whom threatened to leave if the organization was turned back into the hands of one of the consultant co-founders.

That night a caucus of five board members met and identified a slate of candidates for all the executive offices, including Chavis as president, which they all agreed to support. They also mapped out the likely votes of the remaining board members and concluded that the election would be close, with the outcome likely to hinge on three swing votes. They assigned individuals in the caucus to persuade each of the three of the merits of the slate. The caucus held together and swept the election, with its slate taking all the executive positions. We see here the consequences of the absence of an effective institutional mechanism for choosing the board's officers. In desperation it took a flyer on an unknown individual.

Fred Riley, the outgoing president, summarized the accomplishments of the IAQC over the past two years. Membership had grown from 300 in September 1980 to 5,000 in September 1983.[5] Chapters had grown from none in September 1980 to 50 in September 1982. The number of paid attendees at the annual conference had grown from 300 in February 1980 to 1,900 in March 1982. Riley also listed other accomplishments, such as the production of a very professional quarterly journal, agreement upon and evolution of association bylaws, survival, and chapter-run quality-circle conferences. He closed by noting that the glamor was starting to wear off circles nationally and that the real challenges lay ahead.

Attendance at the October board meeting was off again, with only twelve members present, just making a quorum. One board member resigned, citing frustration and new job duties (he was only the second to resign since the first board had been elected). The board for the first time adopted an attendance provision, specifying that any board member missing more than one regularly scheduled meeting in twelve months would be subject to expulsion at the following meeting. It was passed unanimously.

This board meeting was well managed and efficient. For the first time the association had a president who chaired the meeting with authority. However, the revenue situation was reported to be getting difficult. The major sources of the problem were seen as a loss of membership growth, flat material sales, and a falling off in attendees at facilitator training courses. The new president identified the following problem areas: the national organization needed to give back something to the chapters so that they would continue their affiliation; IAQC growth was inhibited by lack of top management support; board members needed to attend chapter meetings in their areas; and the IAQC must continue educating the public about QC circles to assure continued growth.

5. Note discrepancy with the reconstructed figures in table 1.

By the December board meeting, deficits of some $22,000 a month for the previous six months were reported, eating into the organization's modest reserves. The association ran a deficit of $58,000 for fiscal year 1983 (after having had a net income of $147,000 in 1982). Success at the 1983 annual conference was critical to keeping the organization financially sound. Meanwhile, various alternatives were explored to reduce costs and generate additional income. It was in this context that the association made the previously discussed decision to give up its long-held plans to develop its own training materials and opt for seeking bids to supply them, thereby avoiding any up-front costs.

The new president began to flex his muscles in a variety of ways; one of his assistants, a "volunteer" from the company, put pressure on the nominations committee to recruit two or three high-level managers to replace some of the incumbents on the ballot for the next board election and to limit the total number on the ballot to ensure their election chances. While this was exactly the outcome the association needed to improve its management skills and external legitimacy, the nominations committee did not appreciate the strong-arm approach and did not act on the suggestion. This was the first, but not last, case in which the strong-willed new president antagonized some board members. Paradoxically, the participatory style inherent in QC circles often seemed to attract many "Theory X" (Douglas McGregor's term for authoritarian) managers. Chavis saw himself as a doer. He believed he needed the authority to act quickly, without being restrained by the board or the membership, if the organization were to survive.

At the April 1983 board meeting, Chavis pushed through a bylaw change that allowed the board to amend the bylaws subject to alteration or repeal by the members. Prior to this time, the board had only been able to propose changes in the bylaws to the membership. Chavis also developed the habit of appointing and replacing committee members and abolishing and adding committees in a freewheeling manner. Unfortunately, coming on the heels of the Diener affair, this management style tended to recreate feelings of mistrust and suspicion on the board. Notwithstanding, most board members saw no positive alternative, and Chavis was reelected as the following year's president by acclamation.

Other important events took place at the April 1983 board meeting. A new executive director (ED 3) was appointed as a result of dissatisfaction with the performance of the incumbent. For the first time, the IAQC had a director who was an experienced association executive and not simply a QC circle enthusiast. He had other problems, however, and like his predecessor lasted only about a year. By fall 1983 there were nine staff people at the new headquarters office (now located in Cincinnati), including a new assistant executive director. There was a lengthy discussion of chapter relationships and the failure of the national organization to honor its rebate commitments.

Chapter relationships came to loom larger in association business, there being some sixty-five chapters in existence by March 1983. A plan was also proposed for establishing nine geographic regions and electing nine regional vice presidents, who would also be members of the board, replacing nine of the current directors-at-large. The rationale was not entirely clear, but seemed focused on bringing the board closer to the membership and creating a new tier of people capable of holding higher office in the organization. The board endorsed the plan, and the membership approved the regional concept in a mail ballot in October 1983. Once the transition was complete, the board would total twenty-one members. Eleven would be national directors; nine, regional directors.

For the first time, the annual conference in 1983 did not report a growth in paid attendees. Prior to that year, the conference had doubled in paid attendees each year, but in 1983 there was a small decline in attendance. This heightened the financial difficulties facing the organization. One other aspect of the convention bears mentioning. Of the 133 sessions of the three-day meeting that could be classified as either company- or consultant-led, 33 (25 percent of the total) were consultant-led. Clearly, the IAQC had become a major forum for consultants to display their wares, not only in the sales booths reserved for them for this purpose, but at the sessions as well. If the sales pitch was too blatant in the sessions, the staff typically received complaints from attendees. There were a number of such complaints at the 1983 meetings, and those criticized were told that if they persisted, they would not be invited back.

The education committee was reconstituted in early 1983; it now had fifteen members, of whom seven were consultants. Despite the prior agreement to invite bids to supply IAQC training materials, the new committee members introduced some different ideas. One consultant argued forcefully that the IAQC should urge all producers of quality-circle materials to submit their products to it for review and evaluation, with those found acceptable to be included in an IAQC catalogue of approved materials. Vendors would then be charged for space in the catalogue, and the IAQC would receive a commission on sales. Consultants would also submit a portfolio of qualifications to be listed in the catalogue. According to this plan, the IAQC would continue to offer public facilitator training programs, with the trainer free to choose the materials used to teach each workshop from the catalogue of approved materials. The stated objectives of this plan were for the IAQC to generate revenues from material sales and to continue to offer, and receive revenue from, facilitator training workshops. At the same time it was argued that this would establish some standards to assure IAQC members that they would be receiving high-quality materials and services. Finally, an objective would be to "provide a fair and equitable distribution forum for those individuals, consultants, or companies who develop and produce quality-circle materials and literature."

The April committee discussion of this proposal was spirited. The proposal's originator argued that all the IAQC could do, as represented in this proposal, was to set minimum standards and certify all materials that met those standards. (Note the distinction between minimum standards and diffusion of best practices.) He further argued that to become a marketer of any one vendor's materials was inconsistent with the IAQC's role as an information clearinghouse. The argument was that the IAQC should expose everyone to all available materials; it should give consumers a choice and give all consultants an opportunity to get their business. The focus on "freedom of choice" brought into play powerful ideologies to which many were committed. Speakers arguing in favor of the proposal prefaced their statements with words like "in a democratic society." It was also argued that the committee would never be able to choose the one best package, if there was such a thing. It would simply be too controversial. The implicit argument was that since the IAQC could not define best practice, it had to settle for meeting minimum standards.

One opponent of the proposal, a consultant, asked the rhetorical question, "Why do people come to IAQC?" He answered that it was because "they don't trust consultants and want independent assessments of materials." They perceived IAQC screening to be a bargain. From his point of view, the consultants with high-quality training materials benefited from an effective association screening. Another committee member argued that to accept the new proposal would be to abdicate professional responsibility. The IAQC needed to filter the mass of available information to provide service to the membership. Setting minimum standards for certification would provide only the roughest filter for the organization. The membership needed to have its organization setting the highest standards. Notwithstanding these arguments, the proponents of this new proposal were in a clear majority. A number of committee members, especially the consultants, pushed their position even further, arguing that the IAQC should get out of training altogether, but the chair reminded them that it was the board's decision and that the board was dependent on training for revenue.

What were the views of IAQC members on this whole controversy? At these discussions, few people asked; the focus was rather on what was fair to the consultants. On the general matter of whether the IAQC should be in the training business, there was a clear indication from a 1985 survey of IAQC members that the membership preferred that the IAQC "continue to provide training and training materials" (ReVelle 1985:27). Moreover, this sentiment was directly correlated with length of the individual respondent's experience with QC circles; the more experience one had with circles, the stronger the preference for IAQC involvement in training.

Growing Pains

At the September 1983 meeting of the board (thirteen members attending), the issue of association governance came to the fore. The ample agenda and numerous attached memos and reports proliferating from headquarters were testimony to an active staff. Committee chairpersons complained that decisions were being made that sidestepped or ignored the committee structure. From the staff viewpoint, the committees did not function very well; they met too infrequently (typically four times a year at the board meeting) and attendance was erratic. Moreover, the executive committee had been making decisions in the interim between board meetings without what some board members saw as sufficient consultation with the full board.

The issue that triggered a full-scale debate on these issues was the matter of selecting training materials. Although the education committee voted to let instructors pick their own training materials, the executive committee opposed that decision. Instead, it voted to adopt a training package developed at General Electric as the official IAQC training package.

The GE materials were developed out of a large research project within GE and eventually ended up costing GE some $300,000. They shifted the focus of the IAQC training materials to group process activities as opposed to pure problem-solving methods. The GE package was presented to the board as the "leading edge" materials in the field.

The executive committee believed that the tight financial situation of the association required that action be taken quickly when opportunities presented themselves. It had an opportunity to work with GE to gain access to a set of what it believed to be high-quality materials and thereby solve a problem vexing the organization from the start. At one swoop (most excutive committee members thought), it would break the dependence on consultants and provide the association with training materials of which it could be proud. Committee members also noted that the others entering bids (recall that seventeen sets of materials had been submitted) all wanted up-front payment and were not prepared to grant exclusive use of their materials to the IAQC. Moreover, only two had responded with a complete package. One of the consultant board members asserted that he would have been prepared to meet GE's bid, however, and he criticized the whole decision-making process.

The board voted by a large majority to amend the tentative arrangements with GE and directed the executive committee to renegotiate the contract with better terms for the association. It also gave the executive committee, on a much closer vote, the authority to conclude a contract with GE. The executive committee did conclude a renegotiated contract with GE, which was approved by an overwhelming majority at the December meeting. Yet this had been a highly emotional matter for the board, with the opponents hinting at some impropriety on the part of the executive committee. As with the ASQC, we begin to see the organization's past history (in this case, the Diener affair) providing a stigmatizing model.

These were the horns of the dilemma facing the IAQC: to motivate volunteers to operate the committee structure and be active on the board, they had to have a sense that their decisions counted. However, the erratic functioning of the committees, the lack of regular meetings, especially by the board, and the need for quick action to deal with rapidly changing situations led to a shift in the balance of decision making to the executive committee and the headquarters staff.

Much of this tension was simply unavoidable as the organization struggled to find the right balance that would make a majority of people comfortable. One outcome of the board's discussion was that the executive committee agreed for the first time to make the minutes of its meetings available to the rest of the board on a timely basis. The president summarized the discussion by saying: "There has been and is no intent to make decisions outside of required channels. But we do need better communication." Notwithstanding, damage had been done and collective trust had fallen another notch.

Two other matters came up at the September 1983 board meeting that deserve mention. In wrestling with the problem of poor attendance and a bylaw that required the board to remove members who missed more than one meeting, the awkward fact was that the two co-founders were among the worst offenders. Somehow in trying to deal with this problem, the board voted to expel the two co-founders and at the same time to make them directors emeritus with permission to attend board meetings as nonvoting members whenever they chose. One of them, Jeff Beardsley, did become more active on this basis over the next few years, continuing to push the board to pursue his vision of what the IAQC should be. By virtue of his chairing the development committee, he was eligible for and appointed to the executive committee. In 1986 he was elected a regular member of the board. In late 1988 he resigned from the board, citing the difficulty of making board meetings but insisting that he continued to want to participate in shaping the future of the association. Shedding its founder origins continued to be a struggle for the IAQC.

The second matter that came up was a statement by the president that he had become aware that two unions had filed claims with the National Labor Relations Board arguing that employer-established employee-participation programs in the two companies in question violated the National Labor Relations Act by using employee committees to "deal with" employees. Implicit here was the potential claim that quality circles were labor organizations insofar as they influenced the conditions of work. The president informed the board that the IAQC could file a friend of the court brief in which it could argue that quality circles were not labor organizations. The board was also told that the law firm employed by the president's employer would be willing to work on the matter for the IAQC. At its December meeting the board authorized the president to work with appropriate legal counsel to write a brief that communicated a description of quality circles and distinguished them from other forms of employee involvement. This brief would then be presented to the NLRB. The president was instructed to do all this in a way that communicated that the IAQC was not anti-union.

Such briefs were subsequently filed, but it was discovered upon further investigation that one of the briefs had the unfortunate effect of making it appear that the IAQC was taking the side of one of the notorious anti-union firms in the specific case in question. Such had not been the intent of the board. Furthermore, it was discovered that the law firm handling the matter had a reputation for being anti-union. When this was brought to the attention of the board at its November 1985 meeting, it instructed the new president to explore an amendment to the IAQC brief making clear that it was not the intent of the association to take a position on the facts of the specific case. Rather it was its intent to demonstrate that quality circles are not in violation of the NLRA. During this discussion, Chavis (no longer president) stated in an impassioned presentation that he had decided a long time ago that unions were either "hostile to or at best neutral to circles because it undercuts their role on the workplace floor."

All this is significant for what it tells us about the IAQC and its relation to organized labor. By the early 1980s many union leaders were drawing a distinction between quality circles and QWL. QWL was presented as involving unions and workers in a broad pattern of worker participation that included, but went beyond, small-group activity. Union leaders often saw quality circles as stand-alone initiatives used either in nonunion shops to help keep out unions or in union shops to weaken unions. Such fears were not unfounded, as employee-participation activities were advertised by "union avoidance consultants" as part of a strategy to stay non-union (Hughes and Demaria 1979:96). Thus, the initial IAQC action described above could only reinforce such interpretations and indeed some radical union dissidents publicized the IAQC's initial brief in the September 1984 issue of the journal *Labor Notes* (Parker and Boal 1984:7). They urged unions with quality circles to encourage their companies not to use consultants affiliated with the IAQC given its stand on "weakening labor's legal rights."

As reported in chapter 10, 47 percent of IAQC members were in union shops and offices. The danger of being labelled anti-union or having QC circles seen as anti-union was thus a serious matter for the IAQC. It was important for the future of quality circles and the IAQC that they be seen as legitimate among union leaders. Yet the above action showed relatively little sensitivity to the matter. Although some board members had tried to get a union leader to run for the board, they were not successful until 1985, when a union officer ran for board membership and was defeated. However, he was appointed treasurer of the organization in late 1986. Still another union leader running for the board in 1988 was defeated.

By and large, during the early 1980s, the association showed little sensitivity to the issue and undertook relatively few initiatives to recruit and commit union employees to the association. The basic GE training materials sold and taught by the association studiously avoided mention of unions on the theory that it might offend some potential purchasers. It was not until 1986–87 that the IAQC brought in an outside consultant to teach a separate course on "Strengthening Employee Participation in the Unionized Work Organization."

Perhaps most symbolic of this insensitivity were decisions made at the 1985 and 1986 annual conferences, where Coors Beer was officially associated with the conference through various giveaways during the meeting (a Coors employee had become a member of the board). For union activists throughout the country, this was a red flag. From 1977 to 1987 local union publications had prominently featured Coors as a symbol of anti-union activities, and union members were continually being urged to boycott Coors products.

The point of this discussion is not that the IAQC was anti-union; most of the board members were simply naive on the subject, and the matter seldom came to the attention of the board. Nor do I believe that quality circles are intrinsically anti-union, though some companies have certainly used them to that end. Rather, the point is that a new national organization must build legitimacy among its existing and potential constituencies if it is to survive. Unions were one of the IAQC's constituencies, and yet it was incapable of acting to remove simple offensive symbols, much less to take positive initiatives. None of this proved fatal; after all, the IAQC had many members at union shops. Yet the organization was extremely slow in developing and advancing that constituency in a way that would increase their commitment to the IAQC or QC circles.

The May–June 1984 meeting of the board was notable for two events. A new president was elected. He was from the same firm as the previous president, and had been persuaded by Chavis to take the job. Again, the association was forced to bring in an outsider for lack of a credible internal candidate. Chavis stayed on the board (IAQC rules call for past presidents to stay on the executive committee for a year) and the new president, a rather mild fellow, clearly had difficulty getting out of the shadow of his more forceful colleague.

Notable as well at this meeting was the appointment of a new executive director (ED 4). The board, choosing not to engage in a national search, appointed the former assistant executive director. The new director, the first woman to hold the job, also had a background in association activities.

The 1984 conference was a big success, achieving the largest number of paid attendees to date (2,290). That very success led to higher expectations for the 1985 conference and, as we shall see, to new crises. Yet this success did relieve the immediate financial problems of the association. It was increasingly clear, however, that the success or failure of the annual conference (together with the new fall conference after 1984) was becoming the difference between financial success and failure.

Although board members were not aware of it at the time, association membership reached its peak in 1984, at least for the next few years. Membership (see table 1) hit a high of 5,751 in 1984, declined by some 329 members the next year and held relatively steady through 1988. Similarly, any new chapter growth after 1984 was more than canceled out by the growth of inactive chapters. While the organization could not necessarily be expected to predict the future, the fact is that it did not know its current membership figures because of poor record keeping.

The board was told that the corrected figures showed a total membership of 9,482 for September 1984, and by the end of the year it was publicly claiming 10,000 in the association's journal. The reconstructed figures in table 1, however, show the total at the end of 1984 to have been 5,751. One can allow for some inflation of circle membership to account for an additional 1,000 members. Yet even taking this into consideration, the fact that it was off by a magnitude of 29 percent reflects the chaos from which the organization still suffered. Turning over your executive director every twelve months on average was not a way to build a coherent administrative system. Nor could an organization with such misconceptions about itself be expected to do very effective planning.

The association did for the first time set up a strategic planning committee in the summer of 1984. Until then, the board had been so busy either adjusting to growth and demand for services or digging itself out of crises that it had not initiated a significant planning effort.

The September 1984 board meeting was a new turning point for the organization. With the new regional director system now being phased in, and with none of the existing directors allowed to run for these new positions, there were fewer at-large places on the board to accommodate the incumbents. Of the twenty-seven members of the temporarily enlarged board (a transitional phase before the new regional concept was fully implemented), members of the original elected board totaled only nine (not counting the directors emeritus). "Founder board members" were thus now in a clear mi-

nority, and some of the issues that motivated them were not as salient to the new members. Among the twenty-seven, the number
of full-time consultants stabilized at five members (19 percent of
the elected board). Moreover, with some of the bloom off the rose,
the quality-circle boom was slowing down, and the economic incentives for board members to quit their companies and become
quality-circle consultants thus subsided.

The management qualifications of the new board members were
not significantly different from those of the original board members. They tended to be somewhat younger and primarily managers and administrators of their company's quality-circle programs.
Indeed, the regional directors' job description called for them to
service chapters in their regions and answer questions from chapter presidents on how to fill out financial forms and how to get the
membership out to meetings. Such a job description guaranteed
that no high-level executive would seek the post of regional director. There was a certain grass-roots appeal that some of the newly
elected regional directors exploited (most of the regional elections
were contested). Nor was the populist approach limited to the campaigns for regional directorships. In one case, the elected at-large
candidate wrote up his credentials to appear on the ballot as follows:

Quality circle involvement position statement:

This man isn't a famous QC consultant and no, he hasn't written a book
about circles. He's just like you and me—someone with a finger on the
pulse of the baseline worker. His involvement with circles since their conception with the VA has yielded an intimate understanding of the QC concept. This knowledge will translate into action for you.

While successfully appealing to populist feelings, such credentials
hardly provided the skills needed for running a complex national
association. Yet the association's membership regularly turned down
many of the high-level management officials nominated to the board
in the mid and late 1980s. There was a tendency to want people
"just like us" who were "knee deep" in circles.

Until this election, most of the original board members who had
dropped out had done so owing to new job assignments and lack of
company support (I estimate four had dropped out for these reasons). With the new regional director system being phased in,
however, many chose not to run or were forced into runoffs for the

declining number of at-large positions. After the 1986 board election conducted in the summer of 1985, there were only three of the originally elected board members still on the board, plus the two co-founders serving as directors emeritus.

The new regional board members experienced considerable difficulty at their first few meetings (attendance was once again at high levels). They felt they were expected to vote on matters for which back-up data were lacking (for example, budget proposals). This often made them mistrustful and gave them a sense of being manipulated. There also tended to be some faction building, with the at-large directorships being filled by the incumbent board members, who tended to take positions that were opposed by the new regional directors. Rather than dissipating, this sentiment seemed to grow over time. Many of the regional directors believed that the at-large directors were not required to work as hard or did not have the responsibilities that they had.

The regional directors brought to the board a concern for local chapters and members. While true to their mandate, they did not offer any dramatically different ways of organizing the chapters, and many of their concerns were out of step with the fiscal realities of the organization (for example, they tended to oppose dues increases). Once formed, the regional concept created a populist sentiment that was difficult to harness. There was stepped up rhetoric as to how QC circle members and chapters were the "lifeblood" of the organization. Yet, the reality was that the lifeblood of the organization, as it was actually constituted, was the revenue earned by its national conferences. Most board members and officers were reluctant to challenge the populist rhetoric because to do so smacked of heresy.

Organizational Survival in Question Again

The IAQC entered 1985 in moderately difficult economic circumstances. Nevertheless, based perhaps on optimistic projections, spending for the annual spring conference was extraordinarily high. The flamboyant new executive director (ED 4) liked going first class, but the association was once again taken on a long ride. Paid attendance ended up at 1,948 (down 350 from the previous year), and the association was suddenly in deep trouble.

The executive committee was informed that the net income figures for 1985 showed a deficit of $576,678. Reflecting on the size of the net loss, the auditor's report concluded that "these factors, among others . . . indicate that the association may be unable to continue its existence." It was the grimmest moment in the short, tortured financial history of the association. While there was no suggestion of any illegal behavior on the part of the executive director, the crisis illustrated once again the difficulty a volunteer board and executive officers have in retaining control in a rapidly changing situation where sources of revenue are highly variable. Again, these are problems hardly unique to the IAQC (see Naples 1985:77–80).

The executive director (ED 4) resigned in early May. She had lasted just short of twelve months. The four executive directors in the IAQC's short life had served on average less than a year each. If this had been the mid-life of one of those routine muddling-along academic associations that operate in a stable environment, this turnover might have been barely noticed. In a quickly changing environment, a rapidly growing organization like the IAQC was, however, convulsed by these frequent traumatic changes. The office staff was also turning over, and when it wasn't turning over, it was adjusting to a new director. This time, the crisis did not even allow the organization to think about recruiting a new director. It had all too many debts to consider incurring additional ones. The board simply made a senior employee in the office the staff liaison.

The staff, working with the executive committee and the board, developed a crash program for generating revenue and cutting costs. Executive committee and staff members visited eleven companies, to whom over $300,000 was owed, and assured them that the association had every intention of paying in full and was actively dealing with its problems. With few real alternatives, the creditors cooperated, thereby providing breathing space.

Chapters with surplus funds were solicited for donations and loans. Eleven thousand dollars was eventually contributed, not an altogether impressive sum. The relative lack of support reflected the continuing sense of chapters that they were not getting very much from the national organization. Chapter rebates were in fact discontinued once again, and it was not until April 1986 that the board voted to restore them.

A new treasurer with some accounting skills was appointed in September 1985. Not accidentally, he was from the same firm employing the current and past presidents. Both in tangible and intangible ways, support from the president's firm was critical in helping the association through this crisis. One can only wonder what the association would be like if broad-based corporate support was the norm at all times for all affiliating with the association.

An austerity budget was put in place for 1985–86. Survival was literally month to month, with the hope that the fall conference (which had only been run once before and had lost money) would be successful and provide some more breathing space. Board members contributed their time to participate in emergency "fundraising" seminars and training sessions. The 1985 fall conference was a major success, with some 600 registrations. With a significant reduction in IAQC liabilities, the association now had the possibility of making it to the spring conference, which if successful would put it on an even keel again. The 1986 conference was indeed a major success. Although paid attendees totaled only 1,979, the same roughly as at the preceding spring conference, the conference was held in Spartan style, resulting in a drastic reduction in the cost of conducting it. By March 1987 the association was able to publish its fiscal year report (September 1985–August 1986) showing that its debts had been reduced from $405,785 to $10,421.

This was quite a remarkable achievement for a volunteer organization in such a short time and reflected contributions from a variety of constituencies. In the process of recovering from the excesses of the past, however, the association had become more than ever a conference-driven organization. Whatever one might argue to be its impact on the other members, this surely served the interests of the consultants. The IAQC was less and less a factor in the training market, and its conferences provided ample opportunities to showcase consultants' wares.

Out of the Frying Pan . . .

As the association was digging itself out of its deepest financial hole, other issues were brewing that threatened the organization's stability and the IAQC's ability to adjust to a rapidly changing environment. There were board elections to be conducted in 1986 and a new president to be chosen. Although three of the originally elected members remained in 1987, there continued to be significant turnover in board membership; thirteen of the twenty-seven 1985 members were gone by 1987 (with a slimmed-down board of twenty-one in the final phase of regionalization). As one examines the makeup of each new board, there is no indication of any trend toward higher levels of directorship skills, experience, or position. In addition to this continuing handicap, rapid turnover of the board added to the management dilemma. With each annual election, a major learning experience had to occur before board members could begin to provide useful input.

The April 1986 board meeting was well attended, with twenty-five members plus one of the directors emeritus, Jeff Beardsley, attending. The board congratulated itself on the rapidly improving financial situation. The position of staff liaison was redesignated managing director. The incumbent, who had performed admirably under the financial crisis, took on this new role, the second woman to hold the job. No doubt the organization was gun-shy about designating someone executive director. In any case, for all practical purposes, the association had its fifth executive director in six years. One year later, at the April 1987 board meeting, she was promoted to executive vice president. The association finally had a director who could perform without a major disaster, an unprecedented state of affairs. She proceeded to build an increasingly professional staff, but around a limited set of functions.

In June 1986 Beardsley wrote a letter to all board members indicating that he was seeking election to the presidency of the IAQC. He gave his view on several key issues facing the association. On the matter of expanding the scope of the IAQC and changing its name, as was being recommended in draft reports of the strategic planning committee, he suggested caution. He had on numerous other occasions expressed his view that there was nothing wrong with QC circles and that the idea of going beyond circles was misguided. Although he talked about the need for change, his letter, as well as his public and private statements, all suggested a very conservative tone. He also reaffirmed his continuing opposition to the IAQC being involved in training activities. His preferred role for the IAQC was that of conference sponsor.

In a September article in the association's journal, Beardsley wrote a little more bluntly on this subject. He discussed the organization's purpose and its dreams "when we started it." He went on to note:

It is time for the membership to demand that the IAQC live up to its charter rather than change the charter to match the current wisdom of the "experts." Although the charter declares that the IAQC be a clearinghouse of ideas concerning the quality circle process, it does not require nor allow the IAQC to become radicalized by those ideas. In short, the charter does not allow the IAQC to go "Beyond Quality Circles."

Such views are often expressed by founders who see "their" organization turning in new directions not anticipated at the time of the founding. To the extent that they are able to limit organizational change, founders often threaten adaptation to new environmental conditions (Aldrich and Auster 1986). Beardsley continued to fight a rearguard action.

Those who had conceived of the organization as a user organization had one last gasp left. As immediate past president, Chavis still wielded considerable power, and in one of his last acts in the organization he recruited Robert Tallon, president and CEO of the Florida Power and Light Company, for the presidency. This was a company that was building a considerable reputation for itself in its quality-improvement efforts, of which quality circles were one aspect. It suited it to be associated with helping the IAQC. Faced with the opportunity to have the president and CEO of a company with such a national reputation as its head, the board eagerly accepted.

The new president was the first member of the board ever to hold CEO status. Once again, however, the association had been forced to go outside to fill its highest office, testimony to its inability to develop internal succession mechanisms. There had been understandings that the first vice president was next in line for the presidency, but these had broken down periodically for one reason or another.

Tallon displayed the kind of policy thinking that had not heretofore existed on the board. Committees were treated as profit centers, with the challenge of competing for surplus resources. In fall 1986, in conjunction with the board, the president developed a set of presidential charges for each committee. The plan was for committees to put forward proposals for implementing these charges at a subsequent meeting, with each committee implicitly required to show how its plan would be more cost-effective and successful than the others. The full board would decide which initiatives to fund. In this way, it was thought, the board would be able to invest its scarce resources in the most productive fashion. By having the board focus on service delivery to chapters and members in this context, Tallon made it easier for the board to discuss the actual amount of fiscal support provided to this constituency.

The new president also sought to reach out to corporate constituencies through the establishment of a sustaining membership category whereby firms would receive some modest extra benefits (for example, publicity in the association's journal and special workshops at the annual convention) in return for a $1,000 membership fee. By mid 1988, however, there were only two such members. In 1988 Tallon also helped launch "The Academy of the Association," the purpose of which was to recognize outstanding organizations and individuals in the field of quality and participation. It was a way of raising the status of the association by giving recognition to select academy members.

What is important about these two initiatives relative to the Swedish and Japanese experiences described in the next two chapters is that they were made by a volunteer association of individual members in search of a high-status corporate constituency. They are not examples of corporations seeking to pool resources to achieve common goals through associational activities.

There was also a plan presented at the Spring 1987 meeting for making the IAQC an umbrella organization (holding company) with a new name and having it focus on circles as one of several subsidiaries. Other subsidiaries with different, but related, missions would be created by merger. It remains to be seen whether anything will come of this plan.

One additional event at the Spring 1987 meeting points up the recurrence of old issues and the appearance of new solutions. The education committee, following the recommendations of the materials subcommittee, recommended to the board that the IAQC "outsource" its training material requirements. The proposal was to purchase material and training delivery from consultants. "We should become distributors. By going out to consultants, we become more flexible, and have fewer sunk costs than if we had developed programs." This discussion resurfaced because the GE training materials were increasingly seen as obsolete and the organization faced anew the question of whether to develop its own training materials or to acquire them.

There was a difference, however, from the past discussions. First, the IAQC was no longer a major player in the market. There were individual consultant firms that were doing more training in quality circles than the IAQC. Training and material sales no longer provided the IAQC with 61 percent of its budget as they had in 1982; the total was down to 22 percent. Moreover, there were no longer many on the board who were associated with the weaning of the organization away from the consultants. I did not sense from their discussion that board members believed there was much at stake. Thus, unlike in the past, there was little opposition registered to these new proposals. What this meant was that the IAQC would be left with little in the way of core competencies other than running conferences.

As with the umbrella organization concept, what we see here bears a peculiar resemblance to the broader U.S. business environment. With increased outsourcing and a focus on distribution, the manufacturing competence of American companies becomes increasingly weakened. In its place, a merger and acquisition strategy is put forward, since the organization now finds itself incapable of internal growth and development. This strategy, which so many have criticized as containing the seeds of America's economic decline, shows striking parallels to the IAQC strategy.

As a consequence of its decision to become a distributor, consultants would be free to use the association to promote their materials and training, and the association by giving its seal of approval would help remove the taint of commercialism from consultants' products. The notion of promoting best practices was dead; in its place certification of minimum standards came to the fore. One should not be too melodramatic about this. The association was never able to develop its own materials and training. As one long-term observer of the board put it, what we saw at this meeting was not the overturning of an established principle, but rather the dashing of wishful thinking on the part of some of the early board members. He argued persuasively that this outcome was the inevitable culmination of the developments discussed above.

Nevertheless, the idea of association training materials was not entirely dead. In early 1989, the material and education committees proposed a controversial plan to develop new association training materials in cooperation with two large companies. Apparently, there was still some sentiment that resisted the distributor role and all that it entailed.

To further bring matters full circle, at the June 1987 board meeting a new president of the organization was elected. Although he was formally an academic, 75 percent of his time was spent on his consulting business. The association had long resisted one of the consultant co-founders' efforts to become president only to choose as its president a man whose primary reputation was as a consultant. Unlike the older generation of self-made quality-circle consultants, who were not particularly schooled in theories of employee participation and the like, the new president represented a new breed of professional consultants, complete, as one quipster put it, with "Ph.D.'s, books, an established consultant network, good grammar, and tweeds." Whatever the differences between the old and new types of consultants, efforts to establish organizational legitimacy by removing the idea that the organization primarily served consultant interests were dealt still another blow.

The new first vice president, slated for the presidency, was also a consultant. In early 1988 he declined to run, however, and another board member, a mid-level manager from a Westinghouse subsidiary, was selected (the first female president). The IAQC had solved its succession problem through internal choices, but they were a consultant and another middle-management person. The association continued to be unable to draw on corporate resources in support of its efforts on a regular basis.

The "Beyond Quality Circles" Fad

The second major issue facing the IAQC as it came out of the financial crisis was the rapidly changing environment. Quality circles had been the buzz word of the late 1970s and early 1980s. By 1984 references to circles began to diminish significantly in the business press. In their place one began to hear more about creating self-managing teams and designing effective work teams. Consider the following introduction to a 1987 American Productivity Center Seminar entitled "Designing Effective Work Teams":

As a result of the evolution of employee involvement efforts in American business, organizations now clearly recognize the need to move beyond initial technique-driven programmatic employee participation efforts.

While small problem-solving groups–quality circles, employee participation groups, etc. are a good first step and can produce dramatic improvements, it is clear that by using employee involvement strategies as a way to manage your business even greater productivity and quality and quality of work life can be achieved.

DESIGNING EFFECTIVE WORK TEAMS offers you a next step for your employee involvement effort.

It was this sense of a rapidly changing environment and a lack of clarity in IAQC purposes and its future role that led the board to engage in its first systematic planning effort. In fall 1983, well before its most recent financial crisis, the executive director and executive committee formed a strategic committee to plan the association's future. The committee was formally set up in spring 1984. In writing its report, the committee used a variety of information-gathering and feedback techniques. Since, as the first vice president put it in a letter in February 1987, the report became the IAQC's "operating bible," a very brief summary highlighting some key points follows. Commentary is provided to put matters in broader perspective.

The IAQC's current sense of crisis, said the report, did not simply arise from the typical financial ups and downs of a fledgling organization. Rather it grew out of fundamental changes taking place in the marketplace as the QC circle process moved beyond the initial experimental phase in many companies. Membership services were concentrated in those areas appropriate to companies just getting started with circle programs (for example, basic facilitator training). The IAQC had relatively little to offer companies in which large-scale growth had taken place and companies dealing with problems of stagnation and revitalization or working to institutionalize their efforts. Underlying these weaknesses was the difficulty the IAQC had in recruiting a capable staff committed to the organization and in exercising effective management control over its operations.

Dealing with the problem of a narrow market niche, which increasingly accounted for a smaller share of the total market, was more difficult than it appeared. The IAQC had limited resources, much having been squandered by poor management. It was also operating in a rapidly changing environment, one that posed threats to the survival of both the IAQC and the quality-circle movement itself. Above all, the "beyond quality circles" fad was taking increasing hold of American management. For the IAQC to survive it had to position itself properly to respond to these new developments. *The overriding challenge for the IAQC was how to cope with rapidly evolving management interest in the human-resource area.*

The seriousness of this challenge was illustrated by a well-publicized article in the *Harvard Business Review* by Edward Lawler III and Susan Mohrman with the suggestive title "Quality Circles after the Fad" (1985). The authors argued that circles would shortly either die out in the course of an inherently brief evolutionary cycle or develop into more comprehensive participatory forms, represented by self-managing teams. They ignored the fact that the Japanese had sustained circles for over two decades, a long time for a fad, while also exploring other forms of team building. Although there can be no doubt that American management has a tendency to look for the next new cure-all, the way of thinking reflected in articles like Lawler and Mohrman's nonetheless hurt circle activities in many firms.

The report noted that the IAQC's market penetration was precisely in those areas experiencing the most saturation (easy market entry by consultant firms; companies trying to spin off their own expertise), where competition was fiercest, and where the products and services being offered had the most commoditylike character. One of the major consequences for the IAQC was financial instability, deriving from limited and falling demand for its products and a reduced ability to use pricing to raise its revenues. The IAQC's lack of reliable and timely revenue sources flowed from its focus on markets in the most unstable areas. In summary, changing management interests and the IAQC's narrow market penetration interacted to pose the most immediate threat to the IAQC.

The committee proposed that the IAQC respond by broadening its mission to include employee involvement more generally, on the assumption that circles were but one manifestation of employee participation. As one board member was to express the matter at a later date, we see three broad strategies emerging. The first is the incorporation of employee problem-solving groups within a broader framework of an organizationwide improvement process. The second is the expansion of employee involvement in problem-solving throughout other structures such as task forces or value-engineering teams. The third is the evolution to broader forms of employee involvement, such as self-managing work teams. The challenge facing the IAQC is to broaden its mission while not losing its one comparative advantage, a core competency in circles.

The reaction to these proposals by leaders in the IAQC was mostly positive, but a number of those most deeply immersed in circles reacted in a strongly hostile fashion. The two co-founders both wrote letters complaining about the directions being taken. Consultants whose business had already sharply diversified in response to market trends tended to be supportive, while those most heavily reliant on circles for their business tended to respond negatively.

An IAQC membership survey conducted by Jack ReVelle, then the head of Statistical Service at the Hughes Aircraft Company, found that a majority of the membership responded positively to having the association "focus on all forms of EI including quality circles" instead of focusing only on circles. Moreover, ReVelle found a strong positive correlation with the respondents' personal experiences with circles. The longer one's personal experience with circles, the greater the preference for focusing on all forms of EI including quality circles. The results of this survey were published in the association's journal in December 1985, before the board was to make its final decision (ReVelle 1985:26–29). These kinds of data gave the board some additional confidence in the new directions.

The formal report of the strategic planning committee was approved by a unanimous vote of the board in April 1986. In July 1986 the board formally approved as a separate item the mission statement contained in the final report of the strategic planning committee. This statement was subsequently streamlined in February 1987 to read:

The IAQC is an educational organization that serves its members and the nation through addressing all forms of participation. The IAQC will contribute to the growth of state-of-the-art ideas and practices that involve managers and workers so as to:

—Develop individual and group abilities;

—Improve the quality and productivity of organizations;

—Improve work morale, teamwork and communication and;

—Increase participation in workplace ownership and decision making.

The strategic planning committee proposed a variety of specific actions for each area of the organization to implement the mission statement. The most controversial of those proved to be, as one might expect, a name change for the organization. Survey data from the membership showed a slight majority in favor of a name change, but with stronger support for a name change among those with the longest personal experience with circles. Yet even among supporters there was little agreement on what the new name should be, and opponents of overall change were particularly adamant about not changing the name. It was not until June 1987 that the board formally voted to change the organization's name to the Association for Quality and Participation. Many of the planning committee's recommendations became the presidential charges issued to each committee in 1986–87, discussed above. Some recommendations, such as the one that the organization develop a mechanism for generating its own state-of-the-art training materials, were, as we have seen, simply ignored.

In anticipation of the directions suggested by the strategic planning committee and, more important, in response to market pressures, the IAQC had begun as early as 1985 to significantly expand the content of its conferences and journal to reflect the broad employee-involvement theme. It also co-produced a video on self-managing teams. Yet critics of this expanded mission were quite right in questioning whether the IAQC had the expertise to make a significant contribution in this area, especially given the existence of other associations such as the American Society for Training and Development and the OD Network. The strategic planning committee argued that the association did indeed have a contribution to make, but that remains to be seen.

An Evaluation of the IAQC

How are we to evaluate the eleven-year history of the IAQC? The greatest challenge facing small new organizations after their founding is survival, with growth a distant second. By these measures, and they are important measures, the IAQC achieved an outstanding success. With a band of volunteers and an office staff that suffered from high turnover, particularly in the executive director's position, it nevertheless not only survived but grew to a total of 5,605 members (individual + organizational + circles) by 1988. The volunteer contribution, especially during crises, brought forth impressive efforts on the part, not only of many board members, but also of the staff (who worked long hours for which they were not always paid) and chapter-level personnel. As trite as it may sound, it is amazing what individuals motivated by an idea can accomplish. Nor is this simply a matter of board members contributing extra time during a crisis. In late 1983 the IAQC estimated that over eight hundred members were involved in some type of volunteer role beyond simple membership. This included service as board members, committee members, chapter officers, conference workers or speakers, and special-interest-group leaders. The creation of an organization providing the motivation for such an outpouring of voluntary activities is not to be taken for granted. All these services and activities are significant organizational achievements.

The Institute for Policy Research of the University of Cincinnati conducted an extensive member survey for the IAQC in 1986–87 (University of Cincinnati 1987). It found that IAQC members were generally satisfied with the benefits they were receiving and the services provided to them. Members joined to stay informed and believed the IAQC was reasonably effective in meeting that objective. They described the most important benefits provided by the IAQC as the national conference, the *Quality Circles Journal,* and chapter activities, and they reported being generally satisfied with these services.

Yet the limitations of the IAQC's achievements are, in the end, far greater. It has in effect carved out a relatively narrow niche in the market for employee involvement. Its membership is small relative to the number of those that are and could be engaging in organizational changes of this nature. Most organizations actively engaged in employee involvement see little need for the services of the IAQC, and there are many more that are not yet engaged in an active organizational change involving small-group activities. The high annual nonrenewal rate of the organization suggests a rather weak set of links between the organization and its members.

What comes through strongly in the preceding historical account is the way in which the IAQC again and again squandered substantial resources, and in so doing lost opportunities to possibly make a major mark on the way American business is organized. The amateurish nature of the decision-making process—and, in one major case, fraud—defeated the IAQC again and again. The middle- and lower-level management personnel on the board simply lacked the skills and access to resources necessary for running such a complex national organization. For all the strength of voluntary labor, it is typically inconsistent and unreliable. Members' efforts all too often depended on the whims of company superiors who chose to support or not support individual employee involvement with the IAQC. Job changes often led to a withdrawal of services.

After endless discussions and meetings, the drive toward creating an organization that collected, analyzed, and integrated data and fed back best practices to the membership was defeated. In its place was a conference-driven organization moving increasingly toward distribution and lacking a core competency to design and generate its own materials and training. A simplistic interpretation of my argument would cast the consultants as the bad guys. It was they, after all, who gradually wore down the company people and whittled away at what core competencies the IAQC may have had. As appealing as this explanation might appear, however, the matter is far more complex than that for a variety of reasons.

First, it is important to clarify what we mean by the term *consultant*. In large companies, there are internal consultants who are also members of the IAQC, who perform at least some roles quite similar to those of external consultants. Moreover, it is not a matter of being or not being a consultant. A number of board members actively gave lectures, and some provided in-house consulting, while serving as regular employees of their firms. In my operational definition a consultant was an individual who derived 50 percent or more of his or her income from external consulting on a contractual basis for specific firms. Yet many board members whom I have not classified as consultants profited in monetary and career terms from their membership on the board through the visibility and legitimacy it gave them. Many board members thus had economic incentives associated with their IAQC activities. Conversely, a number of consultants devoted considerable efforts to IAQC activities that did not have visible economic benefits. They provided an energy and expertise that was not always available from the volunteer company employees. It is reasonable to suggest, however, that the greater the economic returns, present and expected, from consulting, the greater the expectation that it would lead to specific and associated patterns of action.

With these considerations in mind, we may clarify matters by asking what the ideal role of an association would be in terms of a consultant's economic interests. While many IAQC members may have economic interests in pursuing IAQC involvement, in what systematic directions would consultants like to have the association move?

First, they would like the association to have a high degree of legitimacy in the eyes of its members. Second, the association should ideally minimize transaction costs for consultants by enabling them to contact potential customers and providing a means for them to establish their credentials and secure the customer's business. Association conferences are thus an important element, insofar as they can be structured to highlight the wares of consultant members and bring potential buyers and sellers together at one time and place. Third, association activities should be limited to areas where consultants cannot make a market.

From this description, it is apparent that the consultants associated with the IAQC were not acting in an unusual or unexpected fashion; they were just pursuing their economic interests. It would be surprising if they had acted otherwise. The discussion also shows that the consultants were quite successful by the mid 1980s in turning the IAQC into an "ideal" association from their point of view. They were not entirely successful, however, because of a latent contradiction between the first criterion (maximizing the association's legitimacy in eyes of members) and the second and third criteria (minimizing transaction costs and IAQC competition). To the extent that they pushed the second and third criteria, they made many company-based practitioners suspect the purposes of the organization and therefore its products.

The consultants were also not entirely successful because there was continued modest resistance on the board to fully capitulating to their views. I have already mentioned the proposal to jointly develop new training materials with two large companies. In addition, in early 1989 one of the co-founders criticized the association for bidding on an "in-house" company contract that was in compe-

tition with him. At this time the board was also still trying to resolve the dilemma of how to distribute an association membership
list without sending copies to consultant members who were also
competitors. This was an issue that had been controversial throughout the life of the association. Yet, by the late 1980s, these areas of
contention were essentially peripheral skirmishes rather than core
stuggles. The consultants had clearly won the most important contested turf.

We have here a case in which the consultants in effect took over
the associational alternative and turned it to the service of their
own interests. In this sense, corporations needing small-group-
activities expertise were denied this alternative, not because the
consultants acted improperly—they were pursuing their legitimate
economic interests—but rather because corporations chose not to
pool their resources to best achieve *their* common interests.

We need now to ask a more important question. Why were the
consultants successful? Why were those pushing for a user-oriented
organization ultimately unsuccessful? The answer is that those arguing for a user-based organization were acting on their own individual initiative. They did not have the full corporate weight of
their firms behind such efforts. Their firms as corporate units had
nothing or very little to do with the IAQC.

In this connection the strategic planning committee received a
long letter criticizing one of the early drafts of its report from the
Memphis chapter, one of the very few in which there was a strong
corporate presence. One item in the letter stated:

We find that the Board of Directors is far too heavily comprised of professional management consultants. Our recommendation is to replace them
with professional quality circle or employee involvement practitioners.

They were right about the problem, but not necessarily about the
solution.

To succeed in its mission, the IAQC desperately needed high-
level corporate representatives on the board of directors who would
be capable of delivering the support of their firms and would have
acted to maximize achievement of their corporate interests. This
would naturally have pushed the consultants more to the fringes.
Indeed, in a few sporadic cases, such corporate support did occur
during Chavis's and his successor's terms of office as presidents of
the organization. In both those cases, that support made a strong

contribution to restoring the association to health. Unfortunately, these interventions were not part of a systematic pattern involving a large number of companies, but rather a set of isolated circumstances involving one company at a time. The significance of systematic high-level corporate involvement for diffusing small-group activity will become apparent in my subsequent discussion of the Swedish and Japanese cases.

An alternative model for limiting the role of consultants would have been for the evolving body of knowledge associated with QC circles to have crystallized into a system of professional norms. The association's rhetoric showed that the aspirations of IAQC leaders were for it to become a professional association. Yet the probability of that happening was quite low in view of the vagueness of the body of knowledge associated with quality-circle activities and the ability of consultants to take control of much of that knowledge. This was symbolized by the debate over certification and the inability of the association to proceed with it. It was easier for the consultants to capture this emerging knowledge than it was to create a professional solidarity among the various quality-circle specialties. This has been a common problem in related associations. For example, in 1981 the American Society for Training and Development announced that it was studying the possibility of certifying human-resource specialists. It further stated that the decision awaited the "identification of the core competencies and body of knowledge which underlie the training and development field" (American Society for Training and Development 1981). Had the incipient drive toward professionalization at the IAQC taken place forty years earlier, when the model of professional societies was more clear-cut and the consulting business form was less well developed, perhaps the IAQC would have had a better chance of becoming a successful professional society.

The Liability of Newness

A different slant on these phenomena can be obtained by examining the typical liabilities associated with new organizations, and especially with small new ones. This analysis will parallel the exploration of the liabilities imposed by organizational aging on the ability of the ASQC to adapt to new circumstances. Aldrich and Auster

(1986) list the following factors as the major ones causing failure among small new organizations: barriers to entry, problems of establishing legitimacy, difficulty of creating and clarifying roles and structures consistent with external constraints, and difficulty of attracting qualified employees. We shall consider each of these. The issue with the IAQC was not a failure to survive but rather a failure to achieve its lofty goals as the primary diffusion agent for a rapidly growing national quality-circle movement.

We have seen that barriers to entry were far less significant problems for the IAQC than is often the case for new bodies. Because of the national wave of interest in quality circles, the lack of established competitors, and the relatively low entry costs associated with the generation of materials and training, the IAQC was able to become a force to be reckoned with in the early years of the quality-circle movement. The market was growing so rapidly that almost any credible entry could do well despite a lot of mistakes. And the IAQC did make a lot of mistakes.

Legitimacy, on the other hand, was a much more complex problem for the IAQC. Initially, the two consultant co-founders had in their favor their Lockheed quality-circle experience, which gave them some credibility as one of the early quality-circle success stories. At the same time, their consulting background made their motives suspect to many company employees who were potential members of the IAQC and purchasers of its services. There is some indication that they were aware of the problem and tried to blunt it. From the very first issue of the *Quality Circle Quarterly* in the second quarter of 1978, they described the IAQC as a nonprofit organization (see appendix D). Yet, as I noted, state registration as a not-for-profit organization was to elude the IAQC until February 1981, and it did not receive IRS status as a 501(C) (3) organization until September 1982.

This discrepancy symbolized what was a major dilemma for the IAQC in its early years and, as we have seen, continues to be an issue facing the association. Whatever else the new organization did, it kept the names of Dewar and Beardsley visible and therefore made its links to their consulting businesses visible as well. While this was an asset to the two co-founders, it stood in the way of the new organization acquiring legitimacy. If it was seen by outsiders as just a front for the consulting businesses of the two founders, it would have difficulty achieving its announced objectives. Use of terms like "nonprofit" tended to blur such distinctions. With the shift to an elected board, the association began to distance itself from the co-founders. The repeated rejection of one of the co-founders in his attempts to win the presidency is an indication of the efforts of the board to outgrow the association's origins. A number of influential company employees sought to restrict consultants' influence. Yet with the great economic incentives to join the board and/or to become a consultant, there was a steady stream of consultants either elected to the board or coopted as mid-term "conversions." Despite some slackening of movement in this direction as the quality-circle "boom" faded in the mid 1980s, this culminated in 1987 with the election of a consultant to the presidency, the first since the elected board had chosen a president in 1981. Efforts to shake the image of the organization as serving the interests of consultants and develop a professional image thus met with limited success. If legitimacy was to be found in an image of the IAQC as a professional organization, it has yet to be achieved.

Yet what was most lacking in the efforts of the IAQC to acquire legitimacy was top management participation on the board (not just as an occasional president of the association) and the announced support by major business organizations of the IAQC and its objectives. The IAQC had no friendly parental unit seeing to it that doors were opened and the resources it needed made available. We shall see in the next two chapters that the national organizations in Japan and Sweden did have such support. Recent research on volunteer social service organizations has shown that external legitimacy as measured by supportive relationships with other significant organizations is critical to the survival of new organizations (Singh et al. 1986:171–93). In particular, endorsement by powerful institutional actors can have a strong impact on the success of new organizations. There was a failure to use board membership effectively to co-opt important external constituencies and thereby gain access to more resources. All this would have contributed to establishing organizational legitimacy (see Singh et al. 1986:177). As still another alternative, mergers with existing established organizations also have some potential for producing a similar outcome, but such mergers never became a high priority for either the IAQC or its potential partners.

A broad top management presence on the board or support from friendly influential business associations could have bestowed legitimacy on the organization. It would have reflected shared corporate interests in the IAQC's outputs and encouraged its development of valued assets. Instead, the prominent role of consultants and the squandering of resources and opportunities resulting from mismanagement (and from outright embezzlement), which tarnished the image of the association, showed in the end top management's lack of commitment to the quality-circle movement. Middle and lower-level managers on the board acting on their own initiative simply did not have the contacts and the expertise to operate effectively and thereby realize the organization's dream of leading American industry to a full commitment to quality circles.

A good example of the problem was the association's experience with executive seminars. The failure of these seminars to gain participation by top management reflected both the latter's agenda and the inability of the middle-management board to attract its interest. When the board did briefly attract a top manager to its presidency in 1986, he proposed that one of the leading CEOs with experience in quality circles in each city the seminar was held in be put on the program. As he put it: "If there is one thing CEOs like to do, it is to listen to other CEOs." Whether or not this would have worked, or will work in the future, it shows the benefit of having someone on the board who understands top management's thinking. Without such a presence, the IAQC was hard put to acquire legitimacy among top managers.

Though not a major factor, an additional aspect of the IAQC's quest for legitimacy lay in its insensitivity to union concerns that they be legitimate partners in quality circles in their plants and that circles not be a part of union-busting activities. This was just one additional hurdle that the IAQC failed to jump.

Among the internal liabilities facing new organizations, Aldrich and Auster (1986: 179) also list the difficulty of creating and clarifying roles and structures consistent with external constraints. This clearly proved a major problem for the IAQC and on several occasions almost led to its demise. In its brief existence, the IAQC has witnessed rapid changes in its external environment in terms of competitors for training and materials and the extent of managerial interest in circles. These changes had major implications for its roles, structures, and revenue-generating ability. The organization had enormous difficulty in adjusting to these rapid changes. There is every reason to think that had the board been composed of higher-level, more experienced managers, with access to outside corporate resources and representing corporate concerns, these adjustment problems would have been mitigated.

Another problem faced by new organizations, according to Aldrich and Auster, is the difficulty of attracting qualified employees and training them. They cannot offer much in the way of internal promotion and security of tenure, and training resources are modest. While one can document such problems in the IAQC as well, a prior, more elementary problem was the difficulty it had in simply screening new employees. The lack of resources, and often time, to adequately recruit and select new employees was part of the problem. The other part was the difficulty the IAQC had in applying the proper criteria. The insistence in the early days that executive directors come from a quality-circle background, and giving that priority over management skills, limited the pool from which the association could draw and the expertise it could draw upon. These problems are quite common in new organizations. Moreover, in voluntary associations, we may add to this the unique problem that derives from the difficulty such organizations have in turning down volunteers for jobs. Some of these volunteers may not be qualified to do the job or have personal economic motives for volunteering that distort organizational objectives.

The squandering of resources, the failure of managerial decision making, and the ascendancy of consultants' interests at the IAQC all showed the absence of corporate interest in the fate of the association and, ultimately, in the fate of quality circles. It is for this reason that I said earlier that those who read this historical account of the IAQC as an indictment of consultants will have misunderstood a complex equation. The historical experience of the IAQC as the embodiment of the emergent national infrastructure for diffusing small-group activities in America teaches us a great deal. It failed in its attempt to lead a national diffusion effort above all because it lacked the support of the national business community and the corporate resources that it could have brought to bear on the tasks at hand. Top management in America still was not persuaded that it needed to move in this direction. Those that were persuaded did not deem it in their interests to act collectively with other firms to pool resources to build a national infrastructure that would serve their mutual interests. This ended up weakening everyone's efforts.

Chapter Twelve

The Building of a National Infrastructure in Sweden

Look for a large tree when seeking shelter.
Japanese proverb

Small-group activities in Sweden, as noted in chapter 3, developed as a result of a national consensus: government, unions, and managers, all for somewhat different reasons, committed themselves to the worker-participation movement. They all became actors in the political bargaining process, culminating in key choice opportunities along the way. It was a movement that operated at many levels in many forms. Direct workshop participation through small-group activity was only one of many solutions. It was a solution, however, that had the support of all major actors in the late 1960s. This support was later diluted as the unions explored other directions and the Social Democrats lost their position as the ruling party in 1976–82. It was not until the mid 1980s that a reconstitution of common interests among the various parties began once again to take shape.

The broad level of consensus, especially in the early years, conditioned the emergent national infrastructure in Sweden. This consensus slowly began to emerge in the 1960s through observation of the Norwegian experience with autonomous work groups and experimentation in Swedish companies. Particularly important for the development of the Swedish national infrastructure for diffusing small-group activities were the experiments in the mid 1960s at the Fagersta Steel Company, where the engineering department, headed by Börje Strender, developed changes in work organization and the wage system to replace the traditional individual piece-rate system.

Employer Initiatives

The Swedish Employers' Confederation (SAF) is the largest organization representing Swedish enterprises. In the early 1970s some 30,000 Swedish companies, with some 1.3 million employees, were affiliated to SAF through forty different industry branch employer federations. Through this structure, and as befitting a "peak association," SAF represented its constituent members' interests on a variety of matters. SAF's membership accounted for some 40 percent of all employees in Sweden. Through its leadership role in the highly centralized Swedish collective bargaining system, SAF commanded great respect. When it took a position on a matter of national policy or identified an approach as best practice, it was guaranteed to be taken seriously by its members and other parties to the labor market. There was no counterpart organization in the United States.

In 1966 SAF established a technical department.[1] The initial motivation for setting up the new department was an effort to develop a workable strategy to cope with the problem of wage drift and, more generally, to build up SAF's own competence by adding personnel with production experience. Börje Strender of Fagersta Steel was hired to head up the new department, which came to symbolize SAF's new commitment to work reorganization and small-group activities.

The initial key staff were all former employees of Fagersta Steel. They were also all industrial engineers who had learned enough behavioral science to absorb the new principles of sociotechnical systems. This was significant, because as production engineers with long industrial experience they had strong credibility in industry. SAF's commitment to the new ideas was signaled by the technical department's sponsorship of the 1969 Stockholm "hallelu-

---

1. Thomas Sandberg (1982), provides an excellent description of the emergent national infrastructure. His observations, along with my own interviews of leading figures and additional literature on the subject, serve as the basis for this section.

jah" conference introducing the new ideas on sociotechnical systems, which triggered numerous initiatives in small-group activities throughout Swedish industry.

Consultants from SAF's Technical Department took part in over ten of these locally organized efforts and reported on them in a series of preliminary and final reports published in the first half of the 1970s. They sought to spread new approaches to work organization, including small-group activities, by publicizing each successful effort. Because of the national debate on work organization, there was great pressure on companies to innovate and to make their achievements public. Under these conditions it was hard to treat the new work practices as proprietary information, as many American companies (for example, Proctor & Gamble) have done (Thompson 1987:38–39).

From a scholarly perspective, these reports were often lacking in hard evidence as to the effectiveness of the new work initiatives. SAF's technical department made it clear, however, that it was engaged, not in scholarly research, but in purposeful selection of case studies ("demonstration projects") to advance the diffusion of new work structures. In response to criticisms from scholars in this regard, a SAF official replied curtly that the technical department was not in the business of testing hypotheses and theories, which was why the projects described in its reports succeeded.[2] All this stands in sharp contrast to the Ford Foundation strategy of using scholarly research to diffuse small-group activities.

Companies continued to come to SAF with requests that the technical department follow the changes they were instituting. That led directly to a sharing of company experiences. As the technical department accumulated experience and competence in this area, it began to grow, increasing from five members in 1966 to more than ten in 1970 and fifteen in 1975. SAF worked steadily to incorporate the new thinking into its various training courses (especially those for supervisors and production and industrial engineers). It acted to identify best practices in industry in the area of small-group activities (and other areas as well), generalize from these experiences, and feed back this information to industry rep-

2. H. G. Myrdal, "SAF's rapporter ingen forskning" (SAF's reports are not research), *Dagens Nyheter*, 22 November 1977.

resentatives. It sought to ensure that firm-level solutions would be "guided by imitation of one's neighbor," as mediated by SAF. This was the proven formula for pooling corporate resources in Sweden.

In 1975 the technical department published a report based on the experiences of what it said were more than five hundred participative work structure experiments carried out in several hundred companies (Swedish Employers' Confederation 1975). In 1979, it published its new factories report, based on more than a year's work with the participation of some eighty people, totaling some six hundred pages (Agurén and Edgren 1979). The new factories report had a significant impact on managerial thinking on how generally to approach small-group activities and factory organization.

In an interview with the manager of Volvo's Tuve truck plant in the late 1970s, I commented that many of the truck plant's approaches to implementing self-managing work teams were quite similar to those developed by SAF in its new factories report. The manager insisted, however, that they had not directly learned them from SAF. It was as if these ideas were "in the air." That they were "in the air" is testimony to SAF's strong ability to read the evolving management consensus and feed it back to practitioners. In practice, there was an iterative learning process between SAF and the individual companies.

In 1981 most of the staff of the technical department was spun off from SAF and combined with two other SAF-sponsored organizations to form the Swedish Management Group. SAF, however, at the same time kept a competency in the general area previously covered by the technical department by creating a small new section on "codetermination and cooperation." The Swedish Management Group described itself as a consultant group available for advice and assistance on any project in the field of management. An examination of the board of directors of this new group at the time of its initiation indicates that this was no American-style consultancy. The chairman was Olof Ljunggren of the Swedish Employers' Confederation, and the president was Rolf Lindholm, who had emerged as a leading member of the technical department. Börje Strender of SAF was also a member of the board. The Swedish Management Group was, in fact, a fully owned subsidiary of SAF. It was thus dedicated to serving the interests of Swedish employers as collectively conceived by the employers themselves, quite unlike the free-wheeling consulting firms that characterized the American approach to the diffusion process.

Joint Union-Employer Activities

Also contending for a national leadership role in the promotion of small-group activities were the Development Council for Cooperation Questions and its research subgroup, URAF. The council was formed in 1966 by SAF and the two major union federations, LO (Landsorganisation) and TCO (Central Organization of Salaried Employees, the major salaried workers' federation), to explore methods of promoting cooperation between management and employees that would go beyond the existing work councils. Börje Strender of the technical department was one of the SAF representatives. The council's research subgroup was put on a permanent footing in 1969 and named the Development Council Working Group for Research (Utvecklingsrådets arbetsgrupp för forskning) or URAF.

Managerial motivations for pursuing workplace changes have already been discussed. It was logical for management to seek cooperation from the unions in the context of the high organization rate in Sweden (95 percent of the labor force) and the traditionally pragmatic approaches taken by the parties to the labor market. It was also a strategy for avoiding government intervention. The unions' willingness to cooperate demands some additional explanation.

The highly centralized Swedish union movement has historically been uninterested in direct workshop participation by workers. Centralization developed in the post–World War II period as a combined union and Social Democratic Party strategy in which the union was responsible for increasing workers' share of the national income and following a *solidarisk* wage policy of reducing differences in income among workers (and therefore industries and firms). These objectives were seen as requiring centralized bargaining structures. At the same time, the unions left actual production decisions to the managers of private firms. As a consequence, the unions had become accustomed to centralized solutions to problems, and the role of local union leaders was considerably circumscribed.

The union leaderships' lack of interest in workshop participation also stemmed from the continual struggle of the Social Democrats with the Communists in the local and national unions over many decades. The Communists were strong in many local and national unions, and centralization was a means of minimizing their impact. Employee participation in decision making at the workplace, insofar as it was handled structurally, was channeled mainly through works councils. Yet surveys showed that the rank-and-file workers perceived little benefit from the works councils. URAF was originally established in 1968 as a way of combining shop floor participation with the works councils.

Clearly, the strongest galvanizing force that gave new impetus to union support of direct worker participation in the workplace was the two-month wildcat strike at the LKAB iron mine in December 1969. The well-paid miners were concerned about poor working conditions and their loss of wage advantage compared to other occupational groups (Hammarström 1975). It would be hard to convey in a few sentences the impact of this strike on the Swedish public, government, management, and unions. It attracted enormous media coverage, with surveys showing some 70 percent of the public in sympathy with the strikers. But this was hardly simply a strike against management, for the LKAB mine was state-owned. Moreover, the local union officials were portrayed as both powerless and totally unresponsive to rank-and-file demands. The strike and the public support that ensued were thus as much attacks on insensitive government and union bureaucracies as they were against traditional management. The LKAB strike was followed by a wave of wildcat strikes throughout the country in 1970 and 1971.

These strikes set in motion a national debate on the meaning of work, the proper role of trade unions, what employees had a right to expect from work, and the possibility of restructuring work and authority relationships. Media coverage was intense. Journalists like Göran Palm (1972, 1974, 1977) ventured into the factories and wrote about their experiences. An endless number of TV and radio documentaries and dramas took up the theme of the meaning of work and its impact on individual employees. Newspapers ran series after series on the subject, and it was often the subject of editorials. Left-wing Social Democrats and unionists seized upon the discontent manifest in the strikes to advocate a larger role for workers (Karlsson 1969). This was the period in which radical protest was at its height.

It was in this context that choice opportunities developed.[3] Direct workplace participation by workers seemed to be a means to meet the needs of a disaffected rank and file and to redress authority relationships in favor of the workers. These were powerful factors leading to early union cooperation with management to introduce direct worker participation in workplace decisions. As befitting a national movement, this cooperative activity, reflected in the creation and expansion of URAF, was extended to white-collar employees as well as blue-collar workers and to both the public and the private sectors.

URAF's mission was to make clear what stimulated democratization of the workplace and what hindered it. Its specific objective was to initiate and supervise projects and carry on research. These efforts were anchored in "development groups" at the company level jointly representing management and labor. They had at their disposal the research results of social scientists and technicians associated with URAF. Using these resources, the development groups implemented participatory work structures. Most of their recommendations dealt with autonomous work groups.

Some ten key pilot projects were sponsored by URAF in the period 1969–70, which were reported widely and in a strongly positive manner by management groups and in a cautiously favorable fashion by labor groups (see, for example, Landsorganisation 1976). Yet by the mid 1970s the level of cooperative activity within URAF fell off markedly. Each party accused the other of sabotaging the joint effort and blamed the other for the failure to operate more effectively. It is clear that the employers' federation felt shackled by the cooperative activity and preferred that experimental efforts proceed with strong local control. It also felt that the research focus of URAF slowed down diffusion efforts and that there were strong radical influences from the union side. It was also the case, however, that the employers often had an advantage of superior competence over the local unions that they did not necessarily have on the central level (Hammarström 1978:7). Deriving from a mix of all

3. Andrew Martin provides a good summary of the background factors involved here. He makes a convincing case that union leaders were aware of a number of accumulating signals indicating strong worker dissatisfaction prior to the LKAB strike. For example, LO and TCO had set up internal groups on industrial democracy in 1969 just prior to the wave of wildcat strikes (Martin 1976:6–8).

these factors, the employers' federation increasingly shifted away from cooperative activity with URAF and turned toward local activities, using the technical department to set the direction.

Nor were the unions innocent in regard to the gradual crippling of URAF. As the momentum for change developed, political events required outcomes that were beyond the capacity of the early experiments in shop floor participation. LO was dissatisfied that shop floor democracy had not served as a stepping-stone to its goal of democratizing entire firms. Yet apart from this "official line," it is also clear that many national union leaders experienced acute discomfort with local activities outside their control. At LO headquarters, some initial supporters of the grass-roots decentralization idea were "reassigned."

At its 1971 convention, LO endorsed a historic reversal of its policies when it fully committed itself to the worker-participation movement, demanding that power for workers at all company levels be guaranteed. Although the program adopted at the 1971 convention called for satisfaction of LO demands through collective bargaining, it concluded that such action would be insufficient: "Accordingly, new legislation seems to be inevitable" (Landsorganisation 1972:58).

The new policy symbolized an end to cooperation between SAF and LO in this area. It rewrote the agenda of solutions and changed the locus of decision making. Initially the 1971 LO resolution was used as a bargaining ploy with employers to get them to move faster on expanding shop floor participation. The LO resolution, which TCO also endorsed, did, however, lead eventually to the passage of the co-determination law (Medbestämmandelagen) that came into effect in 1976. The new law provided Swedish workers and their unions with legal authority to bargain collectively over the full range of management decisions. It meant that a company could no longer refuse to bargain on grounds that the matter at issue was one on which it had the exclusive right to decide. It required management to initiate negotiations concerning important changes in operations such as expansion, contraction, and reorganization, as well as individual tasks and working conditions. The legislation itself only provided a framework. The detailed procedures by which this was to happen were left to negotiations between unions and management at the national and local levels.

It was not until 1982 that SAF, LO, and the salaried workers' union association for the private sector (PTK) reached an agreement (the Agreement on Efficiency and Participation) on a framework for implementing the new law.[4] For the first time in a national agreement, the link between corporate efficiency and participation was made. The agreement stressed that the organization of work should be developed to increase companies' strength and competence while simultaneously contributing to job security for employees. Jobs and work organization were to be designed on the basis of employees' needs and their contribution to a sound work environment. The agreement called for workers to be given the right to take part in the planning and design of their own work and to be given needed information about their work, as well as about the financial situation of the company, and for the unions to be involved in planning technical change.

Although the program adopted at its 1971 convention clearly shifted the focus of LO's energies to the legislative route, it by no means abandoned small-group activities. In the same 1971 program, it was noted that the democratic organization of work was a high priority for LO, and that it must be based on principles that met worker needs. It was in this context that semi-autonomous work groups were discussed and described in positive, if cautious, terms (Landsorganisation 1972:66–81). LO recognized that although national legislation was called for, problems relating to the organization of work would undoubtedly call for guidance (collective bargaining) from the unions and employer groups.

How was this recognized in the 1982 agreement between the unions and employers in the private sector? With regard to small-group activities, the agreement stated that "developing the work organization can, for instance, include measures to improve productivity, the introduction of group work, group organization, job rotation or job enrichment." Note that the term *autonomous work group* no longer appears. There is almost no discussion of how these processes should be generated; that is left for the local parties.

One interesting section of the 1982 agreement calls for companies to finance the union selection and training of internal and external "employee consultants" to advance union participation in

---

4. A comparable agreement was reached in 1978 for the public sector.

evaluating the company's financial and economic situation. We see here a union interest in retaining consultants so that workers get access to resources to match management expertise. Again, however, the use of consultants was carefully controlled to meet the needs of the major parties to the labor market.

That it took so long to reach the 1982 agreement after the legislation was enacted in 1976 reflects a variety of considerations, including the more constrained economic environment of the late 1970s and the loss of power by the Social Democrats from 1976 to 1982. With the conservatives in power, employers felt emboldened and were less willing to give in to labor demands; they did not have to fear that labor would bypass the negotiation route and enforce a legislative solution. The 1982 agreement only provided a framework for local bargaining on how to implement the 1976 co-determination law. While most sectors of industry have now concluded agreements, the working out of local agreements has taken longer, and by 1988 was still not complete. The language of legislation and central agreements has proved difficult to apply in local practice.

One of the hallmarks of Swedish trade unionism until the 1971 watershed decision had been that labor and management had been able to agree on and identify particular areas in which their respective interests could be advanced through cooperative action and remove them from the traditional bargaining relationship. Participation by workers in decision making ran the opposite course. It was traditionally a low priority for the unions, which adopted a cooperative approach, reflected in their setting up the works councils and later their cooperation in URAF. Subsequently, participation in decision making became a bargaining issue with the passage of the co-determination law.

With the waning of the cooperative approach in the early 1970s, legislation came to be seen as the key to making worker participation function by expanding the arena for union negotiations. There was a subtle shift from legislation being a means of achieving shop floor democracy and group work, as well as other objectives, to it becoming an end in itself. There was a sharp fall in small-group experimentation in companies throughout Sweden from about 1975 on. As economic conditions worsened, managers worried less about the labor shortage, and the original incentives for experimentation declined. The upward trajectory in small-group experimentation was not resumed until the early and mid 1980s. A variety of factors

were involved in this renewed activity, including the return to pre-
dictability associated with the restoration of the Social Democratic
Party to power in 1982, loss of fear by employers of the democracy-
at-work law, exposure to the Japanese model, and demise of the
wage-earner fund as a polarizing issue between management and
labor. Still another energizing factor was the successful turnaround
of Scandinavian Airlines Systems through a people-oriented approach that stressed decentralization of decision making, less bureaucracy, and a strong customer orientation.

One senses a continuing ambivalence by national union leaders
in the 1980s toward direct participation by workers in workplace
decision making. Many union leaders still see the decentralization
inherent in the movement as a threat to the centralized union bargaining structures that have been built up over the years. Consequently, they see it as an employer strategy to divide and conquer.
Although LO and TCO national officers still endorse worker participation at the workplace, they emphasize the intervening role that
the unions should play. Yet, on the local level the unions tend
to be fairly passive. Consequently, much of the initiative is left to
management.

In one fundamental sense, direct workplace participation in decision making has been a casualty of LO and TCO policy shifts, for
these shifts meant that direct workplace decision making became
only one of several modes of worker participation LO endorsed.
This broadened agenda of solutions brought it into competition
with the movement for board membership for workers and a variety of other representative forms of participation, such as expanded
works councils. Employee representatives on the boards of directors of limited liability companies and economic associations with
more than a hundred employees were mandated by law in 1973
(one of the demands of the 1971 LO congress). In principle, as the
activist scholar Bertil Gardell has argued, participation in various
forms and on various levels of the company is complementary. In
practice, there has often been strong union infighting over the pri-
orities they should assign to the different forms of participation.
The worker-participation movement in Sweden has been multi-
level and taken a variety of forms. This can be directly attributed to
union involvement.

URAF became a casualty of these developments in the mid 1970s.
Two consequences of its demise were first that the unions lost a

base upon which to build further core competencies in small-group activities. Secondly, SAF's technical department emerged in the mid 1970s as the key actor in the national movement to redesign the workplace.

A third instrument for diffusing ideas and practices concerning participatory work structures was the Swedish Council for Personnel Administration (Personaladministrativa Rådet), set up by SAF in 1952. In the early 1960s, it was primarily concerned with personnel questions. It was largely a consulting organization providing services to individual firms through its professional staff and associated consultants (chiefly academics). With the shift in public and employer interest toward participatory work structures in the mid and late 1960s, the council moved heavily into this area.

The council guided several important projects and played an important liaison role between academic research and managerial concerns (see Björk et al. 1973). In particular, one of its researchers, Reine Hansson (formerly of Stockholm University), played a key role by virtue of his acceptability by all parties to the labor market.[5] In the late 1970s, the council had some 350 affiliated consultants, who operated as external change agents responding to company requests for help on a variety of matters, including work reorganization.

Increasingly, however, managers and SAF officials found the council's recommendations (for example, sensitivity training) too abstract and divorced from managerial concerns and orientations. The council had few technical people and thus lacked credibility among plant managers; its ties were rather to personnel departments, which lacked decision-making authority. All this again had the effect of shifting the major thrust of employer initiatives back to SAF's technical department. The main part of the council was eventually merged with the technical department to form the new Swedish Management Group in 1981.

Developments in the Public Sector

One of the distinguishing characteristics of the workplace-participation movement in Sweden is its extension into the public sector, particularly in the approximately forty state-owned joint stock com-

5. Reine Hansson was one of my informants.

panies. Those politically committed to worker participation felt it was absolutely necessary to move the participation movement into the public sector and show that it could work there. The LKAB strike was an enormous embarrassment for the ruling Social Democratic party. The chosen instrument for removing this embarrassment was the Delegation for Company Democracy (Företagsdemokratidelegationen), appointed originally in November 1968 (before the LKAB strike) under the Department of Industry.[6] Its staff was composed of young Social Democratic radicals and academics who were committed to using the public sector to set the norms of participation in the entire private sector.

The delegation developed five projects in which it sought to apply the sociotechnical principles to ensure direct worker participation in shop floor decision making. One of the experiments (Arvika) was generally considered to have been a success and was widely publicized by the unions (Landsorganisation 1976). Three of the projects were considered failures by members of the delegation themselves.[7]

From the beginning, the delegation's activities were extremely controversial. Conceived in a political atmosphere, and with a staff motivated as much by politics as by organizational reform, they required quick and public results. This was incompatible with the slow, painful process involved in introducing and institutionalizing fundamental organizational change.

After LO's 1971 convention, union interest in the bottom-up model of direct participation diminished. At the same time, opposition from the managers of state enterprises hardened; they resented the public attention and the implication that they were doing things wrong. Opposition political parties criticized the poor financial performance of state enterprises, which came under constant scrutiny. Experiments were difficult to conduct under these conditions. Between 1972 and 1974 state enterprises effectively boycotted the delegation and union and political support dried up. It was no surprise that the delegation terminated its activities in 1975.

Although the Swedes have had some success in spreading the

6. A special committee (DEFF) was also set up for employees of the national government. They, however, opted primarily for a formal representational system of participation and will therefore not be considered further here.

7. Personal interview with Olle Hammarström, a former staff member of the delegation, in Uppsala on 17 August 1978.

movement for workplace participation to the public sector, many of the delegation's efforts can be seen to have been counterproductive to diffusion. It relied on external political support to carry through its program, and when the political support evaporated, so did any chance of success. Yet expectations for participation of public employees in workplace decision making achieved and sustained a high level in Sweden. Precisely because there developed a national consensus based on a public debate of enormous proportions, it has been possible to sustain some of the momentum.

In summary, although three major organizational instruments developed more or less outside of SAF, the nature of the developments has been such that they have increasingly played a diminished role in the diffusion of participatory work structures, after having been important in the early 1970s. When they were active, however, they did facilitate a pooling of corporate and union resources.

With the disbanding or playing out of the old organizations, the stage was set in connection with the 1977 co-determination law to create a new organization to deal with workplace issues. In 1976 the Swedish Parliament passed a resolution establishing the Working Life Research Centre (Arbetslivscentrum). Consistent with the Social Democratic Party's majority at the time, a major focus of the new center's activity was research and development in support of progress in the democratization of working life. Although established as a permanent research and development center financed by the central government, the center was under the common direction of the different parties to the labor market, with four union and four employer representatives on the board. In addition to conducting research on the workplace, one of its missions was to diffuse the results of its research. The center has played less of a role than many expected and SAF has been rather cool to its activities, seeing it initially as an instrument set up as a counterweight to its technical department.

An important strategic resource created after the passage of the co-determination law was the Work Environment Fund. This fund, which is financed through payroll taxes on employers, distributes some $80 million a year. Although it focuses on a broad range of work environment issues, a major thrust in recent years has been its program on technology and work reform. This program took as its mission the values on how to handle new technology set out in the 1982 Agreement on Efficiency and Participation between SAF and LO.

Thus, within the overall theme of technology and work reform, small-group activities are once again receiving attention. Representatives of SAF, LO, and TCO, along with the head of the Work Environment Fund, served as the program's steering committee. A strong effort was made in 1987–88 to present the various case studies (some forty companies and public agencies participated in the program) and diffuse their experiences in a series of national, regional, and professional association conferences. Moreover, a new "development council" composed of SAF, LO, and PTK is once again operative under the fund. All this means that progress is being made once again in building up the infrastructure for the centralized diffusion of new work organization ideas. One senses that it is a far more pragmatic effort than that which characterized the heady days of the late 1960s. In that regard, it may in the end lead to a more effective sharing of corporate and union resources to achieve common ends.

Conclusions

The contrast of the Swedish approach to the building of a national infrastructure for diffusing small-group activities with the American approach is striking. First, the small-group-activities movement in Sweden was embedded in a broad approach to restructuring work, one that involves all the major parties to the labor market. The approach stressed direct democratization of work relationships (sharing of power) in its initial stages. Secondly, the Swedish Employers' Confederation chose to support the new movement directly, and worked to gradually shift its emphasis away from democratization per se. SAF's support was manifested in its creation of the technical department, its participation in URAF with the unions (at least during the early 1970s), and its direction of the Personnel Administration Council. More recently, it has cooperated with the Work Environment Fund to rebuild a national approach to work reform.

Throughout the 1970s SAF's technical department was crucial to SAF efforts and was staffed by industrial engineers who had credibility with the industrial firms. Those responsible for new work organization at the plant level were often technical personnel as well. This pairing of competencies meant that small-group activities acquired almost instant legitimacy through promotion by a direct organ of SAF and its knowledgeable staff, who could relate to personnel at the plant level. This even allowed supporters of small-group activities to propose relatively radical ideas and still be assured of an audience.

One cannot help but note the contrast with the United States, where industrial engineers have been most notable by their absence in the small-group-activities movement, and where they certainly have not assumed a leadership role in national organizations or at the plant level. One reason for this difference was the success Swedish employers have had since the early 1970s in introducing new ideas about work organization in the technical universities. The notion of engineering as a social phenomenon with responsibility for introducing social change has deep roots in Swedish society.

Once the sociotechnical system was identified as a promising approach to work organization, SAF and LO pressured for changes in the engineering content of the university system. In 1973, responding to these pressures, Chalmers University of Technology in Gothenberg (the heart of the Swedish west coast manufacturing complex) became the first of the seven technical universities to establish a course on workshop organization as part of the master of science curriculum for civil engineers (including mechanical engineers). It became a required part of the curriculum in 1978. Gradually, all the technical universities came to offer this kind of course. Chalmers added still other related courses over the next decade. These initiatives by SAF represented joint corporate efforts to achieve goals related to small-group activity. SAF not only worked to change engineering education, but along with top management in individual companies also gave strong direction to engineers to pursue work redesign in the early 1970s.

Roger Svensson, an engineer who was among the key people spearheading the movement at the Saab Car Division of Saab-Scania, has described how negotiation of a new rationalization agreement between SAF and LO in the early 1970s pushed him in new directions. The thrust of the agreement was that engineers could no longer think only about productivity increases when they made changes in the workshop. Now they also had to think about meeting workers' needs, such as effects on the work environment and maintaining job security. These were new parameters, and he, along with some other engineers, was prepared to accept the new mission as long as the parameters were carefully specified. Svensson was later to receive national recognition for his contributions in this area in the shape of an award from TCO, the white-collar union federation.

In the case of Volvo Corporation, an informal network focused on changing the work organization and industrial engineering was formalized to a certain extent in the early 1980s in a special "forum for industrial engineering and work organization" (OECD 1984b: 14). The overall conceptual package that tied engineers into these developments, and for which they came to accept some responsibility in many of the large companies, was the sociotechnical systems theory developed at Tavistock. In many large companies, it was a loose alliance of innovative technical personnel, especially manufacturing engineers (*produktionstekniker*), that pushed the movement forward. Sometimes as in the case of Volvo's innovative Uddevalla assembly plant, which began trial operations in 1988, this group allied itself with union leaders to convince management of the need to break new ground.

None of this is to suggest that Swedish industrial engineers have overcome scientific management's explicit separation of execution from planning, with workers expected to execute the orders of a professional management. That heritage is still visible on a daily basis in every major Swedish company. Nevertheless, some headway was made among "forward looking" engineers who responded to managements' direction. That headway represents a critical difference from the development of the small-group movement in the United States, which for all practical purposes proceeded without the involvement of the engineering profession.

Why did the Swedes take such a centralized approach to the building of a national infrastructure? Why didn't they rely on individual firms, consultants, a sense of managerial professionalism, or some combination of these three, as in the United States, to diffuse small-group activities? At the most general level, I would stress that the market has not been elevated as the preferred solution to social problems as it has been in the United States. Simply leaving small-group activities and all the objectives they were supposed to achieve to individual firms or consultants was thus not seen as an attractive solution.

Instead, Sweden has had a history of decision making by centralized unions and employers' associations, as manifested most concretely in the tradition of centralized collective bargaining. Where they have not made centralized decisions, the unions and employers' associations have often sought to influence local decisions through activities on the national level.[8] The historical experience has been one in which corporations and unions alike have appreciated the benefits of pooling their efforts in ways that minimize transaction costs. It is also true, of course, that individual firms did experiment and act to diffuse innovation in their factories and offices, and that there was learning across corporations at the local level, but such local learning across firms was typically a haphazard process depending on personal relationships and chance. This serendipitous character gave it a "garbage can" quality.

To discover more specific historical reasons why Sweden took such a centralized approach to the building of a national infrastructure, however, we need to ask what organizational models were available to Swedish employers. What did they have in their repertoire that helped them appreciate the benefits of corporate cooperation and gave them a willingness to extend such cooperation beyond the obvious area of wage negotiation?

An early predecessor of SAF's technical department was the Industrial Bureau (Industribyrån AB) established in 1912 by the Federation of Swedish Industries (Svenska Industriförbundet). The bureau, in turn, created a special department for factory organization, whose purpose was to help spread the emergent "rationalization movement" whose godfather was America's own Frederick Taylor. The bureau specialized in studies dealing with all aspects of the management of individual firms with time and motion studies and cost analysis receiving special emphasis (De Geer 1978:105). It was initially a subsidiary of the Federation of Swedish Industries, which in exchange for a share of its ownership guaranteed it against

8. To be sure, such centralized activities have also met continual challenges. By the late 1980s the union confederations, for example, were having increasing difficulty in holding their member unions to national wage packages.

losses in its early days. This association was gradually loosened, but its significance for our purposes is to be found in the parallels it has to the structuring of SAF's technical department in the 1960s. It was among the "natural models" available to SAF. Indeed, in the spinning off of the technical department as part of the Swedish Management Group in 1981, there are further similarities.

What the central parties to the labor market endorsed typically commanded a great deal of respect among the participant organizations. This was certainly the case with small-group activities. This is not to deny that there were suspicious managers and union officials at the local level who resisted such initiatives. Notwithstanding, the new movement for small-group activities established its legitimacy from an early point in its existence; its corporate sponsors saw to that. To be sure, small-group activities had to prove their worth, but SAF's technical department and predecessors like the Industrial Bureau had a major advantage over an organization like the IAQC. They did not have to be continually concerned about how to generate revenue in order to survive and how to gain access to high-level corporate officers. They could concentrate instead on their mission of identifying and diffusing best practices.

SAF's technical department was not dependent on a large number of volunteers to accomplish its purposes. To be sure, it needed the cooperation of companies who would volunteer to participate in experiments and to allow the technical department to follow what they were doing. The technical department's central offices were staffed by professionals whose job it was to gather and spread the "word." The reports they drafted, by which they built up their core competencies, were not the product of volunteers who somehow had to find the time for them in addition to holding full-time jobs. Firm-level cooperators with SAF were cooperating as part of their jobs. In contrast, those company employees serving as members and officers of the IAQC who were able to write evaluations of quality circles were quick to turn to the commercial market to benefit personally from their knowledge. Three members of the IAQC board published books on quality circles in the early 1980s, all with commercial publishers.[9]

9. This does not include the consultant members of the board, most of whom also produced pamphlets and/or monographs sold by their firms.

I have noted that consultants were involved in the Swedish diffusion process both as agents of SAF and through participation in the Personnel Administration Council. What was the scope of their activities? A 1972 unpublished survey of SAF members conducted by the Development Council reveals that of the 628 firms judged to be conducting interesting efforts toward work restructuring and worker participation in management, only 45 percent reported using external assistance. Of the 280 firms so reporting, 70 reported working through the Council for Personnel Administration. As a general statement, it may be said that in Sweden there has been a tendency to minimize reliance on outside consultants to initiate participatory work structures (see Kondo 1976). Swedish managers have been extremely conscious of the well-publicized Norwegian experience. This literature stressed that outside consultants too closely supervised the experiments, and that this led to the participatory work structures never being fully integrated into company operations.

The most important observation to be made about the role of consultants in Sweden is that when they were used, their activities were typically controlled and coordinated by the major parties to the labor market. At the national level this control was exercised by SAF's technical department and the Personnel Administration Council. The 1982 Agreement on Efficiency and Participation between the unions and SAF also served to regulate the hiring and use of "employee consultants." The Personnel Administration Council, as seen in the data reported above, was the single major conduit for consulting services in the late 1960s and the 1970s. That many consulting activities have been channeled through the council constitutes a form of quality control by which the council, a creature of SAF, operated as a standard-setting body. Thus, we do not have the situation that we had in the United States of freewheeling consulting firms pursuing their market interests in promoting quality-circle training and implementation. Instead, there is an organized movement, in which the consultants act more as agents of the major parties to the labor market working through central coordinating agencies. These are fundamental differences!

In Sweden, unlike in the United States, we are dealing with corporate instruments (and in some cases corporate and union instruments) and all that this entails. These were neither volunteer organizations nor professional associations concerned with setting standards and individual self-improvement of practitioners. Instead, collective corporate resources were brought to bear on the problem of identifying, evaluating, codifying, and disseminating best practices. All this suggests that the Swedish model was a more efficient one for diffusing innovation, and there is indeed evidence to this effect. It stands in contrast to the more haphazard American model, in which firms, when they acted, tended to do so alone in pursuit of their narrow interests. Nevertheless, we need to be somewhat cautious.

The centralized Swedish model had a top-down quality and the various organizational instruments that were created were not mass organizations that ensured the involvement of large numbers of employees at all levels. There is an elitist quality to the Swedish movement for small-group activities despite all the rhetoric of democratization. To be sure, Sweden is a small nation, with most of its roughly eight million people clustered in the southern part of the country. This served to reduce communication problems. Even so, there is reason to think that a mass organization would have greatly added to the effectiveness of the diffusion process. In this latter regard, the American model, with its chapter organization and grassroots activity, despite all its other weaknesses, should not be treated lightly. SAF had eight regional offices, as well as its member industry federations, but these were not instruments of mass participation. This raises the possibility of combining some of the strengths of the two models, which brings us appropriately to the Japanese case.

Chapter Thirteen

The Building of a National Infrastructure in Japan

Two strings to one bow.
Greek saying

In Japan, unlike in the United States, but comparable to Swedish developments, strong organizations emerged to lead the small-group-activities movement nationally. However, unlike in Sweden, no national consensus emerged in Japan on the desirability of introducing small-group activities. Rather, one principal actor, management, spearheaded the movement. There was no national debate on the subject. A debate did surface among management and technical experts about the proper strategy to pursue, but this was by definition a debate of narrow scope and not always subject to public scrutiny.

Nevertheless, a management consensus gradually developed on the need to adopt decentralized work structures, primarily for blue-collar workers. Nikkeiren (the Federation of Employers' Association) played a major role in legitimating the new ideas on decentralization (see Nakayama 1972). Yet Nikkeiren and other peak management organizations did not play a role comparable to that of the Swedish Employers' Confederation in leading the small-group-activities movement; rather that role was assumed by more specialized organizations.

The Japanese Union of Scientists and Engineers (JUSE) emerged as the major organization leading the diffusion of quality-control circles. There were no serious contenders for this national leader-ship mantle, in part because JUSE had the advantage of playing the major role in evolving the concept and its functions. It created the very name *QC circle*. There are industry associations that have taken an active role in promoting QC circles, the most prominent of which is the Steel Industry Association, which promotes a ver-sion of QC circles called self-management (*jishu kanri*). The active role of the steel association reflects its history as a "national indus-try" that has traditionally cooperated on a variety of matters. That degree of cooperation has not appeared in the postwar competitive consumer industries like the automobile and electronics indus-tries. In recent years some industry associations in the service sec-tor have started their own promotional activities to develop ex-amples based on their own experiences (for example, hotels and the retail trade). Such associations typically hold their own QC circle convention once a year (cf. Lillrank 1988:202). Such industry association activities have not, however, provided serious chal-lenges to JUSE's hegemony, and it regularly cooperates with these industry associations. Alert to its weakness in this area, however, JUSE did begin in 1985 to hold special QC circle conventions for the service sector.

In 1988 JUSE reported on its survey of 590 companies conduct-ing small-group activities in all sectors of the economy. It found that on average 62.4 percent reported conducting QC circles, 12.9 percent self-management teams, 10.3 percent some form of zero-defect activity, and 13.3 percent some other form of small-group activity (1.1 percent did not respond). These figures, however, un-derstate QC circle dominance of the field. Self-management teams are, as noted above, QC circles that originated in the steel industry and have spread to other sectors, such as the construction industry.

Still another seeming alternative, the zero-defect movement, has been promoted for many years by the Japan Management Asso-ciation. It had a different focus, but gradually those promoting zero defects in their firms learned to combine the concept with QC circle problem-solving methodology. In this context, something of a competitive relationship existed between the two organizations. However, JUSE was established quite early in most managers' minds as the premier organization for promoting QC circles and was thus not seriously threatened. In the early 1980s, because of the growing popularity of QC circles, some other organizations sought to enter the market, but they were never serious contenders. The Japan Productivity Center promoted "small-group activities." In private, officials say that these activities are similar to those of QC circles, but they are careful not to use the term *QC circle* publicly to avoid conflict with JUSE.

JUSE is a national nonprofit organization dedicated to providing services to participating Japanese companies in the areas of quality and reliability. It should be kept firmly in mind that QC circles constitute only a small part of its activity. For example, QC circle–related activities (primarily attendance fees for seminars) account for only 18 percent of its total revenues. JUSE has no direct ties to the government. It is composed of university professors in engineering and science and engineers from leading firms.

Unless one reads the preceding paragraph carefully, it might seem that JUSE is roughly the equivalent to the ASQC. The fundamental difference, and it is a difference that goes to the heart of my argument, is that JUSE provides its services to companies, not to individual members. Indeed, JUSE does not have individual members; it has company members, who pay an annual fee to affiliate. Since 1973 that fee has stood at 50,000 yen a year (roughly $140 at the 1973 exchange rate). Only a small part of JUSE's budget has been accounted for by this fee (roughly 2 percent). Most of its revenues come instead from its training and education services (57 percent), publication sales (11 percent), and consulting activities (7 percent). By 1987 JUSE had some 1,800 Japanese company members.

How did this model of company membership come about? Do Japanese companies intuitively have a greater appreciation of the benefits flowing from such arrangements? If they do, it is in part, as with the Swedes, a result of their having pre–World War II corporate models in their repertoire. Prewar Japanese engineering and technology associations had both corporate and individual memberships. The same was true of the wartime Greater Japan Technology Association (Dai Nihon Gijutsu Kai). JUSE elected to have only corporate membership partially out of concern that few people could afford individual membership fees in the face of the drastically lowered standard of living in the early postwar period.

Of the eighty-member full-time JUSE staff in 1988, seven were engineers. Most of its work is accomplished not by this relatively small full-time staff but through a committee structure that involves a large number of university professors and company executives. JUSE has some 250 technical committees, and by the mid 1980s some 1,600 volunteer collaborators served on these committees. Of these collaborators, 35 percent are university researchers and educators, 55 percent are engineers working for private companies, and 10 percent are engineers employed by government agencies. Many of these collaborators also serve as teachers, trainers, and writers for JUSE in its public training and consulting activities.

The QC Circle Center is a unit within JUSE set up in May 1962 to promote circle activity. JUSE provides the center with personnel and office facilities, and the president of JUSE serves concurrently as president of the center, but its activities are entrusted to a board consisting of three chief directors. In 1979 the center received some $40,000 in subsidies from JUSE (at the dollar-yen exchange rate of that time), with 30 percent going for travel expenses, allowances, and honoraria for lecturers and advisors, 28 percent going to its publishing activities, 17 percent for director's and regional chairman's meetings, 11 percent for symposia, and 5 percent for subsidies to chapters. These ratios are similar to those of the mid 1980s.

In addition, JUSE provides a variety of indirect subsidies to the center, including the publication of the QC circle journal, *FQC*, and the provision of education and training for QC circle leaders and members. All these activities contribute to deepening the understanding of circles.

We can see from this description that JUSE and the center are more akin to corporate associations than they are to volunteer professional associations. JUSE does perform some similar functions in terms of providing opportunities for skill enhancement for those taking its courses. Yet there is little in the way of certification activity and no attempt to develop quality specialties as an end in itself. Indeed, Noguchi Junji, JUSE's executive director, argues quite persuasively that one reason for Japan's success in quality control is that it has never cultivated certified quality or reliability engineers; instead, quality control became general knowledge for all engineers.

JUSE does, as we have seen, rely on volunteer collaborators for its committees. However, these volunteers from the private sector and government enterprises participate with the knowledge that their employers are typically members of JUSE and/or the QC Circle Center and therefore strong supporters of their activities. Thus, as "individual volunteers" they are performing a corporate mission. Such participation differs fundamentally from that of IAQC and ASQC volunteers, who act primarily on their own initiatives.

Legitimacy, Engineers, Training Materials, and Training

JUSE is closely tied to business circles. Since 1948, shortly after its founding, the chairman of JUSE has been either the chairman of Keidanren (the Japanese Federation of Economic Organizations), the most powerful business association in Japan, or a former chairman. Furthermore, a significant portion of the intellectual leadership of the QC Circle Center has been provided by Ishikawa Kaoru, its chief executive director, whose father, Ishikawa Ichirō, was the first chairman of Keidanren to sit simultaneously as chairman of JUSE. These linkages have provided powerful legitimation for JUSE initiatives. It is an arrangement consistent with the pattern reported for Japanese trade associations, which are interconnected in a network of peak organizations rather than having the more isolated character typical of American trade associations (Lynn and McKeown 1988).

While JUSE did not receive financial support from Keidanren, Ishikawa Ichirō did help it gain entrée to companies by providing introductions to company presidents where it could plead its case. Ishikawa Ichirō also got company presidents to attend the pivotal lectures by W. Edwards Deming. In these and other ways, he worked actively to introduce quality control to top management and in so doing helped legitimate JUSE. Those who attribute the involvement of Japanese top management in quality control to Americans like Dr. Deming are ignorant of the close relationships that were established between JUSE and top management from almost the beginnings of JUSE (see Cole 1987). By the early 1960s JUSE had acquired a considerable reputation as the place to get information on quality improvements.

The significance of these relationships and JUSE's early success with quality control was that when it began to develop its QC circle activities, JUSE had already acquired legitimacy among Japanese top management. It did not have to fight the battles that the ASQC and the IAQC did. As JUSE was working with Japanese companies to spread quality responsibility to wider and wider circles of employees, it was a logical extension to push for the creation of study groups at the workplace composed of workers and led by foremen.

Private-sector and academic engineers serving as JUSE collaborators played a major leadership role in diffusing QC circles. As in Sweden, and unlike in the United States, high-status engineers were among the strongest proponents of the new ideas; this gave them added credibility. That collaborators in JUSE were able to foster these new approaches to small-group activities testifies to the closeness of engineers and operators in Japanese industry (Okuda 1988). Japanese manufacturing firms tend to place great stress on their newly hired engineers acquiring front-line workshop experience in their early years of employment. They are seldom assigned directly to technical and planning or quality-control sections at corporate headquarters or to the technical staff sections of factories, as is often the case in Sweden and the United States.

These kinds of experiences reduce the social distance between operators and engineers in Japan and make it easier for engineers to engage in the kind of social engineering that we see in the case of QC circles (see Okuda 1983). It is quite astonishing to see what such engineers have accomplished in the absence of a formal behavioral science framework. To be sure, Western behavioral science ideas, as discussed in chapter 7, have been gradually introduced to "make sense" of what the Japanese have been doing. Indigenous developments have clearly taken priority over Western influences, however, especially in the early days of the movement.

In April 1962 JUSE formally initiated QC circles with a new quarterly publication, *Genba to QC* (The Workplace and Quality Control), later renamed *FQC*. This journal, which became a monthly in 1965, served to provide a common language for all those involved in QC circle activity. It was designed to be read by QC circle members and foremen. By the mid 1980s, the number of subscribers stood at 180,000. Ishikawa Kaoru proudly spoke in our 1978 interview about how it initially was priced at 50 yen a month, about the same price as a pack of cigarettes, so that ordinary workers could afford it. "Buy it yourself for the price of one pack of cigarettes a month," was the slogan. The journal is filled with concrete case studies following QC circles through the cycle of identifying a problem, analyzing its possible causes, collecting data, solving the problem, and coming up with a solution. It also includes educational material on particular problem-solving approaches and testimonials. *FQC* serves as the widest medium for information exchange on QC circles.

JUSE and its leaders have played a particularly important role in the "democratization of statistical methods." That is to say, they have pioneered in developing applied statistics that workers educated to high school level can use in their own QC circle activities. Development and application of simple techniques like the fishbone diagram (which allows workers to array possible causes of a problem) and the use of the Pareto diagram (a vertical bar graph ordered according to importance of measurement value) allowed workers to participate in quality-improvement efforts. Value engineering and other techniques used by high-level engineering and management personnel in the West came to be routinely done by blue-collar high school graduates in Japan in the course of their circle activity. JUSE has played a major role in introducing and diffusing simplified versions of these techniques, which must be counted as one of its more important contributions.

JUSE has developed an impressive array of training activities and associated publications. These are important not simply for the expertise they impart but for creating a common language and problem-solving methodology that transcend individual firms and thereby provide a basis for intercompany learning. This gives employees at all levels of many different firms the motivation of a sense of participation in a common social movement.

To be sure, as QC circles grew, companies developed their own training materials and activities. While these company adaptations provide an important opportunity for local invention, and therefore local ownership, the basic JUSE formulas have been retained, so that cross-company communication and learning is not jeopardized. This retention is not simply a random outcome, but rather part of a concerted effort by JUSE. In the late 1960s, with the rapid growth of QC circle activity, the leaders of the movement became

concerned about "unhealthy" divergences from mainline principles. Consequently, they set about creating a standard text. The
product of their efforts, a 75-page text entitled *QC sākuru kōryō*
(General principles of the QC circle), came to be the "bible" of the
movement (JUSE 1970). It functions much the way any "bible"
does; it is the definitive statement of circle goals and methods and,
as such, it evokes the stock phrase, "When in doubt, go back and
study the basic principles enunciated in the *Kōryō.*" One of the
major themes is that QC circles function as a nucleus for companywide quality control (CWQC) at the workshop level. This is in contrast to the United States, where circles have often operated as
independent entities. By being linked to an issue accorded high
priority in Japan, the Japanese QC-circle movement enhanced the
probability of its success. One of the characteristics of CWQC is
that, in addition to QC being performed by each company, it is
"performed organizationally from the point of view of the nation as
a whole" (Kogure 1988:35). The reference here is to various events
external to the firm, such as the Deming prize competition and the
designation of November as quality month. Circles as a firm element in the overall CWQC movement share in this sense of being
part of a larger movement.

There is a dark side to QC circle activity being part of a larger
social movement that deserves exposure. One hears increasing
criticism among leading Japanese managers in the mid 1980s of an
"unreasonable" concentration on quality objectives by firms mobilizing employees to compete for outside awards such as the Deming
Prize and various zero-defect prizes. They say that these campaigns
lead to companies' pushing certain problems under the rug, coerc-
ing individuals, stifling discussion, and isolating those not seen as
cooperative. One employee recounted to me his disillusionment
when, the day after his company won the Deming Prize, all the
carefully kept records documenting quality improvement were
tossed in the garbage. Such outcomes are seen as increasing liabilities in the new age of Japanese leadership, when Japan is struggling to compete in employee creativity and originality.

QC Circle Conventions and Circle
Registrations

JUSE also sought to promote the spread of QC circles through a national registration system that began in 1962 with the establishment of the QC Circle Center. In 1964 it had over 1,000 QC circles registered, and by 1987 registration rose to some 250,000 QC circles. With an average of 8.1 persons per QC circle, the total number of individuals in these registered QC circles totaled over two million.[1]

The significance of this registration activity and of the QC circle conventions was profound; it meant that JUSE welcomed production and office floor workers into the organization and developed a variety of training and recognition activities for this constituency. *It created a mass organization!* This was quite different from SAF's technical department or URAF in Sweden, with their top-down approach, and from the ASQC, with its professional orientation. The IAQC took some weak steps in this direction, but these hardly constituted a significant initiative.

Since quality came to be defined as a companywide issue in Japan, it seemed only natural to the JUSE leadership and its company members to expand their activities to include ordinary shop and office floor employees. There was no professional orientation among quality experts to limit this initiative. Nor did a tradition of centralization of labor-market relationships, as in Sweden, prevent JUSE from building powerful inclusive local networks of activity.

In addition to welcoming workers into the organization, the system of national registration for QC circle members created a sense among workers in different companies that they were part of a larger movement. JUSE developed its specific educational products, such as its journal, *FQC*, as a means of expressing the concerns of the registered QC circle members and meeting their needs. One may imagine that the day after the monthly journal came out, workers in different firms all over the country could be seen studying it for tips on how to improve their QC circle activities. Of course, it did not function this way for all workers, but for those who were committed, it did indeed give a sense of united action.

QC circle conventions, to which diverse companies send circle

1. The actual registration figures overestimate actual membership because they do not reflect deregistrations.

members to present their problem-solving successes, were begun in 1963. Ishikawa Kaoru recounted to me how JUSE originally feared that company officials would not send their employees to such conferences. They were not accustomed to sending blue-collar workers out of their plants. JUSE did encounter some difficulty persuading companies to provide a budget for it, but the problem was soon overcome.

Because of the common framework provided by JUSE's QC Circle Center, workers from different firms were able to communicate and share experiences at these QC circle conventions. By 1987 a QC circle convention was being held once every 2.2 days in Japan. In the early days of the movement, the conventions were an important device for diffusing the movement through the procedure of inviting representatives of companies that had not yet adopted QC circles. This is still true for the service sector. For the manufacturing-related sectors, however, the conventions nowadays serve more to introduce new QC circle members to the broader movement and to reinvigorate existing QC circles by showing off new methods and applications.

The QC Circle Center's conventions are typically paralleled by company, plantwide, and workshop-level QC circle conventions. The functions of the company QC circle conventions are to provide an opportunity for management to display its interest in QC circle activities; to make the QC circle members feel part of a company-wide effort; to pressure QC circles to make greater efforts to achieve results within a given time frame by using QC circle convention deadlines; and to give individual members an opportunity for recognition (cf. Lillrank 1988). They also function as learning centers for rapidly diffusing generic methods and solutions.

The typical hierarchy of presentations would begin with an employees' work section; next would be the factory, then the QC Circle Center's branch or chapter. The most successful of the regional branches advance to JUSE's national competition. Successful company presentations thus provide a stepping-stone to presentations in the outside world at the QC Circle Center conventions. The latter allow workers to get off regular work hours and travel to another city, and therefore often have somewhat of the character of outings. Workers participating in QC Circle Center conventions thus tend to see them as a reward.

By contrast, the idea of allowing hourly workers to leave the plant during working hours to attend educational events continues to be foreign to most American manufacturing firms. It was not until the early 1980s that, partly under the influence of the Japanese, some innovative firms adopted this practice and began sending workers outside the plant—for example, to visit suppliers to discuss quality problems. But even here, these tended to be one-shot affairs devoted to solving a particular problem rather than regularized educational activities.

Grass-Roots Activities

Local network activities are at the heart of JUSE's distinctive success with QC circles. As Shiba Shoji expressed the matter to me in a 1985 interview, the local chapter of the QC Circle Center is at the root of the "creation of a new management culture." What he had in mind is that it is now hard to imagine running a large Japanese firm without such small-group activity.

The QC Circle Center began by building regional branches (*shibu*), the first being established in 1964 and the last, the ninth, in Okinawa, in 1984. The regional branches have representatives from ten companies on their management boards. These representatives offer free service to their regional branch in making plans, organizing, and administering various events.

The presence of such "volunteer" corporate representatives testifies to the overall support that Japanese top management provides for making this infrastructure work. Establishment of the branches was followed by the establishment of thirty-four local chapters (*chiku*). Except for large cities, the chapter boundaries typically coincide with prefectural boundaries. Figure 6 presents a simplified picture of the distribution of activities among the QC Circle Center office, the regional branches, and the chapters.

It is at the chapter level of the QC Circle Center that much of the normal learning about circles and quality control takes place. Each chapter has a senior executive from one of the member companies as its chairman, a board of counselors, and a coordinator, who is often a university professor (Lillrank 1988).

To say that QC Circle Center chapters are roughly equivalent to the chapter or section concepts of the IAQC and ASQC would be grossly misleading; the membership unit for the QC Circle Center is the company, not the individual, so that it is the local factories of

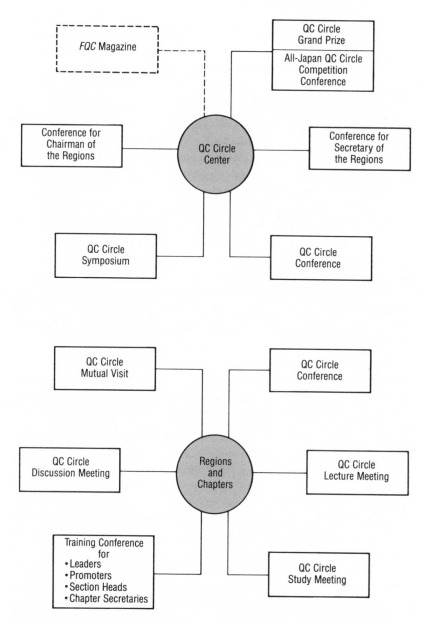

FIG. 6. Activities of the Japanese QC Circle Center, Regions, and Chapters.

national corporations in a given prefecture that typically make up the membership of a chapter. In addition to meetings of higher-level experts, many of the participants in the QC Circle Center's chapters' activities are shop and office floor workers joining in carefully orchestrated events. In contrast, quality-control specialists and leaders of QC circle activity typically comprise and attend the local chapter meetings of the ASQC and IAQC.

Each year, a different registered company member of the chapter is selected by the chapter counselors to take the responsibility for leading chapter activities. For example, in the early 1980s there were 36 companies of the total of 260 company members in the Ibaraki chapter who were designated to run the chapter (all of these are designated *kanjigaisha*), specially selected for the quality of their QC circle activities. From among these specially selected member companies, one company is chosen each year to provide overall chapter leadership. Formally speaking, the leadership role is filled on a voluntary basis, but there is a lot of "peer" pressure from representatives of companies that have previously filled this role for others to take their turn.

Chapter activities are numerous and demanding, and it takes considerable corporate resources and donation of services to staff a section. To begin with, these will include one or more managers to run the chapter, clerical help, and office space. Those running a chapter are, we have seen, part-time "volunteers," but come from the ranks of full-time company employees. There are over a thousand such part-time officers working in the QC Center's branches and chapters. Apart from responding to peer pressure, many companies report that their own QC circle activities were restimulated by assuming this responsibility; this has served as an incentive for companies to take on the chapter leadership role. Still, some companies do refuse to accept being designated a *kanjigaisha*, variously citing the immaturity of their QC circle programs, lack of suitable people to assign to chapter leadership activities, and their firm's difficult economic circumstances as their reasons.

Chapter activities include running QC circle conventions, arranging for factory tour exchanges, and various study meetings. It is through these kinds of activities that local users and potential local users learn from one another. When a company in a given region wants to introduce QC circles or revitalize its QC circle activities, it would typically turn first to the chapter-level personnel for help (see Lillrank 1988). The secretary of the chapter is also expected to aggressively seek out companies that do not have QC circles and try to get them interested through attending QC circle conventions and the like. In sum, chapter activities provide for a local information network among companies interested in or potentially interested in QC circles.

Large numbers of employees, including shop and office floor employees, are involved in these local-level activities. This is particularly the case in the QC circle conventions held throughout the country; in 1986 some 3,652 case reports were presented, and some 140,000 employees attended. The revenue from the QC circle conventions (workers' registration fees are paid by their companies) provide the bulk of chapter income. Viewed from the other side, the benefit of local chapter activities to the worker, and implicitly to the company, is that they give workers hitherto concerned only with internal company matters and specific work processes an opportunity to take a new look at their work from a much wider perspective. They also foster the feeling among workers that they have many co-workers laboring under the same hardships as they push forward with their QC circle activity, and this gives rise to a feeling of social solidarity and mutual development that goes beyond the company. Furthermore, these kinds of joint experiences provide for exchanges and mutual development among QC circle promoters in each company within the chapter (Sugimoto 1982; Shiba 1983b).

Two Days in the Life of a QC Circle Convention

To promote "feelings of social solidarity that go beyond the firm" means creating within each participant a sense of participating in a social movement. So that the reader has a better feel for how this is accomplished, I would like to describe my observation of a reasonably typical QC circle convention I attended in 1978 in the small provincial city of Nagaoka. The QC Circle Center likes to hold its circle conventions in areas not known for their QC circle activities so as to expose as many new companies to circles as possible. The Nagaoka meeting was the center's 710th QC circle convention since it began holding them in 1963; it was sponsored by the QC Circle Center in Tokyo with the backing of the Hokuriku regional branch. The attendance fee was ¥8,500 for registered circle members (about $35 at the then exchange rate) and ¥10,000 for non-members ($40). The QC Circle Center arranged for ten managers from different companies to attend as coordinators (*sewanin*) for the meeting. These individuals, typically with high-level responsibilities for quality in their company, are selected from among JUSE's 1,600 collaborators and contribute their services on a part-time basis with their companies' support. The QC Circle Center covers their expenses and provides a modest honorarium.

The slogans of the conference were "Let's take world quality leadership through QC circles" and "Let's cope with the new age through QC circles." The schedule for the conference was as follows:

Program for Nagaoka QC Circle Convention

4/6/78

9:00 A.M.	Reception
9:30–12:00	Case report announcement of problem-solving presentation
13:00–13:10	QC circle promoters' address
13:10–14:40	Special lecture: "Let's Cope with the New Age through QC Circles" by Mr. Ishihara Katsuyoshi, head, Quality Control Department, Matsushita Electronic Components
14:40–14:50	Break
15:00–17:00	QC circle public consultation panel
17:10–18:40	Social gathering: Nagaoka Cultural Center

4/7/78

9:30–12:00	Case report announcement of problem-solving presentation
13:00–16:30	Factory visit and workshop forum

The conference was attended by 350 people, almost all of whom were production workers, with some working foreman serving as group leaders. Only 25 percent of the participants were from companies without an active QC circle program. Most of this inexperienced group were sent by their companies to get some exposure to QC circles in anticipation of their companies possibly initiating QC circle activities. The average age of the audience was thirty. Companies like to send young workers who have not previously had an occasion to present their QC circle experiences outside their company. Almost all the workers were from the manufacturing and utilities sectors; they appeared at all public functions in suits and ties. There were few women. JUSE officials believe that female workers are reluctant to express themselves in front of males, and they have therefore been running QC circle conferences exclusively for women. Employees were present from competitive companies such as Nissan and Toyota, as well as from their respective suppliers.

The heart of the QC circle convention is the case report announcement of problem solving held on both morning sessions of the convention. Here a worker representing his or her QC circle will make a presentation detailing the problem selection and problem-solving cycle experienced by the group. It will also typically include a statement of the savings or improvements achieved. Most of the savings reported were quite modest. One typical group from Nissan Motor reported savings of ¥416,000 ($2,000 at the then current exchange rate). Often, the presentation was done in rather dramatic, if not melodramatic, terms, with the speaker describing how the group had been thwarted by various obstacles but eventually overcame them.

A second worker served as the prop person for each presentation; since 1975 overhead projectors with elaborate transparencies have become the preferred mode of presentation. Each presentation lasted just fifteen minutes, with a warning bell at ten minutes and a final bell. Few workers went over the limit, and most of those who did were less than a minute over. This indicates considerable rehearsal time. Indeed, JUSE publishes a detailed manual describing appropriate modes of presentation. Thus, the presentations are highly ritualized, though each QC circle tries to find some distinctive approach.

A coordinator chaired the session. Following each presentation, there was a five-minute question-and-answer period. Some typical questions included: When is the best time to meet, during or after working hours? How do you coordinate your "mini circles" with the overall problem-solving effort of the main QC circle? After the question-and-answer session, the coordinator provided a five-minute evaluation, which included complimenting the presentation; providing tips on how it might be improved, or on how the problem-solving effort might have proceeded better if a different path had been taken; or pointing to some important lesson to be learned from this report. The presentation closed with the coordinator giving some token gift to the presenter and with picture taking so that the presenter could show his or her work group, family, and friends visible recognition of the QC circle's achievements. The best presentations stand a chance of being published in JUSE's journal, *FQC*, and the presenters may be invited to the All Japan QC Circle Convention.

It was impressive to watch workers making these presentations. Some, reflecting their nervousness and lack of experience, struggled to express themselves in front of an audience of strangers. They forgot their lines and spoke hesitatingly. Others carried off the whole presentation with aplomb. Regardless of the quality of presentation, however, they were reaching out to people in other companies sharing common interests and experiences and, in so doing, becoming part of a wider social movement.

There were a total of sixty-two presentations at this conference, with four concurrent presentations at any one time. With two people required for each presentation, this means that 35 percent of the total audience made presentations during the course of the conference. This increased the sense of sharing common experiences; it was an audience quite forgiving of weak and nervous presentations, as most of them could empathize, having made similar presentations, if not now, then at an earlier time.

The special lecture in the early afternoon was inspirational in tone. The speaker stressed the requirements necessary for corporate survival as Japan entered a new era. Without such progress, the speaker said, Japan would find it increasingly difficult to export. Those companies that survived would be ones that cut costs and raised quality. QC circles could provide the vital margin by cutting costs. "Cost down" was announced as the new theme for QC circles.

The special lecture was followed by a break and then the QC circle panel discussion. This involved a number of the coordinators sitting on the stage responding to questions solicited from the audience in advance. After each question was answered, the questioner was asked if he was satisfied with the answer, and additional questions on the same topic were solicited. The questions were sorted into four categories—education, theme choice, operations, and staffing—and treated in turn.

A sample of questions asked included the following: How do you avoid ritualism (*mannerika*) in QC circle activities? What can be done about different levels of interest and ability in the QC circle group? How do you handle younger and older workers in a QC circle? How do you integrate new and irregular workers into a QC circle? How do you find suitable themes to work on? How do you find suitable times to meet? How do you combine men and women in the same QC circle? We have differences in QC circles' performances on different shifts in our plant. How do you level up performance in this situation? The company president told us to set up QC circles within each workshop. How should we proceed? How do you select themes in non-production departments? Should we have a unified theme for all QC circles in all workshops? We have a problem of the leader and subleader doing all the work. We divide the work up and give assignments to everyone, but it doesn't seem to work out. What should we do? How do you evaluate QC circle performance?

The coordinators had heard some variant of these questions many times before, and JUSE has numerous publications responding to most of them. The coordinators' responses were thus reasonably straightforward, but they treated each question with great seriousness and attention. At the same time that workers were getting answers to their questions, they were seeing that, regardless of firm, they had basically quite similar problems. Once again, the implicit message was that we are in a movement larger than any single QC circle or firm, encompassing the entire nation (nowadays, there is great attention to the worldwide character of the movement).

That evening a buffet dinner was held in a large room for all 350 participants, coordinators, and JUSE staff. It was designed as a tension breaker to get people to relax, feel at home, and develop a sense of fellowship with the people in QC circles in other companies. There was lots of alcohol, and people stood in front of the main table helping themselves to food and drink. After a short interval, one of the coordinators serving as the master of ceremonies offered a toast of welcome. A blackboard was hauled out and individuals and companies signed up to sing.

The singing started off with a company song from one of the auto companies, and soon covered romantic old ballads, folk songs, and sentimental wartime songs (just recently back in fashion at that time). As time passed and the alcohol took effect, more and more groups signed up for the singing, usually three or four people from the same workshop. Some voices were obviously terrible, but it didn't matter. One company official serving as a coordinator whipped out his old navy cap, which he conveniently had with him (it drew the expected laughter) and launched into a sentimental war ballad. A local company president after a pretense of resistance, was pushed forward by his subordinates and began his song. Other coordinators were also pushed forward to sing. They did so graciously. After two and a half hours of socializing, the social gathering closed with all joining hands in one big circle and singing the national QC circle song (which was written on the blackboard since most did not know the words). It was treated as a serious moment.

This QC circle song capped the theme of the evening and indeed the entire day; through QC circles, it runs, we are all, regardless of company affiliation, participating in a wider social world beyond the workshop. Barriers among workers and firms were broken down and a sense of fellowship established. It was an evening and a day designed not simply for learning specific tactics but to demonstrate solidarity in a common movement, with workers and managers sharing common goals. It was clear from the skill with which they managed the activities that the JUSE staff and coordinators had orchestrated such "spontaneous events" many times before.

The following morning involved a repeat of the announcements of examples of personal experiences. Attendance was lighter, as some attendees chose to wander around the city and relax. For the afternoon session, the participants were divided into six groups and loaded into buses for a factory visit, for which they signed up in advance. I joined the visit to a ball-bearing plant of Nippon Seikō. The factory manager started with a fifteen-minute introduction to the company, the history of its QC circle movement, and its mode of operation. We then took a thirty-minute plant tour. This was followed by a panel discussion involving twelve company workers (eight men and four women). One of the coordinators moderated the session, which lasted for about two hours, with the visitors asking all sorts of detailed questions about both work organization and QC circles in particular.

Once again, we see a situation created in which the participants in the conference were made to confront fellow workers sharing the same kinds of problems. It is hard to imagine a similar exchange of views on work in a Swedish or an American setting. While the IAQC typically has circle presentations at its annual convention, the audience is heavily made up of middle- and low-level management circle experts (especially circle facilitators and coordinators), not fellow workers. An internal staff survey of the IAQC's 1988 spring conference found that only 5.5 percent of the participants designated themselves as "team members." With few circle members in the audience, the circle presentations have somewhat of a "see what the animals in the zoo can do" quality to them. Moreover, the kind of regular factory visit exchanges among Japanese workers just described have few counterparts in the United States and Sweden.

By Japanese management's very willingness to invest in sending its employees to these kinds of events in a regular fashion, workers receive the message that their views and their contributions are important. Moreover, as we have seen again and again, they are told at every turn, in effect, that they are part of a wider social movement. As Ishikawa Kaoru expressed the matter to me, such forums provide opportunities for mutual development: "People doing QC circles are able to jump out of the well and see the broad ocean, thereby getting a bigger view." This is clearly one of JUSE's major contributions, part of a conscious strategy, gradually developed by JUSE. They were driven by a desire to create a mass movement (*taishūka*) is the way Noguchi Junji, the executive director of JUSE, expressed it to me.

In proceeding along this route, JUSE has contributed to enhancing the individual worker's sense of self-importance and dignity. Making the worker the focus of the QC circle convention leads workers to return to their workshops with renewed motivation to improve their QC circle activity. To be sure, many workers are not that motivated to engage in QC circle activities, and many never get sent to such conventions. Moreover, we might anticipate varying degrees of commitment to QC circles even among those who are sent. Overall though, the group that is sent to such conventions is a highly motivated one. To the extent that QC circle success depends upon a cadre of such motivated individuals, JUSE plays a major role in support of corporate objectives.

Chapter Activities

To get a better feel for the scope and character of these chapters, let us examine in detail the activities of the Kanto regional branch (comprising the chapters of Tokyo, Yokohama, Nagano, Gumma, Saitama, Tochigi, Yamanashi, Chiba, Shonan, and Ibaraki).[2] The number of individuals participating in chapter-sponsored events in the whole regional branch rose from 14,000 in 1974 to 36,000 in 1981. If we break this down further to the specific events attended, we find that QC circle conferences accounted for much of the membership participation. Ninety percent of the 36,000 attendees participated in QC circle conferences in 1981. The Kanto branch chapters held a total of forty-five QC circle conferences during the year (averaging five a chapter), and the regional branch held two. Together, these attracted some 32,600 attendees, with the average number of participants per conference being 700.

The remaining 10 percent of those participating in chapter activities attended factory tour exchange meetings, and study meetings for circle leaders, managers, and staff. For all Kanto chapters, this included fourteen leader training conferences, seven quality-circle promoter training conferences, six department and section head training conferences, six factory tour exchange meetings, five member company training conferences, and three other miscellaneous conferences. This breaks down to 4.6 meetings or conferences per chapter per year. In addition, chapter officials are required to attend a larger number of regional branch meetings.

Shiba (1983b) notes that the ratios of those attending QC circle conferences to those attending all other chapter activities was 65 percent to 35 percent in 1974. It moved by 1981 to a ratio of 90 percent to 10 percent. Shiba sees this, along with an overbur-

2. Most of the material on chapter activities to be reported derives from the research report of Shiba Shoji (1983b).

dening of local chapter officials, as a dangerous trend, resulting in the diluting of serious educational activities.

Shiba further reports chapter officials complaining that they cannot meet the new demand in the service industries for circle support because of their heavy burden of current activities. He notes that 89 percent of chapter secretaryships are held by individuals with jobs closely related to manufacturing; he sees this as a problem in responding to the new market demand in the service sector. He is also concerned that in order to accommodate the large numbers of people wanting to attend meetings, the chapters are forced to dilute educational content; he sees this weakening the link whereby experienced circle participants teach newcomers. JUSE officials deny these are serious problems and contend that the organization would not be growing if they were. What problems do exist in this area, they see as the growing pains of a rapidly expanding enterprise.

The critical point here is that this rich local network of educational and learning activities is conducted primarily at the chapter level. The sheer density of interactions is impressive. There is no counterpart in Sweden or the United States. The tremendous amount of learning that goes on across firms, especially among workers who are high school graduates, provides an enormous stimulation for QC circle activities, reinforcing them at every turn.

We can see from the above discussion that JUSE is very much a corporate association providing specialized knowledge, but it is structured as a mass organization and produces mass involvement. In this organizational framework and environment, independent consultants play an almost nonexistent role in the initiation and operation of QC circles. In 1976 one estimate put the number of external organizational development consultants in Japan at a dozen (Kobayashi and Burke 1976:119). While the number has increased since then, independent full-time consultants still play a quite modest role in Japanese economic life.

JUSE has historically designated a number of individual consultants as its representatives, to be assigned to companies requesting help. Typically, it has concluded an assistance contract with the firm requesting help and then paid the consultant costs plus an honorarium. In 1987 JUSE had 660 consultants, ranked into six categories in order of skill (360 of whom had capabilities in QC circles). Consulting services include diagnosis, in-company training programs and instruction, and on-the-spot instructions for implementing and sustaining QC circle activities.

Most significantly, JUSE consultants are not primarily in business for themselves; rather they are part-time volunteers who have full-time jobs with companies, government, or universities. Roughly 30 percent are university professors (engineers); 60 percent are industry personnel and 10 percent are government employees. The academics used to be a much higher percentage of a smaller number of consultants. But as the movement has grown, industry expertise has expanded very rapidly. Most important, as in Sweden, consulting activity is carefully controlled to meet corporate interests. Consultants are the agents of corporate actors rather than freewheeling entrepreneurs as in the United States.

Conclusions

What characterizes the Japanese case? JUSE provided strong guidance and coordination for the emergent QC circle movement. This governance structure allowed companies to share and build upon their individual expertise and, in so doing, to reduce the transaction costs associated with planning, adopting, adapting, motivating, and monitoring QC circle activities. No such organization has emerged in the United States.

JUSE's role exceeded even that of SAF's technical department in Sweden for two major reasons. First, JUSE succeeded because its activities were not contested within the management community, or by the unions or government; it had uncontested legitimacy. What above all sets it apart from the Swedish case and accounted for its success, however, was JUSE's ability to turn QC circles into a social movement. In keeping with the framework described in the beginning of chapter 8, JUSE was able to coordinate the informal interests of disparate individuals in diverse firms through the development of formal organizational activities.

JUSE's success in creating a social movement in support of quality circles is directly related to its QC Circle Center's unique chapter structure. These chapters, with strong management support, involved large numbers of blue-collar workers in regular educational activities. They provided a strong information network that stimulated learning across firms.

JUSE did not by itself create either QC circles or the social movement that drove them forward; QC circles were the results of individual actors at the corporate level forging corporate policy both in support of JUSE and in support of building QC circles in their firms. By correctly reading where these companies wanted to go, involving their personnel in its activities, interacting with them to develop and codify new ideas, training materials, and practices, and ensuring intercompany collaboration, JUSE operated as a powerful catalytic agent. Its accomplishments far surpassed those of its American and Swedish equivalents.

In the early 1960s Japanese companies wanted to find ways to involve workers and foremen in studying how to improve and design new work standards; JUSE and its industry collaborators responded with QC circles. To be sure, QC circles evolved into more than what had been originally intended. The present-day QC circles emerged from a back-and-forth learning process involving feedback between companies and between JUSE and companies. Finally, the development of QC circles must be seen as part of the process in postwar Japan by which the "distribution of intelligence" has been shifted downward to draw on the talents of shop and office floor workers. It is a remarkable achievement that must be recognized as a major factor in Japan's competitive performance vis-à-vis countries like the United States.

TABLE 5. *Comparative Aspects of National Infrastructures for Diffusion of Small-Group Activities*

Organizational Characteristics	United States	Sweden	Japan
Top management support	minimal	high	high
Type of organization	professionally oriented	corporatist[1]	corporatist[2]
Mode of participation	individual volunteer members	corporatist membership	corporatist membership
Structural form	decentralized association; chapter-level organization for experts	centralized association	decentralized association; chapter-level organization with mass participation
Principal strategy	disseminate information through conferences and journals; expert networking	elite researchers identify best industry practices and feed back to practitioners	create social movement through massive training and inspirational activities; develop applied statistics
Consulting activities	autonomous at high level	controlled at medium level	controlled at low level
Engineer involvement	low	moderate	high

[1] Includes a partial role for national labor organizations.
[2] Excludes national labor organizations.

Chapter Fourteen

Summing Up

In the end, we still depend on creatures of
our making.

Goethe

I would like to bring together this discussion by looking at the central characteristics of the respective national infrastructures and reflecting on their significance. These are presented in table 5. Through a comparison of these characteristics, we arrive at a more complete understanding of the evolving national movements for small-group activities in the three countries. This rough comparison of major characteristics does not allow us to provide a precise quantitative parceling out of the causes of success in building a national infrastructure, but it does present us with an overall gestalt. Moreover, it is clear from the preceding analysis that top management support from the major corporations is the key variable that conditions most others.

The United States

In the United States there were a number of potential contenders for leadership of the small-group-activities movement who never did quite leave the starting gate. The direct factors involved in limiting their entry were conflicting organizational agendas, inability to resolve organizational conflict surrounding diffusion versus consulting activities, inability to build local information networks, and labor-management conflict. The most important indirect factor limiting their entry was lack of top management support for small-group activities among America's major corporations.

There were, however, two organizations that seriously contemplated a national leadership role. The first, the ASQC, tried to move in this direction, but failed. Created on the model of the engineering professional society and stressing individual and collective self-improvement, the ASQC could not rise above its origins. Organizations created at a particular time tend to retain their characteristic form long after it ceases to be relevant or adaptive. Homogeneity limited the ASQC's ability to reach out to a new constituency, and bureaucratic inertia stifled those who were prepared to take the kinds of initiatives that might have made it a major player in the circle movement. Consistent with the professional model, the ASQC had individual, not corporate, members. The often unreliable voluntary nature of ASQC members' participation on committees and in divisions further limited its ability to move consistently in the direction of creating a nationally effective organization that would identify, reformulate, and disseminate best practices.

The second organization, the IAQC, was an entirely new body, established in 1978. It both survived, grew, and created an impressive annual conference, a reasonably effective journal, and an extensive chapter organization. Yet in terms of its public mission of becoming the national leader for diffusing the quality-circle movement, it must also in the end be regarded as a failure. Although it created a chapter structure for local information exchange, the chapters were composed largely of individual middle- and lower-level management experts who voluntarily met once a month in the evening. These arrangements limited their ability to ensure information transfer across firms among all categories of employees in a regular and systematic fashion.

The IAQC's national leadership, also composed primarily of volunteer middle-ranking managers, was incapable of establishing organizational legitimacy and gaining access to the kinds of resources needed to give it a central role. Its leadership was primarily made up of human-resource, personnel department, and quality-assurance personnel acting on their own initiative; neither the engineering profession nor union leaders were well represented. The IAQC had no friendly parental unit overseeing its activities and providing entrée and support where needed. Nor did it have a corporate constituency of top management officials who were fervently committed to its goals. In short, the IAQC was not an instrument of collective corporate entities.

This environment provided fertile opportunities for a rapidly expanding community of consultants, whose knowledge, expertise, and discretionary time all allowed them to see association activity as a business investment and to play a prominent role in moving association activities in directions that served their economic interests. The IAQC proved unable to surmount its consultant origins. By the late 1980s the consultants had all but succeeded in making it into an association to minimize their own transaction costs rather than those of corporations pursuing the adoption of small-group activities. The IAQC had become a conference-driven organization, and was rapidly moving toward becoming a distributor of consultants' products.

Ultimately, we can understand this outcome in terms of the failure of American top management to take a leadership role in supporting the IAQC or any other organization that aimed at leading a national movement for small-group activities. For most of the period in question, top management in America was not seriously interested in small-group activities as a solution to its problems. Even when more interest did develop among some top managers in the early 1980s, their firms were by and large uninterested in building a national infrastructure for diffusing these innovations. Without such involvement, the IAQC was left to limp along by itself, relying on inconsistent voluntary labor, subject to a lack of expertise and clout, and shackled by consultant influence. The result was financial mismanagement, including one large dose of embezzlement, and a relatively ineffectual association.

Sweden

The contrast with Sweden is quite striking. Small-group activities, a subject of national debate, were seen in the light of a movement to democratize the workplace. In the late 1960s, all parties to the labor market came to support small-group activities, albeit for somewhat different reasons. The leading national organization for promoting these activities was the Swedish Employers' Confederation and its offspring, the technical department. SAF was Sweden's peak corporate association, unabashedly pursuing the interests of its corporate members. There was no talk of creating a "professional association" in the sense that animated ASQC or even IAQC activities. Neither SAF in general nor its technical department in particular had individual members.

How Swedish managers handled small-group activities following the wave of interest in quality circles in the early 1980s provides a test of Swedish consistency in approaching structure. In 1987 the Swedish Quality Circle Federation was established. Its operating principles and structure are in keeping with our expectations based on how Swedish leaders treated the earlier movement for autonomous work groups. That is to say, they proceeded in corporatist fashion. Only corporations, not individuals, were allowed to become members (in late 1987 there were 130 member companies), and although consultants' companies are allowed to join the association, they are not allowed to be members of the board of directors.

The task of the staff of SAF's technical department involved identifying, reformulating, and disseminating best practices in small-group activities. This was done through following local experiments, distilling key ingredients of success, and heavily publicizing successes. They relied on a set of elite researchers interacting with practitioners at primarily elite corporations. Dissemination was also done through various training activities and seminars. The technical department was staffed primarily by engineers with "grassroots" private-sector experience who could communicate well with their counterparts in industry. This gave their efforts added legitimacy. More generally, as an organ of SAF, the technical department had almost instant legitimacy among managers. With access to SAF resources, the staff did not constantly have to be concerned about generating revenues and gaining access to high-level corporate officers. Managers in private firms did not automatically agree with them, but they could be assured of getting a hearing.

With the department's activities guided by a paid technical staff, there was little need to rely on volunteer labor. In a small nation such as Sweden, such a centralized group could be reasonably effective in communicating its message to all relevant adopters. However, it did lack a grass-roots educational organizational form like the IAQC's chapter system. As a result, it lacked a direct, systematic method of information sharing across local corporate entities and a means of mobilizing shop floor employees.

The two other relevant national-level organizations in Sweden were URAF and the Personnel Administrative Council. URAF, a joint union-management research group, did play a significant role in the early days and provided an important avenue for the building of competence in this area by the union movement. It had the potential to be a contender for the national leadership role. The decline in cooperative labor-management relationships in the mid 1970s led, however, to its being dismantled.

The council, primarily a consultant and research organization, was also influential in the early days. It was originally a creature of SAF and can be said to have provided quality control over consultant activities, which it carefully orchestrated to serve the interests of the major parties to the labor market. The council began to play a diminished role in the small-group-activities movement by the mid 1970s.

The decline of URAF and the council shifted the central national role to SAF's technical department, which issued reports and visions of the future (the new factories project in the late 1970s) that were detailed serious examinations of shop floor organization. Regardless of whether one agreed with them, they were documents that had to be taken seriously. Such a role was quite beyond anything the IAQC was capable of.

All this is to say that SAF developed core competencies (assets) in small-group activities that ensured it of national leadership. Despite the dismantling of the technical department, these management competencies were preserved with the establishment of the Swedish Management Group in 1981. The movement to reestablish a national approach to work restructuring proceeded in the mid 1980s under the auspices of the Work Environment Fund. Again, the centralized corporatist model came to the fore, with joint labor-management participation. These experiences contrast sharply with those of the IAQC, which increasingly moved toward "distributor" activities in a way that guaranteed inability to generate original ideas and expertise.

Japan

This leads us to the Japanese case. Unlike in Sweden, there was no national debate on the subject of work democratization, but Japanese management did gradually evolve a consensus on shifting the responsibility for decision making further down in the organization. QC circles were one manifestation of that process.

There were also, however, a number of striking parallels to the Swedish corporatist approach and its ability to establish legitimacy among the business community. While not an organ of one of the peak business associations, JUSE nevertheless had close ties with the business community, especially Keidanren, so that the legitimacy of its new Quality Circle Headquarters (like that of SAF's technical department) was never in question. As the foremost proponent of quality in Japan, JUSE was able to link the QC circle movement to further success in quality improvement. JUSE had no serious contenders for its national leadership mantle in the diffusion of QC circles. This was the case, in part, because it played a major role in evolving the concept and its functions, constantly developing "new products" in a way that no other national organization was able to match. Like SAF, it had only corporate members, and was thus not limited by the inconsistency of volunteer efforts. There were a lot of voluntary efforts at the chapter level and in committee activities at the national level, but these are strongly supported and stimulated by corporate support (especially at the local level).

In neither SAF's technical department nor JUSE was there any attempt to move toward becoming a professional association. Both were task-oriented in terms of spreading small-group activities. The self-improvement of individuals per se had little meaning for them. As in Sweden, corporate- and university-based engineers in JUSE played a decisive role in linking up with corporate engineers in the private sector to develop and refine the QC circle concept.

Distinctive in the Japanese approach was the stimulation of activities at the local level through JUSE branches and chapters, allowing mass participation in the organization. The voluntary company rotation in running the JUSE chapters on an annual basis is notable. Closer examination reveals that these voluntary activities reflect not only perceived self-interest but also peer pressures from other companies. It involves what Bill Ouchi (1984) has called "serial equity" and is premised on the notion that there are corporate memories. Ouchi refers to this as "clanlike" behavior. Regardless of the term, however, what we see here is a level of collective action among corporate actors at the grass-roots level that was absent in the United States and Sweden. It made possible a sharing of corporate experiences and gave those who were active in its events a sense of participating in a national social movement. This had significant motivational benefits that firms acting on their own in America could not, by definition, replicate. JUSE chapter activities provided a strong, reliable information network that directly and systematically stimulated employee motivation and learning across firms among all categories of employees. The Swedes, even though they proceeded along corporatist lines, did not develop such direct, systematic information sharing across firms.

The IAQC did develop grass-roots activities in its chapter activities, but these were attended primarily by middle- and lower-level management officials responsible for circle efforts in their firms. They were chapters of "experts." JUSE chapter activities, on the other hand, were modes of eliciting mass participation of shop floor employees. JUSE's distinctive organizational contribution to the diffusion of quality-circle activities was its combining of the corporate association form with the provision of specialized knowledge and training to a mass constituency. The organization was structured to ensure mass participation in its activities. It created a succession of special training materials, including creative adaptations of applied statistics for shop and office floor workers. There can be little doubt that JUSE activities building on this foundation were major factors in the successful promotion of quality circles in Japan.

As a leader of this social movement, JUSE stood above the pursuit of private economic interest in a way that was not possible for either consultant firms or individual corporations. Unlike in the American case, consultant activity in both the Swedish and Japanese cases was carefully controlled by the major parties to the labor market. Using part-time consultants from private-sector firms, JUSE managed to harness their experience without jeopardizing its organizational integrity. It also found ways to finance its promotional activities at the national level and its local chapter activities, so that it was not dependent on an ever-increasing role for the consultants. Education and information transfer at the chapter level was financed to a considerable extent through QC circle conventions, with individual attendance fees paid by the employers. These solutions seem quite beyond anything that the Americans could mount.

Final Thoughts

In summary, the professional orientation of the ASQC limited its ability to play a national role in the diffusion of quality circles. The

IAQC, despite some impressive achievements against great odds, failed in its mission to lead a national quality-circle movement. This failure, manifested in the dominant role of consultant interests, reflected above all failure to win support from American top management.

The Swedes had somewhat more success in building an effective national infrastructure relying on a centralized top-down model of corporate associations to accomplish the spread of small-group activities. Volunteer activities and professional development had little currency in this model.

The Japanese, in effect, combined some of the local-level activities of the Americans with the centralized corporate association model of the Swedes. In a stroke of organizational genius, they created a corporate association with a mass constituency. Therein lies one of the central roots of Japanese success and their ability to avoid a faddish succession of management panaceas. Nor was this approach limited to JUSE. The Japan Supervisors' Association (Nihon Kantokushi Kyōkai) set up similar local chapter activities for its first-line foreman members to teach them a variety of managerial skills, including, since 1975, how to manage small-group activities. They claim to have developed this organizational form independent of JUSE. Thus, we see an unconscious patterning of organizational responses to the task of mobilizing and training mass constituencies for Japanese industry. The variety of these kinds of organizations means that companies had a "thick" local network of educational and training activities involving their employees at the plant level.

There is one hint of the Japanese approach and what it could accomplish in IAQC experience. The Memphis chapter was generally acknowledged within the IAQC as its most successful chapter. This was the one chapter that had strong and consistent corporate support (Dover Elevator). Thus, when individual Dover employees took leadership roles in the chapter, they knew they were also doing the corporation's work. Such experiences, however, were the exception, not the rule, in the American case.

JUSE provided the guidance and coordination for QC circles that was lacking in the West. It coordinated the informal interests of disparate individuals and firms through the development of formal organizational activities. In so doing, it built a social movement. Joe Juran (1987:61) makes a related point in discussing the vacuum in Western countries created by the failure of recognized professional quality-control societies to take a leadership role in promoting circles. This vacuum was filled, he says, by company enthusiasts, consultants, journalists, and so on. Such a mixture was unable to provide the broad coordination and guidance needed for the QC circle movement to prosper. Based on my analysis, I would differ only in arguing that the vacuum was created above all by the failure to develop joint corporate action.

I have hypothesized that to the extent that major institutional actors, especially management, become strongly committed to small-group activities as a solution, a well-organized national infrastructure will be created. This hypothesis explains reasonably well the divergence between the American experience on the one hand and the Swedish and Japanese ones on the other. Without the support of any of the major institutional actors, little headway was made in creating an effective national infrastructure in the United States. Conversely, with support from varied institutional actors in Japan and Sweden, significant progress was made toward creation of an effective national infrastructure.

The American failure to successfully create an instrument for corporate collaboration to diffuse small-group activities meant that those individual firms that did have an interest in moving ahead were vulnerable to the garbage can model of decision making. Goals were problematic, the technology was ambiguous, and participation in the decision making to introduce and operate small-group activities often confused. Without a national organization to organize experiences at the firm level on a systematic basis, defining and codifying best practices as one went along, these problems took much longer to resolve. Small-group activities were often abandoned in response to frustrating experiences and unrealistic expectations. Quality circles took on a faddish character. To be sure, some companies persisted and, relying heavily on trial and error, overcame these barriers. The lack of an effective national infrastructure, however, made their task more difficult, increased their transaction costs, and reduced the *probability* of successful outcomes.

The Japanese and Swedish corporations, however, were more oriented to collective solutions to the start up, operations, and research and development costs associated with small-group activities. They

seem to have had a greater appreciation of the economizing benefits associated with collaborative activities than did their American
colleagues. Perhaps the norms, values, and practices in these societies did, in fact, yield greater economizing benefits from collaborative activities than would have been the case in the United States.
These benefits contributed to smoothing the decision-making process in individual firms, thereby reducing its garbage can quality
much more rapidly. This perspective builds on the reality of imper-
fect markets in the flow of information between firms and the need
to supplement them with external mechanisms that smooth the
decision-making process. Firms were guided by imitation of their
corporate peers as mediated by national organizations.

In their comparison of U.S. and Japanese trade associations,
Leonard Lynn and Timothy McKeown (1988) suggest that Japanese corporations are generally more oriented to collaborative research and development activities. This is not to suggest that American firms never cooperate on an industry or national level. This is
certainly not the case. The issue for future research is under what
conditions and in what areas firms are likely to engage in joint
efforts. I can only say with certainty that the willingness to do
so was minimal in the area of small-group activities in the period
under investigation.

To the extent that this collaborative tendency is characteristic of
both the Swedes and the Japanese, we cannot simply attribute the
results to the uniqueness of Japanese culture. Yet if we think of culture as accumulated historical experience, the Swedes and the Japanese share a common cultural orientation with regard to the benefits
of pooled corporate activity. In neither country has the market
been elevated to such heroic stature as in the United States. Simplistic comparisons that put Sweden and the United States in the
same "cultural camp" and Japan off to one side are thus misplaced.

In both Sweden and Japan, there were established traditions of
corporate collaboration. Corporate leaders intuitively appreciated
the economizing in transaction costs that would result when they
jointly pursued small-group activities. It is the American experience that appears unique, at least in this three-way comparison.
This way of thinking is strikingly consistent with the more general
analysis of Philippe Schmitter and Gerhard Lehmbruch (1979) and
their collaborators, who treat Sweden as a case of societal corpo-

ratism, Japan as a case of corporatism acting without labor, and the United States as a case in which the lack of corporatism needs to be explained. This way of thinking is also consistent with the observations of Max Boisot (1986: 145), who notes Oliver Williamson's belief that "federations" among employers are inherently unstable; as a consequence, Williamson focused on markets and hierarchies as being the most stable institutional alternatives for parties conducting transactions. Boisot points out, however, that by confining his analysis to the choices facing American firms, Williamson has limited himself to an environment unsympathetic to the "collusive nature of federative transactions," especially at the microeconomic level. In keeping with that analysis, the data I have presented make clear that Sweden and Japan do not share the American distaste for federative economic transactions.

It is apparent that employers vary in both the extent of their coordinated activity (high in Japan and Sweden and low in the United States) and the shape it takes (highly centralized in Sweden and decentralized in Japan). This variation shows the limitations of an approach that emphasizes only the economic factors involved in assessing transaction costs. Such an approach cannot show why employers in the three countries have varied in their willingness to pool resources to reduce their transactions costs for small-group activity. Rather, we must combine economic, social, and political factors to reflect the real impediments to such pooled activities. Thus, the joint associational experience in the repertoires of each country's managers, the extent of knowledge of small-group activities already in the heads of managers, the role of markets, managements' willingness to include labor and pressures for doing so, and the traditions of centralization and decentralization, among other factors, all vary by country. These variables become in effect "costs" and constraints influencing the managerial calculus as to whether to pool resources and, if so, how such activity should be conducted. Upon further examination, it also becomes apparent that country differences on each of these variables capture a great deal of what we commonly call cultural differences.

What does all this mean for competitive abilities? We cannot assume that such pooled corporate activity will be decisive, thereby leading to the dominance of the Japanese over their American competitors. Many factors are involved in determining overall com-

petitive strength; it is not just a matter of how a firm handles transaction costs (Robins 1987:68–86). Moreover, collaborative activity
that economizes on transaction costs in one situation may lead to
excessive bureaucratic burdens in another. We must be careful not
to overgeneralize from the findings. The fact remains, nevertheless, that Japanese firms seem to have been able to move more
quickly and efficiently in adopting small-group activities and de-
ploying them for competitive advantage when compared to those of
competitor nations. The data presented in the second half of this
book strongly suggest that creation of an effective national infrastructure played an important part in these developments.

Notwithstanding these similarities between Japan and Sweden,
we do need to highlight the fundamental differences that emerged
between these two experiences in this study. In the case of Sweden, disagreements among the major institutional actors about how
best to proceed and the emphasis on a corporatist top-down model
of diffusion detracted from the effectiveness of the national infrastructure. The uncontested nature of management interests and
JUSE's organizational creativity in devising a corporatist structure
with a mass constituency seem to explain the greater success of the
Japanese in building an effective national infrastructure.

One way to think about these findings is that in the period under
investigation the Swedes tried more and accomplished less, the
Japanese tried less but accomplished more, and the Americans
tried less and accomplished less.

Appendix A. Ford Motor Co. Policy Letter

Policy Letter

B-14

November 5, 1979

Subject: Employe Involvement

It is the policy of the Company to encourage and enable all
employes to become involved in and contribute to the success of
the Company. A work climate should be created and maintained in
which employes, at all levels, can achieve individual goals and
work satisfaction by directing their talents and energies toward
clearly defined Company goals.

To the extent practicable, management is expected to operate
within the following guidelines:

.   Management systems, procedures, and practices should take into
    account that human resources are among the Company's most
    important assets and that imagination, ingenuity and
    creativity are widely distributed throughout the entire
    workforce, as are dedication and the desire to contribute.

.   Methods of managing should encourage employe participation in
    identifying and solving work-related problems.

.   Communication programs and procedures should be implemented
    that encourage frequent, timely and constructive two-way
    communication with employes concerning work-related problems.
    Employe work suggestions and ideas should be solicited, and
    employe questions should be answered as completely as possible.

There is no simple or universal prescription associated with human
resources management. All members of management should identify
and evaluate available methods and employ those most suited to
their particular set of circumstances.

* * * * * * * *

The Vice President - Labor Relations and the Vice President -
Personnel and Organization are responsible for interpretation of
this policy.

It is recommended that all Ford subsidiaries and affiliated
companies adopt a policy similar to the one set forth in this
Letter.

Philip Caldwell
President

Appendix B. Ford Motor Co. Directive

B-103

President
November 5, 1979

Chairman of the Board
Executive Vice Presidents
Vice Presidents
Division General Managers
General Managers and Managing Directors,
    Overseas Manufacturing, Sales and
    Assembly Affiliates
Persons Designated by the Above

Directive: Employe Involvement

The purpose of this Directive is to assign responsibility and provide implementing instructions associated with the policy on Employe Involvement (Policy Letter B-14).

The policy provides that the Company will encourage and enable all employes to become involved in and contribute to the success of the Company. A work climate should be created and maintained in which employes, at all levels, can achieve individual goals and work satisfaction by directing their talents and energies toward clearly defined Company goals.

Implementing programs and actions consistent with this policy are key management functions, and responsibilities are assigned as follows:

Staff and Operations Management

It is the responsibility of staff and operations management to:

o Communicate the policy to subordinates in their organizations and ensure that they operate within policy guidelines.

o Develop plans, as appropriate, for implementation and maintenance of actions that contribute to the goals sought in the Policy Letter. Plans for employe involvement projects or programs, including allocation of resources, should be included as part of annual and long-range business planning.

The general process of implementation also should include:

o Analyses of the work situation to determine the extent to which existing practices are consistent with the policy.

o Well-designed experimentation with new and different human resources managing methods where this seems useful and appropriate.

o Evaluation of the effectiveness of programs and actions and sharing of results with other components.

o Review with the Personnel and Organization Staff and the Labor Relations
   Staff, as appropriate, to ensure consistency with existing personnel
   policies, compliance with contractual commitments, and an assessment of
   collective bargaining implications.

Union involvement is critical to the effective implementation of programs and
actions affecting the represented workforce. Unions should be encouraged to
participate, voluntarily, in efforts to involve the represented workforce to
accomplish mutual employe and Company goals. Unions should be kept informed
of planned actions related to involvement of represented employes prior to
implementation.

Personnel and Organization Staff and Labor Relations Staff

It is the joint responsibility of the Personnel and Organization Staff and the
Labor Relations Staff to:

o Interpret the policy and issue, as required, necessary instructions,
   procedures, and guidelines.

o Identify, evaluate, and communicate alternative approaches to involvement
   of the workforce, and provide guidance and assistance as appropriate.

o Review component programs or project proposals prior to initiation to
   ensure compliance with existing personnel policies and collective
   bargaining commitments.

o Act as a clearinghouse for information on employe involvement projects
   conducted within components and outside the Company.

Human Resources Subcommittee

It is the responsibility of the Human Resources Subcommittee to:

o Recommend strategies to management to stimulate implementation of employe
   involvement programs and actions.

o Sponsor executive conferences to inform management of employe involvement
   activities both inside and outside the Company.

o Advise and report on the status of implementation of this policy and
   related activities to the Policy and Strategy Committee.

It is recommended that all Ford subsidiaries and affiliates adopt a similar
Directive.

Philip Caldwell

Appendix C. General Electric Advertisement for Factory Automation

SOURCE: *Wall Street Journal*, 24 October 1984, p. 15.

Yesbutters don't just kill ideas.

They kill companies, even entire industries.

Take the issue of factory automation. The yesbutters have all the answers.

Yesbut we're different. Yesbut we can't afford it. Yesbut our business doesn't need it. Yesbut we're too small. Yesbut we couldn't sell it to our work force. Yesbut we can't explain it to the shareholders. Yesbut let's wait and see.

All the answers. All the *wrong* answers.

The issue isn't factory automation. It's staying in business in a complex and competitive world.

We ought to know. For General Electric has invested *billions* in factory automation and other technologies.

Call the GE Business Information Center at (518) 438-6500, and we'll tell you what we've learned. And tell you about programs, seminars and plant tours that will give you the chance to see what we've done.

For now, here are three points to ponder.

Automation isn't evolution but revolution. It can help you design, test, manufacture—faster, better, more economically than ever before.

Automation is leverage. Payback isn't always the issue. What is important is how you will gain the efficiency you need to survive and succeed in a competitive world.

Automation is a journey, not a step. You can go as far and as fast as you'd like, and still reap the benefits.

We use automation. We provide automation. So between our experience and the products and systems we sell, there's something to be gained by calling (518) 438-6500.

Before the yesbutters yesbut you right out of business.

(518) 438-6500

Appendix D. IAQC Statement of Objectives

SOURCE: IAQC *Quality Circle Quarterly* 1 (2d quarter 1978): 6.

WHAT IS THE INTERNATIONAL ASSOCIATION OF QUALITY CIRCLES?

It is a non-profit organization representing Quality Circle programs around the world.

WHY AN IAQC? WHAT ARE ITS OBJECTIVES?

1. Serve the educational needs of members.
2. Promote the recognition and spread of the Quality Circle concept.
3. Act as a central international clearing house for Quality Circle information.

HOW WILL IAQC CARRY OUT ITS OBJECTIVES?

Issuance of a quarterly publication, "Quality Circle Quarterly".
- Technical articles written by qualified individuals
- Up-to-date current events on Quality Circles
- Reports of government legislation affecting worker participation
- New techniques used successfully by others
- Articles by Circle members
- Special features of interest to:
    - Management personnel
    - Facilitators
    - Leaders
    - Members

Publishing educational materials on the subject of Quality Circles.

Encouraging the development of local chapters.

Sponsoring seminars.

Sponsoring conferences.

References

Agurén, Stefan, and Jan Edgren. 1979. *Annorlunda Fabriker* (New kinds of factories). Stockholm: Swedish Employers' Confederation. Published in English as *New Factories* (1980).

Aldrich, Howard. 1979. *Organizations and Environments*. Englewood Cliffs, N.J.: Prentice-Hall.

Aldrich, Howard, and Ellen Auster. 1986. "Even Dwarfs Started Small: Liabilities of Age and Size and Their Strategic Implications." In *Research in Organizational Behavior*, vol. 8, pp. 165–98. Greenwich, Conn.: JAI Press.

Altshuler, Alan, Martin Anderson, Daniel Jones, Daniel Roos, and James Womack. 1984. *The Future of the Automobile*. Cambridge, Mass.: MIT Press.

American Productivity Center. 1984. "Japanese Modify Management for U.S. Operations." *Productivity Letter* 4, no. 7 (December): 6.

———. 1985a. "Survey Highlights Productivity Concerns, Improvement Efforts." *Productivity Letter* 4, no. 8 (January): 5.

———. 1985b. "Directory of Productivity and Quality of Work Life Centers." *Productivity Brief* 48 (October): 1–12.

American Society for Training and Development. 1981. "ASTD Position on Certification of HRD Professionals." *National Report for Training and Development* 7 (12 June): 1–6.

Amsden, Davida, and Robert Amsden. 1976. *QC Circles: Applications, Tools, and Theory*. Milwaukee, Wis.: American Society for Quality Control.

Aoki, Masahiko. 1987. "Decentralization-Centralization and the Role of Small-Group Values in the Japanese Social System." Prepared for the Japanese Political Economy Research Committee Conference III: The Economy and Culture, Tokyo, January 1988.

ASQC. "Forty Years of Growth and Change." 1986. *Quality Progress* 19 (May): 56–67.

Bendix, Reinhard. 1956. *Work and Authority in Industry.* New York: Wiley.

Berg, Ivar, M. Freedman, and M. Freeman. 1978. *Managers and Work Reform.* New York: Free Press.

Berger, Peter. 1963. *Invitation to Sociology.* Garden City, N.Y.: Doubleday.

Berglind, H., and B. Rundblad. 1978. *Arbetsmarknaden i Sverige* (The labor market in Sweden). Stockholm: Esselte Studium AB.

Björk, L., R. Hansson and P. Hellbert. 1973. *Ökat inflytande i jobbet* (Increased influence on the job). Stockholm: Personaladministrativa Rådet.

Boisot, Max. 1986. "Markets and Hierarchies in a Cultural Perspective." *Organization Studies* 7 : 135–58.

Brumbaugh, Martin. 1946. "Highlights in the History of ASQC." *Industrial Quality Control* 1 (March): 6–34.

Burawoy, Michael. 1983. "Between the Labor Process and the State: The Changing Face of Factory Regimes under Advanced Capitalism." *American Sociological Review* 48 (October): 587–605.

Cartin, T. J. 1981. "Quality Circles Concepts—An American Invention." In *Proceedings of the 35th Annual ASQC Quality Congress and Exposition.* San Francisco.

Cherns, A. 1979. *Using the Social Sciences.* London: Routledge & Kegan Paul.

Cohen, M., J. March, and J. Olsen. 1976. "People, Problems, Solutions, and the Ambiguity of Relevance." In J. March and J. Olsen, eds., *Ambiguity and Choice in Organizations.* Bergen: Universitetsförlaget.

Cole, R. E. 1979. *Work, Mobility, and Participation: A Comparative Study of American and Japanese Industry.* Berkeley: University of California Press.

————. 1980. "Learning from the Japanese: Prospects and Pitfalls." *Management Review* 69 (September): 22–42.

————. 1987. "What Was Deming's Real Influence?" *Across the Board* 24 (February): 49–51.

————. 1989. "Large-Scale Change and Quality Improvement." In Monte Mohrman, Susan Mohrman, Gary Ledford, and T. C. Cummings, eds., *Large-Scale Organizational Change.* San Francisco: Jossey-Bass.

Cole, R. E., and Dennis Tachiki. 1983. "A Look at U.S. and Japanese Quality Circles: Preliminary Comparisons." *Quality Circles Journal* 6 (June): 10–16.

Cole, R. E., and Philippe Byosiere. 1986. "Managerial Objectives for Introducing Quality Circles." *Quality Progress* 19 (March): 25–30.

Cole, R. E., Masami Iburi, and Sharon Jablonski. 1986. "Membership Views on IAQC, Quality Circles, and Employee Involvement." *Quality Circles Journal* 9 (December): 51–55.

Cummings, William. 1980. *Education and Equality in Japan.* Princeton, N.J.: Princeton University Press.

Dachler, H. Peter, and Bernhard Wilpert. 1978. "Conceptual Dimensions and Boundaries of Participation in Organizations: A Critical Evaluation." *Administrative Science Quarterly* 23 (March): 1–39.

Davis, L. 1977. "Enhancing the Quality of Working Life: Developments in the United States." *International Labour Review* 116 (July–August): 53–65.

De Geer, Hans. 1978. *Rationaliseringsrörelsen i Sverige* (The rationalization movement in Sweden). Stockholm: Studieförbundet Näringsliv and Samhälle.

Dickson, P. 1975. *The Future of the Workplace.* New York: Weybright & Talley.

Edwards, Richard. 1979. *Contested Terrain.* New York: Basic Books.

Efficiency and Participation Development Council: SAF, LO, PTK. 1984. *Volvo Kalmar Revisited.* Stockholm: Swedish Management Group.

Eisenstadt, S. N. 1973. *Tradition, Change, and Modernity.* New York: John Wiley and Sons.

Emery, F., and Einar Thorsrud. 1969. *Form and Content in Industrial Democracy.* London: Tavistock. Published originally in Norwegian as *Industriel demokrati* (Oslo: Universitetsförlaget, 1964).

Emery, F., and Eric Trist. 1969. "Socio-Technical Systems." In F. Emery, ed., *Systems Thinking.* London: Penguin Books.

Feigenbaum, Armand. 1960, 1961, and 1983. *Total Quality Control.* New York: McGraw-Hill. 1st, 2d, and 3d eds. respectively.

Frazer, Kennedy. 1981. *The Fashionable Mind: Reflections on Fashion.* New York: Knopf.

Freund, William, and Eugene Epstein. 1984. *People and Productivity.* Homewood, Ill.: Dow Jones–Irwin.

Fujita, Yoshitaka. 1982. "Participative Work Practices in Japanese Industry." In Robert E. Cole, ed., *Industry at the Crossroads.* Ann Arbor: University of Michigan, Center for Japanese Studies.

Goldmann, Robert. 1976. *A Work Experiment: Six Americans in a Swedish Plant.* New York: Ford Foundation.

Goodman, P. 1979. *Assessing Organizational Change.* New York: Wiley.

Grant, W. Vance, and C. George Lind. 1977. *Digest of Education Statistics (1976).* Washington, D.C.: National Center for Education Statistics.

Griliches, Zvi. 1957. "Hybrid Corn: An Exploration in the Economics of Technological Change." *Econometrica* 25 (October): 501–22.

Gunzburg, D., and O. Hammarström. 1979. "Swedish Industrial Democracy, 1977: Progress and New Government Initiatives." In International Council for the Quality of Working Life, ed., *Working on the Quality of Working Life*. Boston: Martinus Nijhoff.

Gyllenhammar, Pehr. 1977. *People at Work*. Reading, Mass.: Addison-Wesley.

Halpin, James. *Zero Defects*. 1966. New York: McGraw-Hill.

Hamilton, Kathleen. 1985. "Volvo's Plan: Small, Alone, Upscale." *Automotive News*, 25 November, p. 2.

Hammarström, Olle. 1975. "Joint Worker-Management Consultation: The Case of LKAB, Sweden." In L. Davis and A. Cherns, eds., *The Quality of Working Life*. New York: Free Press.

———. 1978. "On National Strategies for Industrial Democracy." Paper presented at the Ninth World Congress of Sociology, Uppsala. Pp. 1–14.

Hirota Kimiyoshi, and Ueda Toshio. 1975. *Shōshūdan katsudō no riron to jissai* (Theory and actual practice of small-group activities). Tokyo: Japan Personnel Association.

Hirsch, P. 1972. "Processing Fads and Fashions: An Organization-Set Analysis of Cultural Industry Systems." *American Journal of Sociology* 77 (January): 639–59.

Holden, Constance. 1986. "New Toyota–GM Plant Is U.S. Model for Japanese Management." *Science* 233, no. 4,761 (18 July): 273–77.

Homans, George. 1968. "The Study of Groups." In David Sills, ed., *International Encyclopedia of the Social Sciences*, 6: 259–62. New York: Macmillan/Free Press.

Hughes, Charles, and Alfred Demaria. 1979. *Managing to Stay Non-Union*. New York: Executive Enterprises.

Japan, Ministry of Labour. 1973. *Rōshi komyunikēshon chōsa kekka hōkokusho: Shōwa 48* (Report of the results of the labor-management communications survey, 1972). Tokyo: Labour Minister's Secretariat.

———. 1974. *Koyō kanri shindan shihyō* (Indicators of the conditions of employment administration). Tokyo: Employment Security Office.

———. 1978. *Rōshi komyunikēshon chōsa hōkoku: Shōwa 52* (Results of the labor-management communications survey, 1977). Tokyo: Labour Minister's Secretariat.

———. 1985. *Rōshi komyunikēshon chōsa hōkoku: Shōwa 59* (Results of the labor-management communications survey, 1984). Tokyo: Labour Minister's Secretariat.

Jenkins, D. 1974. *Industrial Democracy in Europe*. Geneva: Business International.

Jensen, Michael. 1983. "Organization Theory and Methodology." *Accounting Review* 50 (April): 319–39.

Johnson, Terence. 1972. *Professions and Power*. London: Macmillan.

Jones, H. G. 1976. *Planning and Productivity in Sweden.* Totowa, N.J.: Rowman & Littlefield.

Jönsson, Berth. 1979. "Various Corporate Approaches to the Quality of Working Life—The Volvo Experience." Paper presented at the Third National Conference on Business Ethics, Bentley College, Waltham, Mass.

———. 1981. "Corporate Strategy for People at Work—The Volvo Experience." Paper presented at the International Conference on the Quality of Working Life, Toronto.

Juran, J. M. 1980. "International Significance of the QC Circle Movement." *Quality Progress* 3 (November): 18–22.

———. "QC Circles in the West." 1987. *Quality Progress* 20 (September): 60–61.

JUSE. 1962. *Genba to QC* (The workplace and quality control) 1 (April).

———. 1970. *QC sākuru kōryō* (General principles of the QC circle). In English and Japanese. Tokyo: Japanese Union of Scientists and Engineers.

———. 1971. *QC sākuru katsudō un'ei no kihon* (Foundation of the operation of QC circle activities). Tokyo: Japanese Union of Scientists and Engineers.

Kalleberg, Arne, and James Lincoln. 1989. *Culture, Control, and Commitment: A Study of Work Organization and Work Attitudes in the U.S. and Japan.* New York: Cambridge University Press.

Kanter, Rosabeth. 1983. *The Changemasters.* New York: Simon & Schuster.

Karlsson, L. E. 1969. *Demokrati på arbetsplatsen* (Democracy at the workplace). Stockholm: Prisma.

Kepner, Charles, and Benjamin Tregoe. 1965. *The Rational Manager.* New York: McGraw-Hill.

Kimberly, John, Robert Miles, and Associates. 1980. *The Organizational Life Cycle.* San Francisco: Jossey-Bass.

Kobayashi, K., and W. Burke. 1976. "Organizational Development in Japan." *Columbia Journal of Business* (Summer): 113–23.

Kobayashi Shigeru. 1966. *Soni wa hito o ikasu* (Sony revitalizes its employees). Tokyo: Japan Management Publishing Co.

Kogure, Masao. 1988. *Nihon to TQC: Saiginmi to Shintenkai* (Japan and TQC: Its reexamination and new prospects). Tokyo: Nihon Kagaku Gijutsu Renmei.

Kohn, Melvin. 1976. "Occupational Structure and Alienation." *American Journal of Sociology* 82 (July): 111–30.

Koike, Kazuo. 1983. "Internal Labor Markets: Workers in Large Firms." In Shirai Taishiro, ed., *Contemporary Industrial Relations in Japan.* Madison: University of Wisconsin Press.

Kondo, Yoshio. 1976. "Common Lines and Differences in the Swedish Job Reform and Japanese QC Circle Activities." *European Organization of Quality Control* (May): 9–16.

Kōshiro, Kazutoshi. 1983. "The Quality of Working Life in Japanese Factories." In Shirai Taishiro, ed., *Contemporary Industrial Relations in Japan*. Madison: University of Wisconsin Press.

Kuznets, Simon. 1966. *Modern Economic Growth*. New Haven: Yale University Press.

Landsorganisation. 1972. *Industrial Democracy*. Stockholm: Landsorganisation.

———. 1976. *Arbetsorganisation* (Work organization). Stockholm: Tiden.

Lawler, Edward, III. 1986. *High-Involvement Management*. San Francisco: Jossey-Bass.

Lawler, Edward, III, and Susan Mohrman. 1985. "Quality Circles after the Fad." *Harvard Business Review* 63 (January–February): 65–71.

Leymann, Heinz. 1982. *Kan arbetslivet demokratiseras?* (Can worklife be democratized?). Stockholm: Management Media.

Lillrank, Paul. 1983. *Small Group Activities in North Europe and Japan*. Tokyo: Social Research Institute of Japan.

———. 1984. *Sociological Aspects of Japanese QC Circles: Discussion Paper*. Tokyo: Social Research Institute of Japan.

———. 1985. "JSC Seminar Report: Prof. Matsui Tamao and Ms. Mary Lou Onglatcko: Quality Control Circles—Their Socio-Psychological Dynamics." *Center News* 10, no. 1 (June): 3–5. Tokyo: Japan Foundation.

———. 1988. "Organization for Continuous Improvement: Quality Control Circle Activities in Japanese Industry." Ph.D. diss., University of Helsinki. To be published in slightly revised form as *Continuous Improvement: Quality Control Circles in Japanese Industry* by Paul Lillrank and Kano Noriaki (Ann Arbor: University of Michigan Center for Japanese Studies, 1989).

Lynn, Leonard. 1982. *How Japan Innovates: A Comparison with the United States in the Case of Oxygen Steelmaking*. Boulder, Colo.: Westview Press.

Lynn, Leonard, and Timothy McKeown. 1988. *Organizing Business: Trade Associations in America and Japan*. Washington, D.C.: American Enterprise Institute for Public Policy Research.

March, James. 1981. "Footnotes to Organizational Change." *Administrative Science Quarterly* 26 (December): 563–77.

March, James, and J. Olsen, eds. 1976. *Ambiguity and Choice in Organizations*. Bergen: Universitetsförlaget.

Martin, Andrew. 1976. "From Joint Consultation to Joint Decision-Making: The Redistribution of Workplace Power in Sweden." *Current Sweden* 84 (June): 1–11.

Mead, W. R. 1984. "Norden: Destiny and Fortune." *Dædalus* 113 (Winter): 1–27.

Meyer, J., and B. Rowan. 1977. "Institutionalized Organizations: Formal Structure as Myth and Ceremony." *American Journal of Sociology* 83 (September): 340–63.

Miller, David. 1985. *Introduction to Collective Behavior.* Belmont, Calif.: Wadsworth.

Miller, R., and D. Sawers. 1970. *The Technical Development of Modern Aviation.* New York: Praeger.

Minami, R. 1973. *The Turning Point in Economic Development: Japan's Experience.* Tokyo: Kinokuniya.

Misumi, Juji. 1980. "Action Research on Group Decision Making and Organizational Development." Paper presented at the Twenty-second International Congress of Psychology, Leipzig.

Mitchell, Ron. 1987. "Rediscovering Our Roots: Quality Circles in the U.S., 1918–1948." *Journal for Quality and Participation* [formerly the *Quality Circles Journal*] 10 (December): 56–66.

Morris, Rosemary. 1981. "Quality Circles Consulting: Marketing Survey Industry Analysis." Unpublished paper. San Jose, Calif.: FMS Corporation. Pp. 1–44.

Mouer, Ross, and Yoshio Sugimoto. 1986. *Images of Japanese Society.* London: Routledge & Kegan Paul.

Nakayama Saburo, ed. 1972. *Zen'in sanka keiei no kangaekata to jissai* (All-employee participation in management: Viewpoints and practices). Tokyo: Japan Federation of Employers' Association.

Naples, Michael. 1985. "Back in the Black." *Association Management* 37 (May): 77–80.

NASA. 1984a. *NASA Productivity and Quality: 1983 Summary Report.* Washington, D.C.: NASA.

———. 1984b. *NASA's Productivity Improvement and Quality Enhancement Initiatives.* Washington, D.C.: NASA.

National Catholic News Service. 1984. "First Draft—Bishops' Pastoral: Catholic Social Teaching and the U.S. Economy." *Origins* 14 (15 November): 337–83.

OECD. 1984a. *The Development and Utilisation of Human Resources in the Context of Technological Change and Industrial Restructuring: Synthesis of the Case Studies in Phase III of the CERI Human Resources Project.* Paris: Centre for Educational Research and Innovation.

————. 1984b. *The Development and Utilisation of Human Resources in the Context of Technological Change and Industrial Restructuring, Phase III: Case Studies in the Automobile Industry: The Volvo Company Report.* Paris: Centre for Educational Research and Innovation.

Okuda, Kenji. 1983. "The Role of Engineers in Japanese Industry and Education." *Journal of Japanese Trade and Industry* (May): 23–26.

————. 1988. *Hito to keiei* (Man and management). Tokyo: Manejimento.

Ouchi, William. 1981. *Theory Z.* Reading, Mass.: Addison-Wesley.

————. 1984. *The M-Form Society.* Reading, Mass.: Addison-Wesley.

Palm, G. 1972. *Ett år på LM* (A year at L. M. Ericsson). Stockholm: Författare Förlaget.

————. 1974. *Bokslut från LM* (Final account from L. M. Ericsson). Stockholm: Författare Förlaget.

————. 1977. *The Flight From Work.* London: Cambridge University Press. An English language abridgement of the two preceding Swedish volumes.

Parker, Mike, and Ellis Boal. 1984. "Will Labor Laws Be Weakened to Permit Expansion of QWL Programs?" *Labor Notes* (September): 7.

Pascale, Richard, and Anthony Athos. 1981. *The Art of Japanese Management.* New York: Simon & Schuster.

Perrow, Charles. 1979. *Complex Organizations: A Critical Essay.* 2d ed. Glenview, Ill.: Scott, Foresman.

ReVelle, Jack. 1985. "Survey Reveals Membership Preferences." *Quality Circles Journal* 8 (December): 25–29.

Rhenman, Eric. 1964. *Företagsdemokrati och företagsorganisation* (Industrial democracy and industrial management). Stockholm: Norstedt.

Rieker, Wayne. 1984. "Quality Circles: QC's Part of a Greater Vision." Presentation at the IAQC State of the Art Forum, Nashville, Tenn., November 29.

Rieker, Wayne, and Harold Kay. 1985. "A Case for Voluntarism: A Case for Obligatory Participation." *Quality Circles Journal* 8 (March): 6–7.

Robins, James. 1987. "Organizational Economics: Notes on the Use of Transaction Cost Theory in the Study of Organization." *Administrative Science Quarterly* 32 (March): 68–86.

Rogers, E., and F. Shoemaker. 1971. *Communication of Innovations.* 2d ed. New York: Free Press.

Rowand, Roger. 1985. "U.S. Lag in Global Technology Cited." *Automotive News*, 8 April, p. 15.

Rubinstein, Sidney. 1980. "QWL and the Technical Societies." *Quality Progress* 13 (April): 28–31.

Sahal, Devendra. 1981. *Patterns of Technological Innovation.* Reading, Mass.: Addison-Wesley.

Sandberg, Thomas. 1982. *Work Organization and Autonomous Groups.* Lund: Liber Förlag.

Schmitter, Philippe, and Gerhard Lehmbruch, eds. 1979. *Trends toward Corporatist Intermediation.* Beverly Hills, Calif.: Sage Publications.

Sethi, S. Prakash, Nobuaki Namiki, and Carl Swanson. 1984. *The False Promise of the Japanese Miracle.* Boston: Pittman Publishing Co.

Shearman, R. W. 1967. "ASQC—Lucky 13 Among the American Engineering Societies." *Industrial Quality Control* 23 (May): 549–53.

Shiba, Shoji. 1983a. "Japan, Today and Yesterday: Its Secret for a Successful Development." Paper presented at the Manila Hilton Hotel, November 25.

———. 1983b. "QC sākuru: Sono kyōdaika to mizukara e no inpakuto" (QC circles: Their huge growth and its impact on themselves). In Takashi Negishi and Yukihide Okada, eds., *Kōkyō keizaigaku no tenkai.* Tokyo: Tōyō Keizai Shinposha.

Shimada, Haruo. 1982. "Japan's Postwar Industrial Growth and Labor-Management Relations." Proceedings of the Thirty-Fifth Annual Meeting of the Industrial Relations Research Association, December 28–30, pp. 241–48.

———. 1988. *Hyūmanwea no keizaigaku* (The economics of humanware). Tokyo: Iwanami Shoten.

Shirai, Taishiro. 1983. "A Theory of Enterprise Unionism." In Shirai Taishiro, ed., *Contemporary Industrial Relations in Japan.* Madison: University of Wisconsin Press.

Singh, Jitendra, David Tucker, and Robert House. 1986. "Organizational Legitimacy and the Liability of Newness." *Administrative Science Quarterly* 31 (June): 171–93.

Simon, Herbert. 1965. *The Shape of Automation.* New York: Harper & Row.

Smith, Robert. 1983. *Japanese Society.* New York: Cambridge University Press.

Statistiska Centralbyrån. 1971. *Arbetsmarknads-statistisk årsbok, 1970* (Yearbook of labor statistics, 1970). Örebro: National Central Bureau of Statistics.

———. 1977a. *Levnadsförhållanden.* Report no. 8. Stockholm: National Central Bureau of Statistics.

———. 1977b. *Statistisk årsbok, 1977* (Statistical abstract of Sweden, 1977). Örebro: National Central Bureau of Statistics.

———. 1978. *Arbetsmarknads-statistisk årsbok, 1977* (Yearbook of labor statistics, 1977). Örebro: National Central Bureau of Statistics.

———. 1981. *Arbetsmarknads statistisk årsbok, 1981* (Yearbook of labor statistics, 1981). Örebro: National Central Bureau of Statistics.

Stinchcombe, Arthur. 1965. "Social Structure and Organizations." In James March, ed., *Handbook of Organizations*. Chicago: Rand McNally.

Sugimoto Tatsuo. 1982. "Genzai no QC sākuru katsudō o bunseki shite" (Analyzing the current activities of quality circles). *FQC* 232 (April): 18–23.

Swedish Employers' Confederation. 1971. *Samtal in Matfors* (Talks at Matfors). Stockholm: SAF.

————. 1975. *Nya arbetsformer* (Job reform in Sweden). Stockholm: SAF. English edition available.

Takezawa, Shin'ichi. 1976. "The Quality of Working Life: Trends in Japan." *Labor and Society* 1 (January): 29–48.

Tanaka Hirohide. 1982. "Nihon teki koyō kankō o kizuita hitotachi—Keimei Yamamoto ni kiku" (People who have established Japanese employment practices: An interview with Keimei Yamamoto). *Japan Institute of Labour* 24, no. 7 (July): 38–54.

Tarter, James, and Staff. 1987. "The IAQC Chronology: A Financial Perspective." Internal IAQC report. Cincinnati: IAQC.

Thompson, Donald. 1987. "Rockwell's Bold New World." *Industry Week*, 15 June, pp. 38–41.

Thorsrud, E., and F. Emery. 1969. *Medinflytande och engagemang in arbetet* (Participation and engagement in work). (Original title, *Mot en ny bedriftsorganisasjon*.) Stockholm: Utvecklingsrådet for Samarbetsfrågor.

Tokunaga, Shigeyoshi. 1983. "A Marxist Interpretation of Japanese Industrial Relations, with Special Reference to Large Private Enterprises." In Shirai Taishiro, ed., *Contemporary Industrial Relations in Japan*. Madison: University of Wisconsin Press.

Tornatzky, Louis, J. D. Eveland, Myles Boylan, William Hetzner, Elmina Johnson, and David Roitman. 1983. *The Process of Technological Innovation: Reviewing the Literature*. Division of Industrial Science and Technological Innovation. Washington, D.C.: National Science Foundation.

Törner, Pär. 1976. *The Matfors Report*. Stockholm: SAF. Originally published in Swedish as *Matforsrapporten* (Stockholm: SAF, 1973).

Turner, Ralph, and Lewis Killian. 1972. *Collective Behavior*. 2d ed. Englewood Cliffs, N.J.: Prentice-Hall.

U.S. Department of Commerce. 1984. *Productivity Improvement: Your Guide to Today's Resources*. Lorton, Va.: National Productivity Awareness Campaign.

U.S. Department of Health, Education and Welfare. Special Task Force. 1973. *Work in America*. Cambridge, Mass.: MIT Press.

U.S. Department of Labor. 1983. *Handbook of Labor Statistics*. Washington, D.C.: Bureau of Labor Statistics.

University of Cincinnati. 1987. *International Association of Quality Circles Membership Survey*. Cincinnati: Institute for Policy Research.

Veblen, Thorstein. 1966. *Imperial Germany and the Industrial Revolution*. New York: Macmillan Co., 1915. Reprint. Ann Arbor: University of Michigan Press.

Vernon, Raymond. 1986. "Can U.S. Manufacturing Come Back?" *Harvard Business Review* 86 (July–August): 98–106.

Walton, Richard. 1975. "Criteria for the Quality of Working Life." In Louis Davis, Albert Cherns, and Associates, eds., *The Quality of Working Life*, vol. 1. New York: Free Press.

———. 1978. "Teaching an Old Dog Food New Tricks." *Wharton Magazine* (Winter): 38–47.

Wareham, Ralph, J. Y. McClure, L. I. Medlock, and Walter Hurd. 1986. "ASQC through Four Decades." *Quality Progress* 19 (August): 47–51.

Weick, Karl. 1984. "Blindspots in Organizational Theorizing." In Douglas Gutknecht, ed., *Meeting Organization and Human Resource Challenges*. New York: University Press of America.

Whiting, Basil. 1975. *The Human Side of Productivity*. New York: Ford Foundation.

Williamson, Oliver. 1985. *The Economic Institutions of Capitalism*. New York: Free Press.

Wool, H. 1973. "What's Wrong with Work in America." *Monthly Labor Review* 96 (March): 38–44.

Yamazaki, Hiroaki, and Matao Miyamoto, eds. 1987. *Trade Associations in Business History*. Tokyo: University of Tokyo Press.

Yankelovich, Daniel, Hans Zetterberg, Burkhard Strümpel, and Michael Shanks. 1983. *Work and Human Values: An International Report on Jobs in the 1980's and 1990's*. New York: Aspen Institute for Humanistic Studies.

Zetterberg, Hans. 1984. "The Rational Humanitarians." *Dædalus* 113 (Winter): 75–92.

Zetterberg, Hans, Karin Busch, Göran Crona, Greta Frankel, Berth Jönsson, Ivar Söderlind, and Bo Winander. 1983. *Det osynliga kontraktet* (The invisible contract). Stockholm: SIFO Förlag.

Index

Compositor: G & S Typesetters, Inc.
      Text: 11/13 Caledonia
   Display: Caledonia
   Printer: Braun-Brumfield, Inc.
    Binder: Braun-Brumfield, Inc.